C000132626

Christian Theosophy Series, No. 2.

THE

PATHWAY OF THE SPIRIT.

A GUIDE TO

Inspiration, Illumination and Divine Realization on Earth.

BY

JOHN HAMLIN DEWEY, M.D.,

AUTHOR OF

"THE WAY, THE TRUTH AND THE LIFE, A HANDBOOK OF CHRISTIAN THEOSOPHY,
HEALING AND PSYCHIC CULTURE;" "INTRODUCTION TO THE THEOSOPHY
OF THE CHRIST;" "CHRISTIAN THEOSOPHY DEFINED;"
"SCIENTIFIC BASIS OF MENTAL HEALING;"
"DIVINITY OF HUMANITY," ETC.

NEW YORK:
FRANK F. LOVELL & COMPANY,
142 AND 144 WORTH STREET.

Dedication.

TO ALL WHO LOOK FOR THE PROMISED "COMFORTER,"

THAT QUICKENING AND REVEALING

"SPIRIT OF TRUTH WHICH PROCEEDETH FROM THE FATHER"

AND GUIDETH "INTO ALL TRUTH";

AND

WHICH IS YET TO BE POURED OUT UPON ALL FLESH

AND LIFT THE WORLD INTO FELLOWSHIP WITH THE CHRIST

IN THE

PERFECT LIFE OF DIVINE SONSHIP AND BROTHERHOOD,

THIS BOOK

IS AFFECTIONATELY INSCRIBED

BY A FELLOW-SERVANT AND DISCIPLE,

THE AUTHOR.

Aco.

There is a spirit in man: and the inspiration of the Almighty giveth them understanding (*Job,* xxxii. 8).

And the Spirit of the LORD shall rest upon him, the spirit of wisdom and understanding, the spirit of counsel and might, the spirit of knowledge and of the fear of the LORD; . . .

They shall not hurt nor destroy in all my holy mountain: for the earth shall be full of the knowledge of the LORD, as the wat·rs cover the sea (*Is.* xi. 2, 9).

After those days, saith the LORD, I will put my law in their inward parts, and write it in their hearts; and will be their God, and they shall be my people.

And they shall teach no more every man his neighbor, and every man his brother, saying know the LORD: for they shall all know me, from the least of them unto the greatest of them, saith the LORD: for I will forgive their iniquity, and I will remember their sin no more (*Jer.* xxxi. 33, 34).

PREFACE.

AS Moses was about to descend from the mount of revelation to carry out the instruction there received for the building of the tabernacle, he was divinely admonished: "See that thou make all things according to the pattern shewed to thee in the mount."

If in the following pages the author seems oracular and dogmatic in the presentation of his message, the reader is kindly requested to regard it as but the earnest desire to be true to the pattern shown him in the mount of vision, and not as an assumption of authority for personal inspiration. Having been caught up in the Spirit to behold with open prophetic vision the ultimate certainty of an emancipated and perfected humanity on earth, and to see that its immediate realization is a divine possibility and provision, through the perfect co-operation of man, he can but sound anew and with emphasis the keynote of the Christ message:

"The time is fulfilled, and the kingdom of God is at hand; repent ye and believe the gospel."

"We speak that we do know and testify that we have seen," the gospel of a present and complete salvation,

salvation from the thraldom and limitations of the
sensuous life and its liabilities, in the realization of the
supremacy, freedom and illumination of the Spirit.
Our appeal is confidently made to the prophetic instinct and spiritual intuition of the reader. Responses
from the divine inmost of the soul, the "still, small
voice" of the Spirit, can be fully trusted. No other
authority is needed. Let but the sensuous mind and
the clamor of tradition be hushed to silence, the voice
of God in a living inspiration will be heard in the soul.

The world is in spiritual torpor, bound in the chains
of materiality and tradition. It needs awakening to
the full recognition of the Christ message, which opens
the true and only door to its emancipation and absolute
redemption. It will be asked: "Does not the church
proclaim that message?" Alas! the historic church
has made the word of Christ of little or no effect
through its traditions. The Christ ideal for man,
whom he proclaimed a child of God, was the perfect
and sinless life in communion and fellowship with the
Father in this world. The Christ promised the present realization of this divine possibility through the
co-operation of man, in faith and unity of spirit and
purpose with the Father. The church has blindly
transferred that ideal and promise to another world
and practically denied its possible realization in this.
In his gospel of spiritual birth and regeneration, the
Christ gave to the world the law and conditions for
the actualization of this ideal and promise, and demonstrated their reality in his own experience as an
example.

There is an arcanum of wisdom and power in that gospel little dreamed of by the world, and wholly misconceived of by the church. Under the personal ministry of Jesus it was opened in marvellous fulness to the understanding and experience of the apostles, and under their ministry to others still. After their departure, however, it was closed again to the world by the misconceptions and misleading speculations of the Fathers. From that day, the blinding fogs of superstition and tradition have been sufficient to keep it hidden, save from a few hated and persecuted mystics of the succeeding centuries. These moral heroes and martyred saints, as living altars preserved the pentecostal fire, and kept to our own time the holy flame from utter extinction. They were "the salt of the earth," living centres of a transforming energy, channels for the continuous work of a divine and heavenly ministry.

Under the swelling tide of spiritual advancement thus secured, the power of ecclesiasticism and anti-Christ at length is breaking. The reopening to the world of the divine arcana, and a great spiritual awakening in the promised return of the Christ in Spirit and power has begun. The transition age from the reign of materialism, selfishness and superstition, to the era of spiritual enlightenment, freedom and brotherhood is upon us. A renaissance of apostolic life and power with its gifts of the Spirit is at hand.

This volume is one of the voices, crying anew, in the wilderness of modern doubt and creedal distraction; "Repent ye; for the kingdom of heaven is at hand."

"The time is fulfilled." "Prepare ye the way of the Lord, make his paths straight." We seek not to build up a new system of doctrine or philosophy, but to open up a new and grander life to man, and make clear, as revealed in spiritual vision, the way and means of its immediate realization.

Reader, in the spirit of a brother we ask you to read with unbiassed mind the volume before you, and to follow sacredly the intuitions and deepest promptings of your own soul which its message shall awaken. These intuitions will thus become the channel of a divine inspiration, which will open to you the secret of "the Word made flesh" in our great Exemplar, by which that incarnation may be reproduced in your own, and in universal experience, for which you are divinely called to labor. "Verily, verily, I say unto you, he that believeth on me the works that I do shall he do also; and greater than these shall he do; because I go unto the Father." The world has been all too slow in awakening to this mighty promise of the Master. The standards of the fathers and all the creeds of Christendom, over which the churches stumble and divide, are utterly worthless compared with the secret of that transcendent life which the Christ promised should be reproduced in all his faithful followers.

Man as a son of God and brother of Christ is, through this higher evolution, to be enthroned in power over all earthly conditions, the absolute master of the world. The demonstration of this reality in the experience of the Christ as the brother of men, was the opened door of entrance upon the regenerate life to all, under his

Leadership and help. "I am the door: by me if any man enter in he shall be saved, and shall go in and out and find pasture." "I am the light of the world: he that followeth me shall not walk in darkness, but shall have the light of life."

The historic church is honestly believed by its devotees to be the body of Christ, and its popes, prelates and bishops a true "Apostolic succession;" and the development of its theology, creedal authority and ecclesiastical power to be an outgrowth or unfolding of the fundamental principles planted by the Christ in the thought and life of the world. Is this true? Why then has not the church become the re-incarnation of the Master's Spirit? Why the decline instead of the unfolding and extension of the Apostolic life, power and spiritual gifts? Can ecclesiastical pomp, power and despotism be a development of or a substitute for these? No greater mistake is possible. These are the outgrowth of another doctrine than the divine sonship and brotherhood of humanity. They are not the unfolding and establishment of that brotherhood under the immediate inspiration of the Father's wisdom and goodness. Practical efforts to secure this result have had to begin outside the church, and often with its direct opposition. They are not the legitimate fruits of the Master's Spirit unfolding in the lives of his followers.

The Christ organized no external church as an instrument to save souls for another world. He taught no scheme of doctrinal theology or philosophy, and left no creed to be accepted as a means or condition of salvation here or hereafter. He did teach in unmistakable terms that man is the child of the living and infinite God, with corresponding divine possibilities inherent within him. He did lift up the ideal of a divine and perfect life for man on earth. He did teach by precept and parable, and illustrated by a living example the law and conditions under which all men may enter into its realization. The salvation he preached was this moral and physical perfection. His ideal church was the realized Fatherhood of God in the actualized brotherhood of man, the enthronement of the kingdom of God—the love, wisdom and perfection of the Father—on earth as in heaven.

The historic church has been true to its ideals and faithful to the work it set itself to do. That work, primarily, was the saving of souls for another world, not the perfection of life in this. Its ideal of salvation has been the rescuing of souls from the eternal consequences in a future world of a fallen condition in this. Its ideal of the kingdom of heaven in the perfect realization of the presence of God has been for the life beyond, the benefits for this world being secondary and incidental. It has been true and faithful to this ideal and work, but such was not the ideal and work inaugurated by the Master; and in his name we call attention to the mistake. His ideal and work were, primarily, for this world, the realization of the presence of God and the kingdom of heaven on earth independent of any consideration of consequences in another world. His motto was, "Take no thought for the morrow, for the morrow shall take thought for the things of itself; sufficient unto the day is the evil thereof."

On the other hand, we are told by the advocates of materialistic agnosticism that this Christ of the gospels is an invention of romance, the fiction of a designing and crafty priesthood, with no just claim to historic verity. Is he? Who then was the transcendent genius to invent the divine ideal, and picture the perfection of a life for which no character of history furnished even the suggestion? Why did so skilled an artist vanish, passing into oblivion—the great unnamed and unknown benefactor of his race? Compare the grandest inventions of modern romance with the simple story of the gospel narratives, and how the ideal characters shrink into puny littleness in the majestic presence of the Divine Galilean. As simple, broken and imperfect as that story is, it has touched and stirred the profoundest depths of the human soul as no other literature has done. In a rude and semi-barbaric age it lifted up the divinest ideal our world has known. The loftiest aspirations of the human race, voiced in its seers and prophets, wer fulfilled and more than actualized in that matchless character; a character, however, not to remain exceptional, but the seed-germ of infinite promise, prophetic of ultimate realization in universal experience. This ideal of priestly origin? The charge is too absurd for serious consideration.

We have here the perfect ideal, and that ideal actualized in practical experience and example, approached by no other character of romance or history. No

higher is needed, nor possible of conception. Its realization in universal experience will bring not only humanity, but the world it inhabits, to perfection. Wisdom that is divine and perfect, taught in precept and
parable and illustrated in example, is here; and, " It
is the power of God unto salvation to every one that
believeth."

No wonder, then, that this record is sacredly cherished, since here man meets face to face with and
touches divinity. "For God who commanded the light
to shine out of darkness, hath shined into our hearts, to
give the light of the knowledge of the glory of God in
the face of Jesus Christ."

Two practical questions arise. First: will the impartial study of the constitution of nature and man,
and of the fundamental laws of being, justify the claim
that man as an embodied spirit and child of God, may
attain physical and moral perfection and live the per_
fect life of mastery over all material and moral conditions in the body, as represented in the story of the
Christ? Second: will the method given and illustrated in the Christ teaching and example secure this
result in universal experience? These questions are
seriously considered in the present volume, which, with
the deep convictions of the author, are now left to the
calm judgment and disposal of the reader.

PART I.

IMMEDIATE INSPIRATION AND KNOWLEDGE OF
GOD, THE SUPREME NECESSITY AND UNIVER-
SAL POSSIBILITY OF MAN.

THE PATHWAY OF THE SPIRIT.

THE REVELATION OF GOD.

Necessity of God-Knowledge.—If God is absolute Being, omniscient and omnipresent, He is the supreme reality of the universe, and all beings and things exist in, from and by Him. A correct interpretation of Nature, life, and the law of human destiny is, therefore, possible only through a correct understanding of the nature and character of God and His purpose in creation. If there is no Supreme Intelligence as the controlling Power of the universe, there is still the supreme Energy, and some original cause or central impulse within and behind the processes of the world which determines the results we see.

Now whether we regard the spring of causation and providence as a Supreme Being of infinite intelligence, will and goodness, or a universal unconscious principle and spontaneous energy, our interpretation of Nature and life will correspond with the conception we hold in this respect; that is, our doctrines of cosmogony and philosophy and of our own being, possibilities and destiny, will correspond with the character

1

and qualities that we ascribe to God, or that which we mentally put in the place of God. There can, therefore, be no perfect science, philosophy or true understanding of life, being and destiny, without a correct conception and understanding of the character and attributes of God. This when attained is true Theosophy.

God Known Through Revelation Only.—How can this practical knowledge of God be obtained? Obviously, only by direct revelation of God to man. The study of nature through the senses—the "scientific method"—does not, and as we shall show, cannot reveal God. Some of the strongest and clearest minds have been led by this study and method into utter materialistic agnosticism. "Canst thou by searching find out God? Canst thou find out the Almighty unto perfection?" Is such a revelation possible or probable? If God, as such, be a living reality, yes; if not, there being no supreme revealing intelligence, the problem, under the present limitation of the human faculties must remain an insoluble mystery; a fruitful source of conjectural and undemonstrable speculation.

If, however, the processes of the visible world are the immediate manifestation of a transcendent, divine activity, under the direction of a supreme intelligence and will, holding a moral as well as a physical government and control, then man as a moral and spiritual being, is entitled to a direct intercourse with and instruction from his moral Governor. Without this he can have no certain knowledge of the divine will and purpose concerning himself; and only to the extent of such knowledge is he responsible for non-conformity. Hence there must in the nature of the case be some condition under which such revelation of and from the divine is not only possible but certain, if in truth God be a supreme lawgiver, and man is under His moral government.

What the Moral Nature of Man Involves.— That man is a moral and accountable being, no rational mind will dispute. But do we fully realize all that this fact involves? Moral accountability in man involves, of necessity, a moral law and government over him; otherwise he could be accountable to no law above or beyond his own will and pleasure. But universal experience testifies to an innate sense of some necessary restraint upon the exercise of these, independent of such as contact with society imposes. This restraining sense is an unmistakable, inward and ineffaceable recognition of a supreme law of right or righteousness.

Divine Intelligence Necessary to a Moral Government.—A moral law based upon such deep and far-reaching discriminations in the sphere of motive and conduct, cannot be the automatic operation of a blind principle like that of gravity, chemical affinity, etc. Such a basis of necessity involves not only a supreme standard of integrity, but a supreme intelligence as arbiter or judge of the relation of motive and conduct to the law. Without this the talk of a moral government would be meaningless. Man would be left to learn only from experience what is right and what wrong; or rather, what is best for himself, and this

would be expediency, not moral law or principle.
With the subtle relations that exist between man and
man, and between the daily habits of the individual
and his own supreme nature, ages of experience would
be necessary under the limitations of his intelligence,
for him to arrive at a knowledge of the absolute right,
admitting right to be an absolute principle *per se*.
But if as we claim, this supreme law of his life relates
to man personally, not to a principle of blind necessity,
but to infinite wisdom, justice and goodness, he may
receive immediate instruction and guidance from the
Divine parental government.

**This Revelation of God's Will Must Be Sought by
Man.**—As a morally accountable being it is left for
man to seek a knowledge of his relations to the moral
and spiritual life—the kingdom of God—as it was left
for him as a rational being to learn his relation to the
physical world, and by the proper exercise of his
powers to acquire a knowledge of that world. If he
choose not to seek a better understanding of his relation to his physical, social and moral environments, he
must suffer from the results of his indifference and
ignorance, until awakened by experience and the better example of others to the wiser course.

**The Moral Nature Necessitates the Recognition of
God.**—The moral nature which calls for righteousness,
thus necessitates the recognition of a Divine Being
whose economy and government are absolute perfection, whose will concerning man is the infinitely perfect way of life for him, conformity to which will
make him perfect as the Divine is perfect. Without

this divine sanction, that is, the discriminative intelligence and judgment of absolute wisdom, justice and goodness, there would be no basis for a moral law and order. The very terms would be without significance. So too the reason and moral sense, without a divine intelligence and judgment to which they stand related, would be evanescent lights "which lead but to bewilder, and dazzle but to blind."

The reason and conscience, then, are the sure, though finite expression of the infinite wisdom and goodness come to this limitation in man. Yet because they are a ray of the Divine, focused in the misty envelope of materiality and sense, they are capable of kindling from within by a divine inspiration, and thus to unfold and shine forth—the brightness and glory of the divine. If it were not so, there could be, as we have said, no absolute standard of right, truth or justice; and man would be left wholly to expediency as the only principle on which to base the law of his life and conduct. That which he thought would bring him the most pleasure—his only standard of good—would of necessity be the governing motive of action. Might, as brute force or superior cunning, would make right. The ruling law of the animal would be the law of humanity, and any high order of human society would be impossible. But man has a supreme sense of right and wrong, *per se*, even though he may not know absolutely what is right in a given case.

The Moral Sense Rooted in Divinity, not Expediency.—If we ask: Whence this universal sense of right and wrong? Philosophers tell us that it is a faculty

established through hereditary impressions from ages
of experience in successive generations, the ultimate
root of which was expediency; and that the varying
standards and ideas of right and wrong are wholly a
matter of education. But is this an adequate explanation? And of what value is this universal and deeply
rooted moral sense, if there be no universal principle
of right as such, and no moral law and order which it
involves and to which man is related by it? It is
clear then, that if there is no moral principle of right,
per se, man is not a moral being and expediency is
the only law of the personal life. The doctrine of
righteousness—conformity with an absolute law of
right—on which religion, Scripture, and all supposed
inspired teaching are based, is a delusive superstition,
and martyrdom for supposed righteousness' sake an
act of supremest folly. The blotting out of moral distinctions, and the idea of a divine sanction and condemnation which the denial of a moral principle involves, puts the highwayman, the bank defaulter, the
petty thief, and every moral and social outlaw, on a
level of merit with the moral hero and martyred
saint. Why then should men, even rogues themselves,
honor the one and despise the other? But one answer
meets the question; justice, mercy and goodness are
strictly moral qualities, and are meaningless terms to
any but moral beings. The fact that all men, even
those who violate them, recognize the binding force of
these principles, proves the moral nature of man, and
thus his relation to a divine economy and government,
which through obedience links him to Divinity. As

the inspiration of these principles has been strong
enough in men and women to lead thousands to self-
sacrificing lives and even to martyrdom, their divine
reality and origin find absolute demonstration in these
examples. No such inspiration is possible from expediency.

**Moral Qualities Attributes of Spiritual Being
Only.**—As these transcendent qualities that distinguish
humanity and differentiate man from the animal kingdom are the expression only of the attributes of a
moral and therefore spiritual being, they relate him to
a corresponding moral and spiritual kingdom. But a
transcendent moral and spiritual kingdom, as such,
would in turn, be empty and meaningless without
the enthroned presence of a Divine Being, the enthroned perfection of wisdom, goodness and power on
the plane of the universal, eternal and absolute.

Direct Intercourse with God.—This vital relation
between the sphere of the human and the Divine, or
man and God, renders free and unrestricted communion with the Divine not only possible, but necessary.
Necessary for the realization of the ultimate possibilities of man, and for the fulfilment of the divine will
and purpose in his being. "The time is fulfilled and
the kingdom of God is at hand," said the Master.
That is to say, the time has come for man, as a moral
and spiritual being, to turn from his absorbing attention to the mere things of flesh and sense, that perish
with the using, and seek the higher and imperishable
treasures of the Spirit. It is time for him to awake to
the realization of his own spiritual nature, as a child

of God, and enter upon an earnest study of his relations to the spiritual kingdom, under the immediate
inspiration and guidance of the Father, that he may
"know the things freely given to us of God."

This does not involve the utter ignoring of the things
of the fleshly life; for, said the Master, "Your heavenly
Father knoweth that ye have need of all these things,
but seek ye first the kingdom of God and His righteousness, and all these things shall be added unto
you." The things of the outward world and the sensuous life are as much the free gifts of God, as are
the things of the Spirit, and are to be as gratefully
accepted and honored in their legitimate use. But we
dishonor God when our interest in them becomes par-
amount to the demands of the spiritual nature, which
calls for divine communion and fellowship, that we
may walk in spiritual supremacy and unity with God
in all things, which is the only rational and true life of
a child of God. Through this realization of God, man
rises to the higher plane of the spiritual life, and
dwells in such unity with the Father that every function of the body as well as every activity of the mind
in its relation to the outward world, will be under the
guidance of His wisdom and so brought to the full
realization of His purpose in them.

Thus will man walk with God in the Spirit and under
His inspiration, while in the full normal exercise of all
the fleshly activities, and of the mental powers in the
study of the outward world. Only thus will the development of science, art, government, invention and all
the legitimate industries of life, be brought to perfec-

tion; because thus only can they be carried out in the spirit and to the end for which they were ordained of Him. "Use this world as not abusing it," is the counsel of inspired wisdom. It is the absorption in the things of the sensuous life and the perversion of its functions, or the indulgence of the selfish spirit in them, that constitute "the lust of the flesh, the lust of the eyes, and the pride of life." To overcome temptation and avoid perversion, man needs the guidance of a higher wisdom than his own, and the inspiration of a higher motive than that which springs from the sensuous life of the natural man. There must be the complete transfer of the centre and spring of motive and inspiration, from the plane of the natural to that of the spiritual man, from the sensuous to the spiritual life and understanding. This is the first step in the process of regeneration, and the casting out of the selfish spirit, announced by the Christ as a universal necessity in human experience.

The Kingdom of God.—The kingdom of God is the kingdom of truth and righteousness, found by man only through supreme loyalty to God in the life. This loyalty of the heart to God is possible only through that love which is awakened by the realization of His love and Fatherhood to us. "We love Him because He first loved us." Truth pertains to the knowledge of all things and of our relations to them, physical and spiritual; while righteousness pertains to the right use of this knowledge and of our powers in its pursuit.

Perfect knowledge of all truth is impossible without divine illumination, and this is attained only through union of the soul with God. Conscious union with God is a state of righteousness, and love is the only uniting power, because this alone secures the spontaneous yielding and allegiance of the heart. Since true wisdom is the right use of knowledge and of our powers in its pursuit, it can be attained only through righteousness in the life. Hence the importance of the right attitude of mind and heart from the first, that all needless mistakes may be avoided and true progress hastened. All divinely inspired teaching couples truth and righteousness together, and makes righteousness the basis of all divine realization, and this is impossible save through the recognition of and allegiance to God as the Father of human spirits.

The Throne of Power and Government Within yet Above the Soul.—The principles of truth and righteousness—the essential elements of the kingdom of God—are implanted within all men and belong to their moral nature, as the controlling principles and law of the spiritual life. The evidence of this is the fact that the binding force of the obligations of truth and right are acknowledged and felt by all. It is this which causes an eternal prompting from the spirit within to seek their realization in the outward life.

The blind impulses of the animal nature and sensuous life, ever tempt man to disregard these inner promptings of the spiritual nature, which thus graciously links him with the divine, and makes inspiration, illumination and divine realization possible to him. If he yield to these temptations against the protest of the Spirit, he will be led into the various excesses and perversions which have to so great an extent characterized the life of man. He thus repeats the tragedy of "the fall," so fitly symbolized in the story of Eden. But if he resolutely turn and follow the leading of the Spirit and obey its law, he will receive immediate power from the Divine to overcome the temptation and bring his life to the highest degree of perfection in all its relations with the inner and the outer world. In this he will follow the example of the Christ as a loyal child of God, and rise to fellowship with him in the realization of the perfect life.

This opportunity comes to all, and each must individually meet and overcome temptation and rise above its power in the strength of the Divine, through the spirit of allegiance to and dependence upon the inspiration and help of the Father. There is no other door of entrance, or pathway to victory and attainment of the divine and perfect life. It is the strait gate and the narrow way that leadeth unto life, found by so few. The transformation of "the natural man" into the "spiritual man," lifting him from the plane of the sensuous life and its limitations to the higher level of the spiritual life in the realization of its freedom and power, constitutes regeneration.

Representative Types.—Adam and Christ are representative characters; and whether historic verities or symbolic, represent the certain possibilities of man. Adam represents the natural man subject to the temptations of the sensuous life. In Eden—symbolic of innocence—he represents the childhood of all men. Driven out of Eden—yielding to temptation and fall-

ing from innocence—he represents all who have thus
yielded and fallen into sin, and who has not? "The
voice of the Lord God walking in the garden," point-
ing out the right and warning against the wrong, is
the intuition and prompting of the Spirit, which, in the
period of innocence, is clearly heard by all. "In the
cool of the day," also, when the heat of desire and the
fire of passion have spent their force in forbidden indulgence, "the voice of the Lord God" is heard in the
accusing conscience, saying, "Adam, where art thou?"

The animal nature knowing no law but indulgence,
when lifted to the plane of human life and associated
with the higher human powers as it is in man, becomes
"more subtle than any beast of the field which the
Lord God had made." This is the tempter, symbolized by "the serpent," which disputes and antagonizes
the voice and law of the Spirit. Pleasure is the end
and aim of the sensuous life and the highest reach of
the animal nature, and to the animal organism, unrestrained indulgence is legitimate. The human organism, however, was made for the higher and nobler
activities of a rational and moral being, whose law is
duty, not pleasure, *per se;* while the animal nature
was given to serve not rule the body. In the performance of duty, and the victory over temptation and the
selfish spirit of indulgence, through allegiance to the
law of righteousness, man rises to the divinest joy and
beatitude of his being, because it lifts him into oneness
and fellowship with the Divine.

The Christ, on the other hand, represents the spiritual man who through loyalty to the leading of the

Spirit from the first, and by the power of its inspiration held his innocence and unity with the Father, until the work of regeneration and final victory was complete, and he attained the perfect life of permanent illumination and spiritual supremacy above the sphere of temptation and the possibility of sin and disease.

Possible to All.—What is thus represented in the story of Christ, represents the possibility of all through the power of an immediate inspiration and strength from the Father, which is promised to and secured by all, through faith in, and allegiance to the leading of His Spirit in the life. The parable of the prodigal son, given by the Christ, represents again these two types of life. To the eldest, who remained with the father from the first and never violated one of his commands, he said: "Son, thou art ever with me and all that is mine is thine." The prodigal took the gifts which that father had divided unto him, turned from the father's government and spent his substance in self-indulgence and riotous living, until dead and lost to the father. When, however, he had spent all, "he began to be in want," and found that "no man gave unto him." "But when he came to himself," and remembered the father in his goodness and providence, and "arose and came to his father" in penitence, faith, and the spirit of true allegiance, he received the immediate welcome and forgiveness of the father, who "said to his servants, bring forth quickly the best robe, and put it on him; and put a ring on his hand, and shoes on his feet; and bring the fatted calf, and kill it, and let us eat, and be merry; for this my son was dead, and is alive again; he was lost and is found." He was restored at once to full communion and fellowship with the royal household, through no other expiation or atonement than a return through repentance and faith and the spirit of restitution, love, and loyalty to the father. Here, too, is symbolized the law and conditions of the forgiveness and restoration of every prodigal and sinner. These are the legitimate and necessary outcome and results of the being and moral government of God as the immediate Father of mankind.

And again, if God, as supreme Spirit, intelligence and power, is the animating life of nature, then His immediate Fatherhood of men, and all that this relation involves, is the legitimate and logical necessity; since man is the ultimate product of the life in nature, and thus the immediate offspring of God who is that life. As the immediate offspring of God, he necessarily partakes of and holds potentially within his being the essential nature and attributes of the Father. This again implies and involves all that inspired teaching has clearly suggested and positively affirmed. Man as a spiritual being and child of God, cannot be true and loyal to the Father's nature within him, only as he comes under the immediate inspiration and uplifting power of the Father's Spirit. Nor is it possible for the unbroken continuance of this, without the unfolding of all the attributes of the Father's nature, until they become embodied in the victorious, illuminated, and perfect life of His child.

Man's Necessity, God's Opportunity.—Enough has been said to show the supreme importance to all who

have consciously violated the law of purity and truth,
of seeking reconciliation at once, and unity with God
in the Spirit—the true centre of motive and inspiration
—that they may henceforth walk with Him and He
with them in the inspiration and guidance of His wisdom and goodness in all the relations of life. Man at
his best needs this immediate inspiration and guidance
of the Father's wisdom, as surely as childhood needs
the better understanding and guidance of earthly
parents. For while man as a moral being has the implanted sense of right and wrong, the actual knowledge of what is right or wrong, as with truth and
error, is of necessity a matter of education. Shall he,
then, in this higher education be left wholly to the
blind impulses of the animal nature and the results of
his experience from their indulgence? Or shall he
obey the inner promptings of the Spirit to seek the
immediate help and guidance of Him who sees the end
from the beginning, and from whom he derived his
sense of right and the inner prompting to do it? Shall
not the righteous One whose omniscient wisdom only
knows the absolute right, give all needed guidance
and help to the children of His love and providence?
"Shall not the judge of all the earth do right?" He
certainly will, but this does not absolve man from the
necessity of personal co-operation, nor of desiring and
seeking the needed revelation and help.

The innate demand of the soul for truth and right,
is itself the divine promise of its completest satisfaction, when man in the exercise of his moral freedom
turns to the true and direct source of his supply in

God. This divine promise of spiritual illumination and guidance, found faithful and assuring utterance in the inspired words of the Hebrew Psalmist: "I will instruct thee and teach thee in the way which thou shalt go: I will guide thee with mine eye." Is not this the promise of direct guidance by the eye of omniscience? And again, in the inspiration of Isaiah: "And, therefore will the Lord wait that he may be gracious unto you; and therefore will he be exalted, that he may have mercy upon you; for the Lord is a God of judgment: blessed are all they that wait for him. . . . He will be very gracious unto thee at the voice of thy cry; when he shall hear it, he will answer thee. . . . And thine ears shall hear a word behind thee, saying, this is the way, walk ye in it, when ye turn to the right hand and when ye turn to the left."

The divine promise and the supply are perfect, waiting only the true mental and moral attitude of man for him to enter into the divinest realization in personal experience. Hence divine inspiration and guidance should be, and in the nature of things must be, the first step in the higher education and realization of man as a moral and spiritual being under a divine government.

Reason, Philosophy, Revelation.—Men have unduly exalted reason and philosophy, and in their earnest protest and reaction against superstition, priestly assumption, and ecclesiastical despotism, have too often forgotten the grandeur of the moral law, and the revelation of God, which it makes possible to man. In so doing, they lose sight also of their own possible attainment in truth and righteousness, or perfection of being under such revelation and guidance.

Revelation Open Equally to All.—Let not the moral law and divine revelation here pleaded for, be confounded with any special Bible of the world. Our plea is for the law of God written in the soul of every man; and for the immediate revelation of God which this makes possible to each soul through the gateway of the spirit which is in man, and which connects all men with God. "There is a spirit in man, and the inspiration of the Almighty giveth them understanding." "In God we live, move, and have our being." He is the inmost life and potency of all things and beings, as well as the overruling intelligence and providence. Hence all things and beings exist and subsist of necessity in, from, and by Him. God is therefore as universal in His presence, power and manifestation as nature; and as vitally active in the simplest processes of the physical world, as in the most exalted activities of the moral and spiritual realms.

> "As full and perfect in vile man that mourns,
> As in the rapt seraph that adores and burns."

The revelation of God cannot be limited to any place, book, man, or class of men, but must of necessity be as universal as His presence and influence in the world, and specifically adapted to the actual necessities of each individual portion of His creation, from the worm to man, and from man to seraph. Man is distinguished from the rest of creation by a self-conscious personality, with a moral sense of his relation to a

2

divine order and government; and it is, therefore, the privilege and the duty of each soul to seek and attain immediate communion with the Father through His own spirit. The doctrine of the necessity of some intermediary between the individual soul and God, is a pagan superstition, based upon ignorance of God's Fatherhood.

The revelation of God to man, and to each soul is simply a matter of man's own individual recognition, attention, desire and faith. Seers and prophets have become such by this means alone. Some of these having come to the open vision or clear hearing of the "Word of God," have faithfully recorded their experience and delivered the message of the Spirit which may have been opened to them for a particular people or for the world; but this can be neither a revelation nor an authority to another until its truth is recognized by his own soul. This, it will be seen, is the final authority of the truth itself, and to the individual that perceives it, is vested in his own recognition of it, not in the medium through which it was presented, or brought to his attention. The experiences and revelations of others may awaken our attention and interest, and lead us to listen, but the truth that we perceive in their revelations and experiences, is the response of our own souls, which is the revelation of God within us of so much of the truth as we are thus able to receive. Hence, the object of all inspired appeals from one soul to another, is to awaken and call forth the revealing power of God, or the spirit of truth in every individual. But if we stop in the recognition of another's inspiration, and it does not bring a corresponding revelation in our own souls, its mission to us is defeated.

The stopping in the letter of the Bibles of the world, —in which the exalted experiences and words of inspired wisdom of the world's seers and prophets have been preserved—has tended to blunt the spiritual impressibility and hinder rather than help the development of inspirational power in those who thus accept them in the sense of an external and arbitrary authority, for which they were never intended. The authority is not in the book, though it contains never so much of truth in external statement, but in the unwritten word of God in the soul that recognizes and receives it. God revealed in the soul will recognize and respond to the word and manifestation of God wherever found. There can, therefore, be no external oracle of divine authority for man. He must know the word of God in his own soul, or it has no divine authority for him. The object, we repeat, of all divinely inspired writing and appeal is to help men to this.

The principle here disclosed exposes the absurdity of any individual, or class of individuals, claiming to be oracles of divine revelation and authority for others, or of being the exclusive custodian of God's truth for the world. "God is no respecter of persons." His presence penetrates, and His Spirit and providence embrace all alike. No power or personality can stand between the individual soul and God. Hence no man nor body of men can become vested with divine authority to coerce the soul of any man into the accept-

ance of that which the word of God in His own spirit
does not make true or right to him. God Himself,
does not coerce the will of one of His children. Having made that will eternally free, He does not confer
upon another a power He Himself will not exercise.

Revelation—Spiritual and Personal.—All experience tends to bring us face to face with the supreme
fact that the knowledge of God is not acquired through
the study of external nature, nor through books, nor
from any external source whatever; but that it is
wholly a matter of inward personal revelation and experience. The inspired words and experience of others
may be used as hints and helps toward our own attainment, but can never be made a substitute for personal experience. When we accept them as authority
in an external and arbitrary sense, and do not enter
into their spirit and power through a corresponding
inward experience, which makes them true to us, they
become a hindrance and a curse instead of a help and
blessing. Man can find God only through the gateway of the spirit in his own soul. In the ordinary
conditions of the sensuous life, however, men need to
be awakened to the recognition of their higher possibilities. Their attention must be so aroused and concentrated in desire and faith—true prayer—that they
will not turn from the seeking until the spiritual impressibility is sufficiently awakened and established to
bring the needed revelation and experience. Divine
inspiration and permanent illumination are secured in
no other way. In spontaneous trances, and in the
ecstatic stage of the magnetic trance, this exalted ex-

perience is sometimes temporarily realized, because mental action in all other directions is for the time fully suspended, and the attention abnormally aroused and concentrated on this experience. On awakening from the trance, in such cases, and the attention becoming again absorbed in the things of the sensuous life, this inner experience is generally lost to memory.

When, however, as is sometimes the case, a clear memory of the experience is brought over to the outward life, the divine impressiveness of that holy season rarely loses its influence on the entire subsequent life of the individual. The spiritual illumination and heavenly communion thus temporarily enjoyed under abnormal conditions, may become practically a normal and permanent experience, through the persistent cultivation of spiritual impressibility and inspirational power under the proper conditions. He who would attain full and permanent illumination, however, must make it the supreme object of life. The western seeker after God, may learn a lesson in this respect from the Hindoo devotee, whom he too often despises. "The kingdom of heaven is like unto a merchantman, seeking goodly pearls: who, when he had found one pearl of great price, went and sold all that he had, and bought it." The absorbing attractions of the sensuous life to the natural man, must be absolutely subordinated to the higher demands of the spiritual nature. The activities of the mind and the pursuits of life must be conducted under the motives and inspirations of the spiritual life, if we would enjoy the blessing of divine communion and heavenly fellowship.

Man a Co-worker with God.—The moral freedom with which man is endowed, and the personal responsibility which this involves, render the seeking of divine inspiration and realization not only a necessity, but a wise and beneficent provision; since through it he becomes a co-worker with God, and a participant in the working out of his own destiny. The relation also, which binds man to man in the indissoluble ties of a common origin, brotherhood and possible destiny, renders it incumbent upon all who have reached the higher experience to do what they may to help others to its realization. In this view, the revelation of God to man depends as much upon the attitude of man toward God as upon God's attitude and relation to him. Hence were this impressibility to divine influence universally cultivated, the direct inshining of the divine wisdom and goodness, the immediate revelation, guidance and help of the All-Father, would become the supreme reality and joy of universal experience.

Objection to Divine Revelation Considered.—It may be objected, that we cannot assume the existence of a sphere of Divine intelligence and goodness with which to seek communion before it is demonstrated to us, since successful seeking confessedly demands entire faith and unreserved committal at the outset. To this we reply, that, in the nature of the case the only possible demonstration is in the revelation itself, and this must be personal to each soul. If, as we claim, the Divine Spirit is the animating and all-encompassing reality of being, there is a portion of the Divine nature focused in the inner life of every man, which not only qualifies him for receiving such revelation, but will in every case respond to the Divine touch in full personal recognition, when the proper attitude of the mind and heart is taken toward God. "Verily I say unto you, whosoever shall not receive the kingdom of God as a little child, shall in nowise enter therein."

Man need not necessarily assume the Divine existence in order to seek its demonstration in a personal revelation, but he must not assume the opposite. Let him come absolutely unbiased, in the teachable spirit of a child, ready to welcome in all humility the manifestation of the Father's Spirit to his own. Let him still the materialistic reasonings of the sensuous understanding, and enter the holy stillness of his own inner life, and calmly listen to the voice that will then surely speak to him. His own spiritual intuitions will thus assert themselves, and he will gladly welcome the revelations from the heavenly and divine, that will certainly come to him. The issues involved are too momentous to be ignored or slightingly passed by. There is no one yet too learned in the things of the outward world, to refuse to sit at the feet of the humblest seer of spiritual realities and listen to the testimony of his experience. His philosophy may be unsatisfactory, but his experience will not fail to stir a responsive chord. As a mere working hypothesis, however, it is certainly as easy and consistent to assume the existence of a Divine being and providence behind and over the processes of the world, and with this, the moral and spiritual nature of man and the possibility of divine communion and revelation, as to assume the contrary. It is quite as strong and reasonable an *a priori* position. Every hypothesis must be judged by the results of its working. The one that meets and explains the most completely all the recognized facts of observation and experience is nearest the truth.

Important Facts Ignored.—There is one class of the facts of experience bearing especially upon the question of Divine existence and revelation, that are either entirely ignored by both materialists and pantheists, or if recognized, are regarded as possible delusions and not of sufficient importance to constitute a factor of the problem. We refer to the exceptional experiences of the seers and prophets of the Spirit who have testified from personal experience to the revelation of God in their souls, and whose exalted and consecrated lives under its inspiration have been the living witness of the truth of their testimony which, in many cases, received the seal of martyrdom. As questions of fact these experiences cannot be disposed of by ignoring them. The more they are studied, the more urgently do they appeal to and awaken our better nature, and the more important grows their demand upon our attention. The study of man from the standpoint of his moral nature necessitates, as we have seen, the recognition of a spiritual constitution which relates him to a spiritual kingdom and a Divine government. This is the only consistent deduction from the supreme facts of human experience, and furnishes the only key to the understanding of those higher exceptional experiences of inspired souls, and of their instruction to us concerning the way of reaching a corresponding experience. The earnest but fruitless effort of both the materialist and pantheist to find the secret of life without Divine revelation or the recognition of God, but serves the purpose of emphasizing the need of such revelation, since this is the only absolute demonstration of His Being, possible to man.

Divine Revelation the Only Basis of True Philosophy.—Revelation from God is the only possible satisfaction to a rational and moral being, since it is the only source of any true knowledge or understanding of His will and purpose in creation, and so the only basis of a true philosophy of nature and life. Every attempt to account for the phenomena of life and intelligence without the recognition of an original self-existent being as the giver of life and intelligence, has proved an utter failure. It may well be asked, How can life proceed from that which has not life? or intelligence from non-intelligence? or the feeling of moral obligation under a binding sense of right and wrong, where there is no moral law or eternal and unchanging principle of right in the constitution of things? And how could a principle of moral righteousness exist in the nature of things independent of the moral order of a spiritual kingdom and divine government, to which man as a moral and spiritual being belongs?

Theism a Logical Necessity.—Life, intelligence, and moral sense are not inherent attributes of matter; if they were, man could by some possible arrangement and correlation of material elements bring forth their manifestation. Man can analyze and determine the constituent elements and proportions of protoplasm, the simplest form in which life is manifest; but when he has rearranged these elements in the most accurate proportions and relations, his failure to reproduce the life, reveals his utter impotency in this direction. He cannot, indeed, by any chemical test even determine the difference between living or dead protoplasm. The beginning and manifestations of life are dependent upon conditions beyond the power of man to provide, invent or determine. Sensation, intelligence and moral quality proceed only from life, and as none of these, including life, are inherent attributes of matter, they necessarily belong to that which is not matter. And since these qualities are manifest only under organic conditions in and through matter, yet are not attributes of matter, they necessarily belong to that which is the organizing power over matter, and thus transcends it. To this invisible omnipresent something which is not matter, and which transcends matter, yet is manifested in and through matter—as life, sensation, intelligence, and moral quality—we can give no better name than spirit.

Accepting spirit, then, as the organizing power in nature, and the omnipresent source of life, intelligence and moral quality, we have all that is essential to the recognition of that which men have called God, and can say with Jesus that "God is Spirit." Man is the product of the operations of this life of Spirit in nature, and being the effect he will never be able to fully analyze and comprehend the cause and conditions which produced him. As a rational and moral being, however, he is the child of intelligence and goodness, and partakes of the nature of his source. He is capable, therefore, of being inspired and enlightened from and communing with his divine parentage, through his inner life which unites him vitally and organically with God. Hence, only through revelation can man know God, and the fulness of this knowledge will be determined by the measure of his personal realization of God in his own life and experience. Theism in its broadest conception, as the basis of a philosophy of nature, life and human experience, is the only hypothesis that adequately meets the requirements of all the facts involved. Both materialism and pantheism, in denying or ignoring the existence of an overruling intelligence and Divine government, are obliged to ignore the moral law and order, and the moral nature of man which relates him to that order, and thus to frame a philosophy that does not embrace all the facts of human experience, nor meet the necessities of man.

Mistake of Theologians.—The moral and spiritual nature of man which relate him to a moral order and Divine government, makes, as we have seen, Divine revelation both a universal necessity and possibility. Hence, as this divine relation is personal to each soul, the revelation itself may and must be immediate and personal to each and all. The theologians who claim that the Bible is the only direct and authoritative revelation of God and of His will possible to man, are nearly as far astray as the agnostics themselves. They really stand almost if not quite as much in the way of each man's seeking the necessary personal rev-

elation for himself, since they practically and in the
most dogmatic spirit deny its possibility. The power
of dogmatism over the mass of men is almost supreme,
whether wielded on the side of truth or error.

Experience the True Test.—If God has been revealed to one human soul, He may and ought to be
revealed to each and every other soul. Indeed, as
already shown, there can be no revelation of God, but
that which is personal and experimental. Who can
know practically anything of the nature of a mother's
love until it becomes a personal experience? So of all
spiritual realities. The statement of a truth, however
correct and authoritative, is but testimony, not in itself revelation. To the individual nothing is revealed
that is not made known to him. Nothing can be absolutely known until realized in personal experience, hence
true revelation is experimental knowledge. Theoretical
and inferential evidence and acceptance of the truth of
anything is not sufficient for perfect knowledge; it must
be experimental to be practical. The realization of God
in personal experience, is, therefore, the only real knowledge or revelation of Him possible to man. The firmest
intellectual conviction of the truth of another's experience is belief, not personal knowledge of its truth, for
where knowledge begins belief ends.

However genuine may have been the experiences
recorded of Moses and Elijah, or of Paul and Jesus,
those experiences can be of no practical service to the
world unless they lead others to seek and attain the
realization of a corresponding experience. Because
this has not been done by their followers—owing to

the blind teaching of theology that these exceptional experiences and inspirations of the Bible characters were to be accepted as substitutes and authority for others—scepticism concerning the reality and possibility of these things prevails in the world to-day. The false teaching and the spiritual impotency of the church itself, is largely responsible for the prevailing agnosticism of our age.

The Nature of True Faith.—Belief is not necessarily faith, as this word is used in the New Testament, and especially emphasized by the Master. Belief may be only blind credulity based upon traditional prejudice and wholly fictitious and arbitrary authority; this is superstition. Such belief is more of a hindrance than a help to the attainment of a personal knowledge or demonstration of the truth, because it leads to contentment in the mere belief. To all such the question of Christ to Pilate is especially applicable and significant. "Sayest thou this of thyself, or did another tell it thee?" And, again to the Jews, "Why judge ye not of yourselves what is right?" True faith is that inward assurance based upon an intuitive recognition of a truth which prompts the believer to seek its realization in personal experience. It was such faith to which the Master referred when he said, "All things are possible to him that believeth."

The soul animated by such a faith has the inward assurance that what has been experienced or attained by one, may, under proper conditions be essentially reproduced by others. Once believing in the reality of another's experience however exalted, he will not

rest content until what has thus been suggested, or
its equivalent, becomes also a personal experience.
The Bible records thus accepted, may and will be made
the mightiest stimulus toward the uplifting, advancement and final emancipation of the world in the transfiguration of man universal.

The Biblical Appeal.—The object of the appeal of
all Bible inspirations is to arouse the spiritual life in
man, and lead him to seek Divine inspiration and guidance. The Christ, who stands at the head of all the
sons of God who have found the Father and rejoiced
in the light and blessedness of personal communion
with and immediate revelation from Him, asked no
one to rest in the assurance he gave, of the existence,
Fatherhood, love and providence of God, but to make
the demonstration of their truth in personal experience the supreme end and aim of their being. "My
doctrine is not mine, but his that sent me; if any man
willeth to do his will, he shall know of the doctrine
whether it be of God or whether I speak of myself."
He gave his followers clearly to understand that the
kingdom of God he preached was not a set of doctrines to be accepted as a system of truth by the intellect, but a new and higher life to be attained in personal experience. It was his startling and abrupt
announcement of this truth to Nicodemus—that the
kingdom of God could not be revealed save as it was
realized in the personal life—that shattered the rabbi's
traditional ideal of the kingdom, and led him to look
within for that which can never be found or derived
from without.

The Master's Supreme Legacy.—Among the last words of the Master to his immediate disciples, after having done all in his power during the three years of his personal ministry to awaken within them some adequate conception of the kingdom of God, and the higher life of the Spirit it opened to them, and to enkindle a desire for it, he said, " I have yet many things to say unto you, but ye cannot bear them now. Howbeit when he, the spirit of truth, is come, he will guide you into all truth, . . . and will show you things to come." "The Comforter, which is the Holy Spirit, whom the Father will send in my name," "whom I will send unto you from the Father, even the Spirit of truth, which proceedeth from the Father, he shall teach you all things and bring all things to your remembrance, whatsoever I have said unto you." " He shall testify of me: for he shall receive of mine, and shall show it unto you. All things that the Father hath are mine: therefore said I he shall take of mine, and shall shew it unto you." As the Father held no secret from the Son who dwelt and walked in such perfect unity with Him, neither would He from any other of His children under like conditions. The Father gave "not the Spirit by measure unto him;" because he gave himself in unreserved and holy consecration unto the Father. The Christ clearly affirms that the same revealing "Spirit of truth which proceedeth from the Father," would, on the same conditions, inspire and illuminate them as it had him. And this promise was to all his faithful followers, no exceptions being given. " I am the light of the world [example for the world]; he that followeth me shall not walk in darkness, but shall have the light of life." Thus in the last hours of his earthly teaching, as the richest legacy he could leave his followers, he points them to the immediate inspiration and guidance of the Divine Spirit in their own souls—for which his external teaching had prepared them—as the supreme and only source of revelation, the illumination of true wisdom, the true Theo-Sophia.

The Kingdom of God Within.—Nature is external, but God is internal to man and to Nature. Only through the internal of his own being, therefore, can man enter into the kingdom of God and find communion and fellowship with the Divine. This once fully attained he may then study and interpret Nature and all the relations of life and experience in the inner light of the Divine omniscience. He will thus and thus only attain to the true understanding of God, and the final mastery of Nature and life, over which as the child of God, he is destined to achieve and hold dominion. The universe is but the birthplace, nursery, schoolroom, playground, and workshop of the human soul, as the child of the Eternal, and therefore in the true order of things is placed under his feet, to be mastered and ruled over by him as he enters into his kingdom or unfolds in the realization of his true being as the child of the Divine love, wisdom and providence. "For there is nothing covered, that shall not be revealed; and hid, that shall not be known."

Men Led, not Driven to Listen to Truth.—The ignorant and the vicious may very properly be physically restrained to prevent their harming themselves and others, until through appropriate means their better nature is aroused and they can be persuaded, not forced, to seek and listen to the voice of God in their own souls. This act performed in the spirit of brotherly kindness, would be but the carrying out of the law of brotherhood to the salvation of both the social order and the individual member. This is the only principle upon which prison discipline should be founded and conducted. On this principle, every penal institution and reformatory would be turned, as they should, into hospitals and schools for the spiritual healing, moral education and civil and industrial training of their inmates.

The idea of retaliation or punishment in any form should be banished forever from the thought of man. It is a relic of barbarism and savagery. All reform as well as all divine revelation must come to the soul of man through the spirit which is in him, connecting his life with the Divine. When this tremendous fact is once fully realized in all its divine significance, men recognizing the secret spring of the Father's Spirit in the life of the most abandoned and hardened of His children, will appeal with such boldness, directness and certainty from the spirit of a brother to the heart of a brother, and from the love of the Father to the heart of His child, that the divine from within will respond, the fountains of the great deep will be unsealed, and the cleansing and healing waters of the Spirit will break forth in power to cleanse and restore the wanderer.

3

The Key to Missionary Success.—The law and principle thus applied to the reform of the vicious and criminal classes, applies with equal if not greater force to all missionary work for the spiritual awakening and regeneration of men in all ranks, civilized and uncivilized, who have not yet been brought to a realization of their relation to God and their real duties and privileges under this relation. In this work no appeal to arbitrary authority of church, creed or book is admissible. The appeal must be made directly to the authority and word of God in each soul. The Christ, our great exemplar, appealed only to this. This only will arouse the true sense of personal responsibility and awaken an unquestioning response in the soul. The recognition of the actual brotherhood, equality and privilege of all men before God is an absolute necessity. All men, therefore, should be appealed to and persuaded as the children of God and brethren of Christ and of each other, to turn at once and seek the immediate revelation of the will of the Father and His help each in his own soul. The moral sense and the Spirit of God in the souls of all His children will respond to the appeal from the heart of those who are themselves alive in the Spirit and love of the Father. Spirit responds to spirit, and hearts to genuine sympathy.

Right and Wrong Use of Scripture.—The lives of inspired men and the words of inspired wisdom recorded in all true Scripture should be pointed to for example, instruction and encouragement in the way of life, not as arbitrary authority. "Every scripture inspired of God," said Paul, " is also profitable for teaching, for reproof, for correction, for instruction which is in righteousness: that the man of God may be complete, furnished completely unto every good work." Used in this way, the Bibles of the world instead of enslaving the souls of men and retarding their real spiritual awakening and growth as they have been made to do in the past, will become of priceless value in the spiritual education and advancement of the race. Being written in and from the Spirit, they appeal to and tend to quicken and call forth the spiritual life in men.

The love of truth and righteousness thus enkindled, the spiritual illumination and power to perceive and do the right, are evidences of the soul's activities under the immediate inspiration and authority of the Father's Spirit. But when a book containing a record of inspired words and experiences is presented to the soul as an external standard of arbitrary authority to which an unquestioning submission is demanded, whether the truth it contains is perceived or not, it becomes an instrument of a most blighting despotism, and a curse to both priest and people. When the letter of a book is assumed to be the word of God, an external oracle of divine authority over the reason, intuition and conscience of the soul, instead of appealing to these as the final authority of the truth of the message, it becomes an instrument of spiritual death instead of spiritual life for which it was given. Both the priest who ministers at the altar of religion, and the people who call for spiritual instruction at his hands, are thus enslaved and blinded by the letter, and lose the spirit which enlightens and saves. "For the letter killeth, but the spirit giveth life." "And if the blind lead the blind, shall they not both fall into the ditch?"

Once deny the inward voice of the living and omnipresent God in the soul of every man, and assume, believe and teach that His last and only spoken word to men is confined to a book, and you have effectually shut off access to God even through the book. If there is nothing of kindred nature in the living soul to recognize and respond to the inspiration in and behind the message of the book, then there is nothing in the book for that soul. But if the message of the book be inspired of God, and there is that in the soul which recognizes, responds to and unites with the spirit and inspiration of the message, it can be nothing less than the inspiration of the same living God in the soul that responds. Only on the recognition of this truth can the Bibles of the world be made the instruments of spiritual education and advancement. Deny the power of a present living inspiration to men, the power of the unwritten and unutterable word of God in every soul, to meet, interpret and properly use the true word that has been written or spoken, and assume the absolute supremacy and arbitrary authority of the written word over the living soul, confining the right of interpretation to a chosen few, and you have assumed the prerogative that belongs to God alone. You have effectually shut the door of the kingdom to priest and people alike.

This is precisely what the Christian Church has done, Catholic, Greek and Protestant. They have locked the door and held the key, neither entering themselves nor allowing those to enter who would. Whenever any in the church have found the key and entered in to drink of the living waters of the Spirit, they have met only with the anathema and ostracism of the church itself. The fiercest persecutions, the most cruel martyrdoms, and the fiendish tortures of the Inquisition itself, have been the legitimate fruits of this false assumption and the ecclesiastical despotism it involves and necessitates.

No Arbitrary Authority from God.—No divinely inspired soul has ever yet demanded the arbitrary acceptance of his word of testimony and appeal. Whenever such a demand is made, its real source in the human and earthly is at once revealed. "Where the Spirit of the Lord is there is liberty." The claim for any book or prophet, as the infallible and only inspired oracle and authoritative Word of God to man, is fictitious, wicked and absurd. The Word of God comes to emancipate, not to enslave. The spiritual experience of one soul, even of the Christ, is possible in its essential features unto all. So taught the Christ. "Verily, verily, I say unto you, he that believeth on me the works that I do shall he do also; and greater than these shall he do; because I go unto the Father."

When this truth of a present living inspiration, possible to all men, is universally recognized, and the divine experience and testimony of illuminated souls are brought to the attention of all men under this recognition, the prophetic words of an ancient inspiration, with which this paper began, will become literally fulfilled. "After those days, saith the Lord, I will put my law in their inward parts, and write it in their hearts and will be their God, and they shall be my people. And they shall teach no more every man his neighbor, and every man his brother, saying, Know the Lord: for they shall all know me, from the least of them unto the greatest of them, saith the Lord: for I will forgive their iniquity, and I will remember their sin no more."

PART II.

CHRISTIAN THEOSOPHY DEFINED AND ILLUS-
TRATED, AS DISTINGUISHED FROM THE THE-
OSOPHY AND OCCULTISM OF ANTIQUITY AND
THE FAR EAST.

And this is life eternal, that they might know thee, the only true God, and Jesus Christ, whom thou hast sent.

O righteous Father, the world hath not known thee: but I have known thee, and these have known that thou hast sent me. And I have declared unto them thy name, and will declare it; that the love wherewith thou hast loved me may be in them and I in them. (*John*, xvii. 3, 4, 25, 26.)

No man hath seen God at any time; the only-begotten Son, which is in the bosom of the Father, he hath declared him. (*John*, i. 18.)

God, who at sundry times and in divers manners spake in time past unto the fathers by the prophets, hath in these last days spoken unto us by a Son. (*Heb.* i. 1, 2.)

WHAT IS THEOSOPHY?

Theo-Sophia.—The term Theosophy, from two Greek words, *theos* "god," and *sophas* "wise," signifies God-knowledge, or wise in the things of God—Divine wisdom. As defined by Webster, it is "A direct, as distinguished from a revealed, knowledge of God, supposed to be attained by extraordinary illumination, especially a direct insight into the processes of the divine mind, and the interior relations of the divine nature." "A theosophist," says Vaughan, "is one who gives you a theory of God or of the works of God, which has not revelation, but inspiration of his own for its basis." "In this view," says another, "every great thinker and philosopher, especially every founder of a new religion, school of philosophy, or sect, is necessarily a theosophist."

The Ideal of Philosophy.—This higher wisdom and mastery has been essentially the ideal of attainment and effort held by the sages and philosophers of the race from time immemorial. Awakened minds in all ages have sought to penetrate the arcana of Nature and wrest from her, if possible, the secret of life and destiny. They have sought a knowledge of her occult forces and secret processes, to gain if might be, a mastery of the world and of the conditions of life and immortality.

To this end mystics in all times have endeavored to

quicken and exalt the soul's powers of perception and will, by the suppression of the fleshly activities, and the subordination of the body to mental development and supremacy. This has led, especially in the East, to the most severe and extreme austerities of asceticism, self-denial and mortification of the flesh, through which the desired mental supremacy and illumination were supposed to be reached.

Through such effort it is believed that the esoteric wisdom, adeptship and occult science claimed for the ancient Magi, were attained. A corresponding claim for a secret "Brotherhood of Mahatmas" in the East, as still holding the treasured wisdom and occult science of the past, is now being seriously presented to our western world, in the name of Oriental Theosophy.

The hidden knowledge and occult power believed to have been thus attained by the few, has been and still is held as too great and sacred for the common mind, and is thus kept by the Adepts as the treasured wisdom of the ages, to be yielded up only to such as through initiation and discipline become prepared to receive it.

Origin of Priesthoods.—Out of this supposed necessity of initiation and preparatory discipline, have sprung the sacred temples of the past with their secret rites, ceremonies and initiatory degrees, with corresponding orders of initiates, from the neophyte to the Adept or Hierophant. From the initiates have sprung also the various orders of priests and teachers to stand between the masters and the common people as interpreters of the sacred mysteries.

This system of interpretation and the symbolic and figurative language in which it has ever been given, instead of enlightening the common mind, has but tended to mystify and bring it in subjection to priestly authority and domination. This mystification and subjection of the common people to arbitrary author- ity has ever proved the fruitful source of the most de- grading forms of mental slavery, ignorance and super- stition.

Thus on the results of what was at first claimed to be original and independent inquiry and research, have been based the most stupendous monopolies of knowl- edge and the most despotic autocracies of priesthood. All this, also, in the name of religion; for on this basis have been established all the great religions of the world save Judaism, Christianity and Mohammedan- ism. These three differ from the others in the fact of a special claim to divine revelation as their basis and authority. All the other prominent systems of relig- ion and philosophy, are supposed to be the result of human discovery or invention independent of a divine revelation or inspiration. Hence Theosophy, as it comes to us from remote antiquity and the far East, is called the "archaic *Wisdom Religion*, the esoteric doctrine once known in every ancient country having claims to civilization." By its modern devotees it is specifically defined as, "The Wisdom-Religion taught in all ages by the sages of the world."

Fundamental Differences.—Here begins the funda- mental difference between both the claim and esoteric teaching of the Eastern Theosophy, and that which constitutes the Theosophy of the Christ. The first is based upon the loftiest attainment and apprehension of the human mind by its own unaided effort; the latter upon the highest development and activity of the human powers under divine inspiration and enlightenment. The deeper esoteric understanding of the things of God (first or governing principles) involved in each, is claimed in both cases to be the result of illumination. In the first, however, the illumination is supposed to be self-induced and self-contained; in the latter, the direct result of a divine leading and influence helping the seeker after God and opening to him the mount of vision. The knowledge and wisdom reached by the first, is, therefore, considered strictly human, the result of unaided human effort; that of the latter, as the wisdom and knowledge of God, reached by man through the help of a divine inspiration and enlightenment, crowning him with the "Gifts of the Spirit." It is undoubtedly true that "God helps those who help themselves," so that every seeker after the highest truth must receive more or less of divine help; yet when the soul starts out by ignoring both the fact or possibility of such help, it must to some extent at least shut out its blessing from the life.

The Theosophy of the Christ.—Christian Theosophy, then, is that understanding of the nature of God and of man, of life and of destiny, opened to the world in the divinely illuminated life and teaching of the Christ and his inspired Apostles. The New Testament, in which that life and teaching is recorded and preserved to us, is its standard Scripture and text-book.

The special claim for the pre-eminence of the Christian Theosophy and its superior means of attainment as well as the more perfect and immediate realization it makes possible to man, is based upon the recognition of Jesus as the Christ, who, through the divine anointing and illumination, was the first to attain the supreme realization or conscious union with God, in a single earthly experience. All other teachers confessedly fell short of this; hence his word and experience are of supreme authority to the race. Having lived the perfect life of personal mastery through spiritual supremacy in the flesh, he thus opened and demonstrated its possibility for all, as well as the law and means of its attainment to all. Being the first to achieve this result, he became thereby the Supreme Teacher, leader and helper of His brethren, "the way, the truth and the life" for his race. If this claim for the Christ and his Theosophy be just, its truth and saving power will sooner or later become the universal recognition and glad experience of mankind.

The Claim Disputed.—The advocates of the Eastern philosophy dispute the claim that Jesus reached his attainment in a single incarnation; while some deny his existence altogether. Such as accept the essential truth of the story of his life, however, claim that he was, like other Avatar's of the past, an incarnated "planetary spirit." He had, therefore, passed through many incarnations before attaining that degree of spirituality which enabled him to accomplish what he did in his last incarnation; and furthermore,

that he must have been initiated and trained in the
secret brotherhoods of the East to which he might
have had access in early life.

This explanation is necessary to the claim of Oriental
philosophy; for if Jesus attained his divine realization
in a single earthly experience, and from his altitude of
vision taught men that the same was possible to all,
then the fundamental doctrine and claim of that teaching is proven false.

The Reply.—In reply to this explanation of the
Oriental Theosophist, it need only be said that Jesus
was too royal a nature, and too loyal to truth not to
acknowledge the source of his exceptional wisdom and
power. This he did in unmistakable terms, "The
words I speak unto you, I speak not of myself; but
the Father that dwelleth in me, he doeth the work."
"Believe me that I am in the Father, and the Father
in me: or else believe me for the very works' sake.
Verily, verily, I say unto you, he that believeth on me,
the works that I do shall he do also; and greater than
these shall he do because I go unto the Father." On
one occasion, when speaking in the temple, in the presence of neighbors who evidently knew of his early
history, so that if he had actually been under the
training of eastern Adepts, the fact would have been
known to them, we read, " and the Jews marvelled, saying, How knoweth this man letters having never
learned? Jesus answered them, and said, My doctrine
is not mine, but his that sent me, If any man willeth
to do his will, he shall know of the doctrine, whether
it be of God, or whether I speak of myself."

His Doctrine Opposed to Orientalism.—This doctrine of God as the living Father of man and the indwelling of His Spirit in the souls of His children to guide and instruct them as they are obedient to His leading, which on all occasions was emphasized by Jesus, is diametrically opposed to the thought of God as entertained and taught by the modern interpreters of Oriental Theosophy, as will be seen from their own declarations, quoted in another place.

The Oriental doctrines of re-incarnation and Karma belong together; and each is a necessity to the other. But the doctrine of forgiveness and immediate restoration taught by Jesus and especially emphasized in the parable of the prodigal son, absolutely antagonizes these doctrines.

Differing Ideals Involved.—Here, then, are two opposing ideals for man involving different methods of attainment, and based upon different conceptions of God, both of which are claimed to be the teaching of illuminated minds. The illumination in the one case is believed to be attained through the immediate inspiration of omniscient wisdom, the other being reached by the unaided effort of men who deny the existence of a supreme intelligence and the possibility of such an inspiration. Which shall we accept—not necessarily as an arbitrary and final authority, but as a basis of study and effort, and the most reliable guide in the study? If both claims are allowed, we have Divine inspiration as the basis of one teaching, and human speculation as the basis of the other.

Discrimination Needed.—These differing claims are

not thus set in sharp contrast for the sake of exalting one to the detriment of the other, nor to appeal to any prejudice in favor of one or the other. Let each claim stand on its own merits. "Every tree is known by his own fruits," said the Christ. This discrimination has not always been made in Theosophical studies, and the result has been much confusion of thought in the matter. Theosophy is properly thought of as the higher wisdom, "the understanding of God." But the words God, Deity and Spirit do not mean in Oriental thought what they do in the New Testament and in Christian thought. The Eastern conception of God, Spirit, etc., is mostly pantheistic, which does not admit of the recognition of an intelligent superintending Providence, though there is recognized a universal law of harmony which maintains the general equilibrium and holds all things to a common order.

Under this ruling conception, any degree of illumination that enabled the seer to penetrate by occult vision into the secret processes of the cosmic order, and comprehensively observe and classify the working and results of the great law of evolution, would not be regarded as the result of a divine inspiration, but altogether of his own mental supremacy. On the other hand, under the Theistic conception, which admits of the possibility and the probability of immediate inspiration and revelation from the Deific mind, such illumination and occult vision would naturally be regarded as the result of divine inspiration, especially if it had been sought as such. It is simply a question, whether the Christ and his apostles and the Hebrew and other prophets, were mistaken in the nature and source of their inspiration. It is also a question, admitting the Theistic doctrine to be the correct one, whether the prejudgment of the Eastern mind against the reality of a supreme Intelligence and direct providence, and therefore the possibility of a divine inspiration, would not of itself be sufficient to shut his mind to such inspiration, even though he should attain a high degree of psychic development and occult power and insight.

A Safe Leader.—It would appear that unless the claim for the supreme realization of Jesus through divine guidance and help be proven a myth, and the teaching accredited to him a fallacy, that his leadership, doctrine and method must prove the most direct and helpful possible to us. It is for this reason that we seek to set them forth in clear, full contrast with the highest and best the world presents outside of him. If we succeed in this, we shall help the earnest seeker after the higher realization to intelligently choose that course which shall most speedily and surely secure him the divinest results in personal experience. The fundamental difference in the basic teaching of the Christian and the Oriental Theosophy, necessarily involves a corresponding difference in their ideal of attainment, as well as in their means and methods of realization.

The True Method.—Allowing the claim of Theosophy under whatever name, Oriental or Occidental, Aryan or Christian, as holding the key to the higher wisdom and attainment, it must be borne in mind that justice cannot be done its study without the recogni-

4

tion and observance of the following important considerations:

First; since the higher wisdom and understanding
can be reached only by interior and exceptional processes, Theosophy has of necessity a twofold character; it is both exoteric and esoteric. It must have an
external form of doctrine and method for neophytes, as
well as its internal understanding and higher esoteric
wisdom mastered only by initiates or Hierophants.

Second; as the esoteric wisdom can be reached only
through the opening of the higher understanding by
inward illumination and personal spiritual realization,
it cannot be exoterically taught or apprehended. The
external teaching of Theosophy is therefore of necessity
confined to the symbolic and philosophic presentation
of doctrine as oracularly given by the Masters or Illumi-
nati; and its study to the consideration and practical
application of the laws, conditions and methods to be
observed in securing the needed illumination.

Thus the exoteric teaching and study of Theosophy
is seen to be a first necessary step in opening to the
mind the higher ideal of attainment proposed, and to
awaken interest and desire, and thus prepare for and
lead to practical effort at realization.

Third; this practical effort, as experience has shown,
is best made under the guidance of such as have attained some degree of illumination and personal realization. The esoteric wisdom and personal realization
attained by inspired souls can, however, never be
directly imparted to others, even by the most fully
illuminated. They can only demonstrate its truth and

reality through personal experience, and by precept and example lead men to and help them in practical personal effort at realization.

This was all the Christ could do. He said to his immediate disciples even at the last, "I have yet many things to say unto you, but ye cannot bear them now. Howbeit, when he, the Spirit of truth, is come, he will guide you into all truth: . . . and he will show you things to come." "These things have I spoken unto you, being yet present with you. But the Comforter, which is the Holy Spirit, whom the Father will send in my name" [the Christ or anointing Spirit], he shall teach you all things, and bring all things to your remembrance [recognition and understanding], "whatsoever I have said unto you." In these words the great Teacher himself announced the necessity of turning to and depending finally and only upon the true interior and spiritual method of reaching the higher knowledge and wisdom.

Here also he defines and names the revealing or illuminating Spirit, "The Comforter which is the Holy Spirit," "Even the Spirit of truth which proceedeth from the Father." He also points out the necessity of this illuminating or revealing Spirit, to interpret and bring to the understanding of his disciples, even the significance of his own words and teaching to them. When this revealing Spirit is come to you, "He shall take of mine and shall show it unto you. All things that the Father hath are mine: therefore, said I, that he shall take of mine, and shall show it unto you." In these words he intimates, or rather

boldly asserts, that no secret of the Father was held
from his illuminated soul, yet such could not be exoterically taught, or directly imparted by him to
them. He could only lead them to and prepare them
for the immediate inward revelation from the Father,
as he himself had received it.

The Keys of the Kingdom.—In this specific instruction the Lord Christ gave to His immediate disciples,
and to all that should follow, the keys of the kingdom
which He had promised them, and for which his previous teaching had prepared them. In this also is
shown the great truth so stoutly emphasized by
George Fox, the modern apostle of the "inward light,"
that "no man can understand inspired Scripture only
as he is in the same spirit from which they were
given."

The fatal mistake of Christian theology has been in
attempting to formulate and teach the esoteric wisdom or things of the Spirit, to the external understanding by external methods. The historic church from
apostolic times thus stopped in the exoteric or external, and became entangled in "the letter which killeth," and so failed to reach "the Spirit" which "giveth
life." "Can the blind lead the blind? shall they not
both fall into the ditch?" These significant words of
the Master have found abundant illustration and fulfillment in the church that bears his name, especially
in the blinding curse of its ecclesiastical despotism,
which demands, in the name of God's anointed, the
blind acceptance of speculative opinions on purely external and arbitrary authority.

Theologians have forgotten that "if any man have not the Spirit of Christ, he is none of his." He who has the "Spirit of Christ" will dwell and walk in such unity with the Father, that he will receive immediate inspiration, and in due time permanent illumination from his Spirit. The Christ Spirit is the anointing and illuminating Spirit of the Father's love and wisdom which the great Teacher promised should be realized in the experience of all his faithful followers. Whoever receives and comes to possess that Spirit, as did the Master, shall be as the Master in realization, insight and mastery. "The disciple is not above his master: but every one that is perfect shall be as his master," were the words of the Christ.

No Arbitrary Authority.—Neither the Christ nor Apostolic inspiration were to be accepted as the final revelation and authority to others; nor their realization and experience as a substitute for personal experience in others, as theology has taught, but rather as examples and encouragement for all, and a divine call unto each and all to follow their example. "He that followeth me," said the Master, "shall not walk in darkness, but shall have the light of life." "He that believeth on me, the works that I do shall he do also."

Until this discrimination between the external and internal, or the sensuous and spiritual understanding, the letter and the spirit, is kept in mind and observed, and the necessity of spiritual illumination and personal realization to the higher understanding are recognized and sought for, no real advance can be made in the study and practice of Theosophy, whether

Oriental or Occidental. This is the key to all genuine Apostolic insight and experience, whether Christian or Aryan. "The natural man receiveth not the things of the Spirit of God: for they are foolishness unto him; neither can he know them because they are spiritually discerned."

The Spiritual Understanding.—Spiritual discernment and esoteric wisdom are secured or acquired only by the awakening and coming forth of the spiritual nature—latent in all—through the process of what in the New Testament is called "regeneration," under the immediate influence of the Divine Spirit. This emancipates the soul from the bondage of flesh and sense, and the limitations of the sense perception and understanding, by opening the intuitions and inspirations of the spiritual nature, and lifting the whole man through transformation into the freedom and power of the spiritual life.

Other Claims to Revelation.— Reference has been made to Judaism and Mohammedanism also as claiming a Divine Revelation for the basis of their religion. Allowing all that they involve, neither of these claims necessarily implies, as many suppose, a final and all-inclusive revelation. In no case has this ever been claimed by a single genuine seer or prophet for his own inspiration. The claim of infallibility and finality for any prophet, book or church, is a fictitious assumption of theologians and ecclesiastics. The Christ himself affirmed the possibility of his followers reaching a higher attainment than his own on earth. Divine inspiration is in no sense miraculous as will be shown;

it depends upon the spiritual impressibility of the individual receiving it. This, like every other function of soul or body, may be developed and perfected by cultivation and exercise, or repressed and blunted by neglect and sin. It has, however, without doubt been spontaneously exercised, like other powers of the soul, in total ignorance of this law, giving rise to the idea of special favoritism on the part of Deity.

Divine Revelation Progressive.—Divine inspiration is of necessity an experience of degrees; hence revelation of and from God is correspondingly progressive, depending upon the degree of spritual impressibility, and what may and should be the ever-increasing receptivity and enlarging capacity of the soul to receive and appropriate. The extent of divine revelation to man, then, depends upon the advancing degrees of spiritual inspiration and corresponding illumination reached by him, from the humbler seers and prophets up to the full illumination of the Christ, "The Word made flesh." Therefore, without denying a divine inspiration and some degree of spiritual illumination to any who may claim it, we may without presumption—with the record of the world's prophets before us—place Jesus in position among these illuminated sons of God as a sun among the planets. The light that has been fragmentary and partial in others came to full perfection in him. Hence all of genuine illumination and personal realization of the divine, ever sought for by others, was fulfilled and included in his illumination.

The True and All-Inclusive Theosophy.—The attainment of esoteric wisdom under any teaching or method is confessedly a thing of degrees, depending upon the advancement of the individual seeker. The Oriental method ignores divine help and sympathy; while the Christ method recognizes and adopts it. If the Christ conception of God in His Fatherhood and providence is truth, and his experience of direct communion with and illumination from the Father's Spirit was a reality, and as claimed by him an example for all, then there is no presumption in the claim of superiority for his method, and no argument is needed for its defence. If, on the other hand, it is assumed, that the Christ and his Apostles were mistaken as to the nature and source of their inspiration and power, still their method under this conception was preëminently successful, and its results in their divinely exalted and consecrated lives stand out in marked contrast above any other in the world's history. This of itself is presumptive evidence of the truth of their claim.

If the Christ claim is true, the method he presents for its demonstration in personal experience is consistent with the claim, and opens the door of its possibility to all, since under it man is not left to his own unaided effort, but is assured of the co-operation of a divine sympathy and help. Since, then, the Christ method demands as radical personal effort, self-denial and consecration as a basis for the divine sympathy and help as the most austere Orientalist can possibly exact; and since this promise of divine co-operation on these conditions tends to stimulate and exalt the faith of the seeker, whether it is based in truth or delusion, it certainly has this advantage over that of the Oriental, which denies to the seeker this divine assurance.

Again, as the only possible demonstration of the truth of either claim is in personal experience and the fruits of that experience before the world, simply as claims upon the world's attention, they stand upon an equal footing. The Christian claim has supreme advantage in the hope and faith it encourages, and the lofty examples it presents in the lives of the Master and his Apostles, and in all his faithful followers, and their practical work in and for the world. It is an undeniable truth that no one can follow faithfully the example and teaching of the Christ—which were consistent one with the other—without becoming both a better and a wiser man, with no possibility of being made worse, and that if divine guidance and illumination are possible to man under any teaching, they will be the most effectively secured under the leading of the Christ. Hence we do not hesitate to claim that the esoteric wisdom and divine realization promised in the Theosophy of the Christ, embraces all and more than is possible of attainment under any other teaching.

Truth Its Own Defence.—It is not denied that a high degree of illumination, mental supremacy, and personal mastery may be and have been attained by the processes adopted by certain Eastern mystics, without the recognition of and personal dependence upon a divine sympathy and co-operation. Striking and well-authenticated facts with the principles and explanation of these experiences will be fully and fairly presented in another place. We cannot afford in this important study to ignore any fact of experience bearing upon the higher powers and possibilities of the human soul, and the mastery of its environments in the present world. The undoubted attainment in occult science and mastery by a class of Eastern Adepts throws a flood of light upon the higher psychic powers of man; and, as we shall show, it is impossible for properly prepared minds to follow their science and practice faithfully without achieving the most remarkable results in personal experience. We do not here refer to the study and practice of magic and magical arts, nor any form of necromancy or sorcery; but to the deep search into the mystery of being, and the lofty and consecrated effort after the highest realization and the true science of life by the real Magi and Sages of the East. Nevertheless, with the open example of the Christ and his victorious life before us, and his supreme testimony of having found the living God and Father of men, through immediate revelation and personal communion, and the confession of the Eastern Adept that he has not found the God and Father of the Christ, we shall insist that the Eastern ideal and method fails, as it ever must fail, of reaching the highest attainment and perfect result, which can only be found through the following of the Christ.

It is not difficult to show the reason and justice of the claim made by the Master for himself, when from the altitude of his divine experience and perfect attainment he said, "I am the way, the truth and the life; no man cometh unto the Father but by me."

While his life and work before the world, as contrasted with all others, was the demonstration of the
truth of this claim, he bids all demonstrate it in their
own experience by coming to the Father through the
following of his example and instruction, assuring
them, that they shall thus "have the light of life," and
do the works he did. That this has not been demonstrated in the experience of the great mass of his pro-
fessed followers was no fault of the Christ, nor evidence
that his promise may not be made good in universal
experience. We claim and hope to show that his doctrine and method have not been fairly tried, because
neither understood nor applied by the church that
bears his name.

A few faithful souls in all the centuries since the
Apostolic days have held the key and have entered, in
greater or less degree, into mystic fellowship with
their ascended Lord in this divine realization, but
such have ever received the ban and persecution of the
church. Nevertheless the time is at hand when the
world will awake to the true message of the Christ,
and catching a glimpse of his divine doctrine and
method, enter into the realization of its life and power.
The spirit, power and process that made Jesus what
he was, will do the same essentially for all men who
will faithfully follow his example under them.

Continued Ministry of Christ.—The recognition of
the still active sympathy and special ministry of the
ascended Christ, who in his parting promise assured
his followers, that to the end of time he would be
with them in spirit and power to help all who opened

themselves to his ministry, is a precious source of comfort and courage to the true Christian Theosophist. This promise implies also, that all who have risen into fellowship with him in the after-life, constitute a mighty brotherhood of Spirit in active sympathy and ministry, working in his name for the universal awakening and spiritual emancipation of men on earth and in the spheres. Nor will this ministry cease until all souls in all worlds are brought to the knowledge of the Father in the realization of their own divine sonship and brotherhood with that of all men. In this recognition of a divine and angelic sympathy and direct ministration in all human effort after divine realization by Christian Theosophy, and its denial by the Oriental, lies the fundamental difference in the character of the two.

The Basis of all Philosophy.—The conception which men hold of the nature and character of God, or of the "Cause and Providence of all that is," to which this name or its equivalent is given, is the basis of their philosophy and the inevitable key of their interpretation and understanding of nature and life. Hence man's thought of God necessarily determines his philosophy of his own nature, possibilities and destiny. One must correspond with the other. The doctrine of Jesus concerning the immediate divine possibilities of man was based upon and the logical result of his understanding of God, as not only the Supreme Being and immediate controller of all things, but also as the immediate Father of mankind. As the immediate Father of men, His nature and attributes were of necessity engermed potentially in the human spirit. On this basis alone rests his exalted ideal of attainment possible to man, as well as the law and method of its divine realization. Having demonstrated in his own experience the essential truth of this doctrine of God and man, it became the inspiration of his lofty enthusiasm and the burden of his message to the world.

The New Ideal.—After the opening of the heavens unto Jesus at his baptism by John, and the permanent spiritual illumination that followed, through which came his final mastery over temptation and self, we read that, "He returned in the power of the Spirit into Galilee, preaching the gospel of the kingdom of God, and saying, The time is fulfilled, and the kingdom of God is at hand." He thus began his public ministry by proclaiming the advent of a new kingdom as at hand; that the new kingdom was to be brought forth under a divine ministry through human effort and co-operation, and thus dependent upon that co-operation. Hence, he called upon all men everywhere to turn from their absorbing attention in other things, and give themselves heart and soul to the bringing in of the new order. This, he affirmed, would secure to them the true riches, and all that was essential to make life perfect; the time was fulfilled and the world was ready for and in need of its administration.

But what was the nature of the kingdom which this newly illuminated prophet announced as at hand and for which the time had come? Was it a new theo-

cratic government for the Jews as the chosen people
of God—an external and local kingdom among and
perhaps over the other kingdoms of the world, for
which the Jews were looking? or was it a new order
and kingdom of life, which, in its evolution and establishment, should embrace the entire humanity? In
an unbiased study of the Master's life and teaching
from the standpoint of modern enlightenment, we may
see what it was difficult and perhaps impossible for
men at that time to see, that the latter suggestion
was really what was involved in the Master's promise
of the new kingdom.

A New Cycle of Evolution.—The evolution of life in
the world had risen through successive cycles of activity, each marking the development of a new and distinct kingdom, up to the level of self-consciousness in
man—the vegetable, animal and human, three distinct
kingdoms or levels of life above the mineral.

The self-conscious, progressive intelligence of man,
however, while he recognized his position and supremacy over all the kingdoms below him, was still mainly
circumscribed to and concerned in his relations with
the world that was external to himself; yet having a
dim, haunting, prophetic instinct of something higher
and beyond. Out of this sprang his conceptions of a
possible state of existence beyond death, and out of
the speculations thus engendered, came most of his
systems of religious thought and worship. In the inspired souls of seers and prophets this blind spiritual
instinct had here and there expanded into a more or
less clear and open vision of the diviner realization

possible to man in the flesh, and ultimately to be his in actual experience. These being exceptional experiences and prophetic, were necessarily misunderstood by the masses; so that when the long-prophesied Messiah appeared to open that higher kingdom of life to men and inaugurate its beginning, he was misunderstood and rejected by the favored people, the very children of the prophets, who ought to have welcomed and entered heartily with him into the fulfilment of his mission.

Rejected by the Rabbis and leaders of the people, a little band of disciples from the common classes were finally inducted by him into a good degree of understanding and experience of the new and higher life he came to open to the world. These, after his cruel martyrdom, following his instructions and under his spiritual guardianship and leading, faithfully labored, in the face of the most bitter opposition and persecution, and finally of martyrdom, to carry forward the work he had begun. As the Master himself was misunderstood and misjudged, it is not strange that his disciples in turn should be misunderstood and misinterpreted by after generations in the church they planted. Thus the original "gospel of the kingdom of God," announced by the Master for realization in this world, has for more than seventeen centuries been interpreted by the church that bears his name to mean salvation in the heaven and from the hell of another world. On this huge misconception has the mistaken work of the historic church been founded, and the real work of the Christ neglected by his would-be followers.

Turning from the speculative doctrines of theology, and reading with unbiased mind the life and words recorded of the Master, no one can now mistake the purport of his message. His gospel was for this world and the present time, in fulfilment of all millennial prophecy; not a future world nor a future age in this world. It was to be realized there and then; and still to be realized here and now. "Take no thought for the morrow; for the morrow shall take thought for the things of itself. Sufficient unto the day is the evil thereof." "The time is fulfilled" was the new watchword, "and the kingdom of God is at hand,"—may be realized at once. To-morrow is born of to-day; surely, then, if to-day is made perfect we need have no fear or care for the morrow. "Now is the accepted time, behold now is the day of salvation." Salvation is realization; hence an insurance ticket of safety for another world is not a present salvation, nor the realization promised by the Christ in this world; nor the fulfilment of millennial prophecy in the enthronement of the kingdom of God on earth as it is in heaven, through the advent and work of the Christ. With the advent of the Messiah the time had come for the fulfilment of this prophecy in the beginning of another cycle of advancing life, by the evolution of its deeper, latent and yet unexpressed functions of spiritual consciousness and power.

Thus far each successive kingdom of life had been characterized by a new and higher type of organism for the embodiment and expression of its functions. But the ultimate and highest possible type of organism had been reached in man with the birth and organic embodiment of his intellectual and moral powers, though imperfect in development, because of the yet imperfect development of the embodied spiritual man. For the next cycle of evolutionary activity and development, therefore, no other or different kind of organism was needed, this being capable of indefinite improvement and ultimate perfection through the further evolution and organic expression of the engermed powers yet latent in the spiritual man it embodied. All that was yet needed was the quickening and bringing forth of the divine germ of spirituality, potential in the human spirit as the offspring of God. This would spiritualize, illuminate and exalt all the powers of man, soul and body, and lift and expand his consciousness from the plane of the sensuous life and the outward world, to the recognition and realization of his corresponding relations with an inner spiritual kingdom, the veritable kingdom of God. The awakening and bringing forth of the latent spiritual life to organic activity and supremacy in man, would so transform the character of the individual and social life, by bringing them under the higher law of the divine and heavenly, as to constitute a new and distinct kingdom or order of life, the long-prophesied order of the sons and daughters of God in the earth.

The Higher Realization Begun.—Jesus having reached the full realization of this divine estate, stood not merely as its prophet, but its representative in actual illustration before the world; and the transcendent beauty and power of that life were manifest

5

from the first. "And they were astonished at his doctrine, for his word was with power." "And they were
all amazed, and spake among themselves, saying,
What a word is this! for with authority and power
he commandeth the unclean spirits, and they come
out. And the fame of him went out into every place
of the country round about." "And Jesus went about
all the cities and villages, teaching in their syna-
gogues, and preaching the gospel of the kingdom, and
healing every sickness and every disease among the
people." "And great multitudes followed him, and he
healed them all."

Dwelling in the power of the new life himself, he
authoritatively announced the possibility of its immediate realization by all, saying, "The time is fulfilled,"
and called upon men to enter at once upon the work
of regeneration that was to secure it. Let nothing
stand in the way of its attainment, nor divert attention from the effort. "Be not anxious therefore, saying, What shall we eat? or What shall we drink? or,
Wherewithal shall we be clothed? (For after all these
things do the Gentiles seek:) for your heavenly Father
knoweth that ye have need of all these things. But
seek ye first the kingdom of God and his righteousness; and all these things shall be added unto you."

The Christ Basis of Faith.—From the altitude of
his opened spiritual vision, the great Teacher recognized the life in nature, that mysterious energy that
"clothes the grass of the field," and builds up the
structures of the organic world; and the wisdom and
goodness in that mysterious providence that feeds the

sparrows and all the moving forms of life, as the immediate manifestation of the immanent God and Father of men. To this evidence of the omnipresent Father he pointed as the true basis of human faith, saying, "Behold the fowls of the air: for they sow not, neither do they reap, nor gather into barns; yet your heavenly Father feedeth them. Are ye not much better than they?" "Consider the lilies of the field, how they grow; they toil not, neither do they spin; and yet I say unto you, that even Solomon in all his glory was not arrayed like one of these. Wherefore, if God so clothe the grass of the field, which to-day is, and to-morrow is cast into the oven, shall he not much more clothe you, O ye of little faith?"

To his illuminated soul, God as infinite Spirit, was not only immanent and working in, but also holding direct and immediate providence over all the processes and conditions of life and being, so perfect that not a sparrow falls to the ground without His notice, and the very hairs of our head are numbered before Him. He recognized all the normal processes of life in creation and providence as the manifest expression of the Father's will, and hence that man should will to do His will and only that, and thus be one with Him. He recognized the will and purpose of God in creation, and in man as His child, to be infinite good-will, which fulfilled or brought to realization in man through his co-operation, would make him perfect even as his Father in heaven is perfect. In this recognition of man as the immediate offspring of God is necessarily involved the recognition of the essential spirituality

of his being, partaking potentially of the nature and
attributes of God, and inherently capable, therefore,
of unfolding into all the perfection of being and supremacy that characterize the Father.

Not Anthropomorphic.—There is no anthropomor-
phism involved in this conception and teaching of
Jesus concerning God, as some have supposed and
affirmed. The conception of God's Fatherhood and
man's divine sonship and possible communion with
and revelation from God, based upon the spiritual
nature of both, eliminates all anthropomorphic defini-
tions and limitations, and opens the sense of the
boundlessness of the Father's nature and kingdom,
and the inherent boundless possibilities of man as His
child.

In his constant reference to God as the omnipresent
life and energy of creation, Jesus did not attempt the
impossible feat of defining or explaining the nature
and substance of God. Naming a being or thing does
not necessarily define or explain it, though the name
should give the best possible representation or expression of the thing named. Who knows anything of the
absolute nature of oxygen or electricity—much less of
Spirit, from their names? To define successfully the
nature and substance of Deity would bring Him within
the compass and analysis of the human mind—an obvious impossibility.

The Esoteric Statement.—In the twofold affirmation
of Jesus, that " God is spirit; and they that worship him
must worship in spirit and in truth," both the exoteric
and esoteric character of the teaching involved are

clearly implied. In the first clause—"God is spirit"—
is implied the invisible, transcendental and incomprehensible nature of His substance and Being; and is
given as the only full and final exoteric statement
possible of God as a Divine Being, and the One omnipresent life and reality of all that is. It implies, also,
that while the Divine presence and activity in all the
processes of creation and life are immediately manifest
to the senses and intellect of man, and should be recognized as the true explanation of being; yet the
transcendental nature and actual Being of God in His
omniscient wisdom and eternal goodness, is infinitely
above all His manifestations to the senses and intellect, and so beyond and above their perception and
analysis.

The Esoteric Method.—The second clause—"And
they that worship Him, must worship Him in Spirit
and in truth "—implies that while God as actual being
and the Father of mankind may not be revealed to
man through the senses, nor the pure intellectual apprehension; yet that man may have immediate access to and revelation from God through his own inmost and spiritual nature, which relates him to God
as child to parent. It is, therefore, through love and
loving in the personal realization of this divine relationship, not through philosophy and thinking, that
man is to have open access to and revelation from the
Father, and thus hold a living and unbroken communion and fellowship with Him.

The law of the Spirit, and of the spiritual life and of
all spiritual relations, is the law of love, sympathy and

ministration. It is the law of the life of God in man and of its immediate spiritual activity in the soul. It is, therefore, the law of brotherhood and fellowship, the true law of man's relation to man. Hence the words of the beloved disciple, "Beloved, let us love one another: for love is of God; and every one that loveth is born of God, and knoweth God. He that loveth not, knoweth not God; for God is love. . . . He that dwelleth in love, dwelleth in God and God in him." Thus man can know God only through love; and when this is actually awakened toward God in the realization of His Fatherhood, it is of necessity correspondingly awakened toward man as brother, because the brotherhood of man is involved in the Fatherhood of God. Hence, also the loving Apostle adds: "We love him, because he first loved us. If a man say, I love God, and hateth his brother, he is a liar: for he that loveth not his brother whom he hath seen, how can he love God, whom he hath not seen?" "No man hath seen God at any time. If we love one another, God dwelleth in us, and his love is perfected in us. Hereby know we that we dwell in him, and he in us, because he hath given us of his Spirit." "We know that we have passed from death unto life, because we love the brethren. He that loveth not his brother abideth in death." "Hereby know we the spirit of truth and the spirit of error." This is the esoteric law of all true spiritual illumination, revelation and personal realization—the law of all real and permanent mastery.

A New Life Involved.—When the Jewish Rabbi

came to inquire of Jesus concerning the doctrine of the kingdom of God he was preaching, the Master replied at once, that unless a man was born of the Spirit, he could obtain no practical knowledge of God or of His kingdom. It must be experimental. It can be acquired only through a living experience. It is simply and necessarily a matter of personal, spiritual realization. We may make and accept the exoteric statement that God is Spirit, and we may intellectually understand and believe that as such He is the invisible, all-pervading life, energy and controlling intelligence of creation; but we can have no actual realization of this truth and of its power in our lives, except through personal contact and sympathetic union with God in and through our spiritual nature. This is an inward esoteric or spiritual activity and experience.

To accommodate the external understanding, the exoteric statement is made, that God is the indwelling and essential life and intelligence of the universe and of man. The reverse order of statement would be the esoteric understanding and the actual truth. "In Him we live, move, and have our being." All things exist in and from Him. All that which constitutes creation is but a manifestation or expression of Him; yet He is infinitely more than is expressed. "For the invisible things of him from the creation of the world are clearly seen, being understood by the things that are made, even his eternal power and Godhead."

The Higher Understanding.—The statement " God is spirit " does not imply a Spirit, a Divine Individuality among yet over other individualities, but is made

in the ultimate and exalted sense of Supreme Spirit—
Impersonal, Universal and Limitless Being. All principles of being including that of personality, inhere of
necessity in the original, divine and all-embracing
Spirit, or they could not become manifest in external
expression or individual embodiment. Hence the twofold principle of sex which comes forth in divided embodiment in men and women, seeking to become re-
united in their blended lives, shines in the divine nature
as the omniscient wisdom and infinite love—Father
and Mother Principle—which makes the all-Father one
with His creation. To the spiritual understanding
God is the all-embracing unity and harmony of being.
Hence the masculine terms "Father" and "Him" are
used only for the convenience of external speech, not
in any sense of the limitations of personality and sex
as applied to a human father, since both the father
and mother nature are included in Him as the all-
embracing One.

Spiritual Freedom.—The illuminated soul becomes
emancipated from the limitations of external defini-
tions, and the sense of limitation as applied to personalities and things, when dealing with great spiritual
realities. The Divine Spirit is recognized as the exhaustless fountain of all life, the potency of all energy,
the principle of all order and law, the light of all intelligence and wisdom, the immediate inspiration of all
love and sympathy, the Ego and consciousness of all
personality, yet infinite and exhaustless in His own
being, He ever remains, so far as "the creation" is
concerned, the infinitely unexpressed. Hence the Im-

personal and Divine becomes personal only to the consciousness of the human personality, because of the individuality and limitations of the human powers that thus reflect and express that which on the plane of the infinite is necessarily and always Impersonal.

"God is no respecter of persons." The very Impersonality of His Being makes the manifestation of His love, wisdom and justice as universal, impartial and all-embracing toward the beings and things of His creation, as is the influence of the sun upon the planets of its system.

The Spiritual Standard.—Pure Spirit, even in man, is universal, impersonal and impartial in its nature and manifestation. Herein is the standard by which to estimate the measure of our attainment in spirituality. When the individualized faculties of the soul become quickened in the spirit which constitutes their essential life and power, and so lifted in their activities above the dominance of sensuous impressions, they become the organs and channels of a pure spiritual activity and expression, and the soul is raised above all local attachments, personal considerations and preferences, and so above all partiality of discrimination and judgment. It then stands for universal love and impartial sympathy, and for absolute and impartial justice to all.

The Apparent and the Real.—To the exoteric understanding, the physical world seems the only real and substantial world; and sensuous experience from contact with its apparently solid realities the only experience worthy of practical attention and seeking;

while the realm and things of the spirit seem too intangible, visionary and unreal to be grasped and made practical in experience. Esoteric enlightenment and experience, however, reverse all this and show the opposite to be the actual truth. It is seen that all that constitutes materiality is the result of activities that are invisible and spiritual in nature and origin. The very grossest elements of matter being reducible to invisibility—which indeed is their primordial condition—are, for their condensation or precipitation so to speak, and their combinations into visible substance and formations, entirely dependent upon the operation of invisible forces, under the control and direction of a supreme Intelligence and Will.

Thus, in the higher understanding, the supposed materiality and substantiality of the things of the physical world, are found to be the actually temporary, dependent and unstable things and states of being; while the realm and things of the Spirit are seen to be the only permanent, changeless and indestructible realities.

True Life Only in the Higher Realization.—The realization of this in personal experience, constitutes that true and permanent state of being, called in the Theosophy of Jesus the "eternal life."

This higher permanent realization is reached only through the awakening of the personal consciousness to the reality of the spiritual nature, and the indestructible organism of the soul as the temple of God, and conforming the life and voluntary activities with the moral order of the divine economy, through unity of spirit with the Father. To the higher spiritual perception and understanding, the physical world and physical states of being are but circumscribed points of limitation in the play of special forces within the boundless sphere of spiritual energy and activity, and subserve a specific purpose and function in the universal harmony and working of the divine economy.

Individualization of the Human Spirit.—It is through the processes of the physical world thus instituted, that Spirit becomes finally individualized and embodied in special organisms, which give birth to a personal consciousness. It is by this process the eternal Father brings forth children to Himself, bearing His image and likeness, not in external form, but in essential nature and attributes. Man is thus brought forth under material limitations, and his spirit individualized and awakened to consciousness, first on the external and physical plane which gives him an established sense of personality and being, differentiated from all other forms and states of being. Can we conceive of any other conditions under which this result would have been possible? Can we conceive of a more appropriate starting point of a personality and consciousness thus born to a career of endless development in personal realization?

The Spiritual Organism.—In this individualization man becomes the embodiment of spiritual substance and principles in a living, indestructible organism, of which the physical body is the external form and also the mold and instrumentality of the individualization and differentiation. The substance of the spiritual organism, of which the physical body is the material mold and physical counterpart, is of such an elastic and ethereal nature that it will ever yield and respond to every demand of the unfolding life of the soul, as it seeks to expand the consciousness of being and to enlarge the scope and sphere of its organic activities and powers.

In this individualization of the spiritual organism and the soul's powers under the conditions and limitations of materiality, out of which springs the consciousness of differentiated personal being, the whole organic world from plant to man is made to play a part. The ascending gradations of living structure in the physical world culminating in the human body, serve a similar purpose in the evolution of man that the blade, stalk, and rudimental ear of corn serve in the evolution and final development of the full corn in the ear. Thus the blade typifies the vegetable kingdom; the stalk, the animal; the rudimentary ear, the human body with the first primary consciousness of physical being; and, finally, the full ripened corn in the ear, typifies the perfection of the indestructible spiritual organism and the higher consciousness of spiritual being as a child of God in the flesh.

The Inward Oneness of Man With God.—The human spirit in its differentiated consciousness of personality and limitation, is not a spark, so to speak, struck off and separated from the Divine Spirit by its association with matter—as something outside of and antagonistic to Deity. All things, including matter, exist and have their legitimate place and function in the divine economy and are a necessary part thereof. While man is thus differentiated from the Father in consciousness of personal being, through the individualization of his soul and its powers in a living organism, his spirit is not really separated from the Father's, but is actually so much of the Father's Spirit, specialized within the limitations of an organism brought forth for this purpose.

The personal consciousness is thus the specialization of life, intelligence, affection and moral sense,—attributes of spirit—in, through, and by an organism which serves both to individualize and embody them. Yet though the personal consciousness is held to the necessary limitations of the organism that gave it birth, and its first awakening is on the plane and within the circumscribed sphere of the physical senses, it has an inherent capacity for endless expansion; because it is rooted in the boundlessness of the Father's being, and is itself the specialization of the Father's Spirit under these limitations. Hence the organism thus brought forth as an instrument for the individualization and development of the soul's powers and consciousness, must of necessity be not only indestructible, but divinely adapted to meet this eternally progressive demand of the soul. The perfect adaptation of means to ends that characterizes every department of the divine economy, makes this supreme end of creation an absolute certainty.

Individual Immortality.— The necessary limitations of an organism in which the human soul becomes individualized and embodied as the offspring of God, however ethereal and progressive that organism may be, will forever hold the embodied soul to its differentiated individuality and personal consciousness. The physical body being but the organic matrix used in the formation and establishment of the indestructible spiritual organism, is of necessity temporary in nature and character. It serves a purpose in the primary evolution of the soul and its permanent body similar to that of the husk in the evolution of the corn—"the full corn in the ear." Hence the actual necessity and service of the physical body, and the outward world to which it relates the soul, can hardly be over-estimated, however temporary that service and necessity may be. Without these, so far as we can perceive, there would be no birth of immortal souls in indestructible organisms, for an endless career of unfolding life and progress in the Father's kingdom. Let, then, the physical body and this rudimentary sphere of our primary education and discipline in the school of the senses be duly appreciated and honored, by using them to the ends for which they were ordained and thus honored by the Father.

The Second Birth and Spiritual Consciousness.— When the personality has become fully individualized and established in relation to the things of the outward world, and the powers of attention, reflection and will are sufficiently disciplined through sensuous experience to realize personal responsibility, the soul is ready for the kingdom of God. "The time is fulfilled," and the attention should be at once fully aroused and directed to the higher activities and experiences awaiting the soul in its relations to the things of the Spirit. It should be made to realize its privilege as a child of God of entering into the full illumination, freedom and power of the spiritual life in the flesh.

The Power Conferred.—This ideal and promise of spiritual supremacy in and over flesh and sensuous limitation is no fiction given to mock and delude the seeker after God. We have its perfect demonstration in the living example of the Master. We see his experience reproduced to a remarkable degree in his apostles and immediate followers; and also in all from that day to this, to the full degree in which that example and teaching have been followed. The realization of the spiritual life through divine illumination and communion, gives the higher understanding of and power over all physical relations and conditions. All that is external and sensuous becomes subordinated to the higher law of the spiritual and divine, when this becomes the law of the personal life. The realizing sense of unity with God in spirit and purpose, gives that sense of impersonal being and oneness with the All, which renders personal and selfish considerations and the spirit of exclusiveness and condemnation absolutely impossible. Contact with the outward world and its multiplicity of objects necessarily awakens the sense of individuality among other individualities; while intercourse with men gives the sense of personality and responsibility in relation to other personalities. But the spiritual consciousness, awakened and established by oneness with the Father in spirit, and

the sense of impersonal being it gives, holds the soul
when in contact with the outward world, and in intercourse with men, above all external and partial considerations, and all personal or unjust discriminations.

While an external world of environment and society
are necessary for the individualization, discipline and
education of the soul, conscious communion with and
inspiration from the impartial Spirit and all-embracing love of the Father are equally necessary to over-
rule and direct that experience and discipline to the
perfection of the personal life and character. "All
things work together for good to them that love God."
When the soul has finally attained that degree of divine serenity and harmony of life as its permanent
state, the entire organism, including the body, will
partake of the supremacy of that enthroned harmony,
and be held secure against any possible disturbance or
physical disease. "They shall take up serpents; and
if they drink any deadly thing, it shall not hurt them;
they shall lay hands on the sick, and they shall recover."

The Ideal Life.—This perfect life as exemplified by
the Christ and his Apostles, Christian Theosophy prom-
ises unto all through faith in and fidelity to the example and teaching of the Master. The immediate inspiration, illumination and transforming power of the
Father's Spirit, is promised to all consecrated effort
after this attainment. Man thus becomes endued with
wisdom and power from on high, through which he is
given an intuitive knowledge of the occult forces of
life and the personal mastery of his own organism and

environments. He is then qualified to overcome and "cast out" all manner of physical and moral evil from the lives of men, and help them into the light, freedom and power of the spiritual life in the body. In other words the true disciple is to live the life and do the works of the Master and thus "be as his Master."

Christian Theosophy proclaims this higher life of freedom and supremacy to be possible of attainment in the earthly life of every one who has come to the full estate of the natural man. Great intellectual attainment is not required. While this is valuable in itself, the pride of human understanding is indeed one of the greatest hindrances to true spiritual realization. "Verily I say unto you, whosoever shall not receive the kingdom of God as a little child, he shall not enter therein." The humble, child-like spirit of dependence upon and faith in the Father, coupled with supreme desire to know and do His will, are the essential qualifications. On one occasion, after rebuking the spirit of pride, haughtiness, rebellion and self-sufficiency of certain cities that had resisted his teaching and appeal, "Jesus answered and said, I thank thee, O Father, Lord of heaven and earth, because thou hast hid these things from the wise and the prudent, and hast revealed them unto babes. Even so, Father; for so it seemed good in thy sight."

Karma and Re-incarnation.—The Eastern Theosophy recognizing no divine sympathy and help, does not embrace in its practice faith in and dependence upon a Divine power. Its dependence is upon human effort alone, the specific development of intellect and

6

will. Recognizing no Divine love and sympathy, it sees no principle of forgiveness; and hence no healing and restoration save through personal expiation. This is based upon the unalterable law of Karma, or law of consequences. As a man sows so shall he reap. And as in their pantheistic conception of Nature, the soul cannot attain to an individual spiritual existence until it has worked itself free from every taint of materiality and sense, and freed its Karma from all necessity of further expiation in connection with matter, repeated physical incarnations are deemed a necessity and the only hope of final immortality.

The Infinite Contrast.— Immediate forgiveness, restoration and healing, through repentance, faith and the spirit of restitution and reformation, was the distinguishing characteristic of the Christ message. This was based wholly upon the divine sonship of man and the absoluteness of the love and power of the all-Father, whom giving does not impoverish nor withholding enrich.

All material conditions and personal aberrations are as nothing before the supreme law and omnipotency of Spirit, the absoluteness of the Divine life and infinite love of the Father. The quickening, renewing and healing power of the Father's Spirit when thus invoked, overrules the law of "Karma," breaks the wheel of necessity and emancipates the personal life, setting the imprisoned captive free. "The Spirit of the Lord is upon me because he hath anointed me to preach the gospel to the poor; he hath sent me to heal the broken hearted, to preach deliverance to the

captive, and recovering of sight to the blind, to set at
liberty them that are bruised, to preach the acceptable
year of the Lord." These words the Lord Christ affirmed were literally fulfilled in his personal experience
and work.

A Mistaken Philosophy.—The Eastern Magi and
their followers, blinded by a mistaken philosophy and
zeal, are honestly misled in their supposed necessity
for repeated earthly incarnations, and the long and
severe discipline of asceticism, austerity and mortification of the flesh. This is not the spiritual way either of
attainment or of deliverance from sin. God is the living, sympathizing Father of men; Love boundless and
quenchless is the absolute law of His life and His government. The resources of His kingdom and providence are infinite and exhaustless. Man is indeed the
child of God and heir to His divine perfection of being
and character. In his essential being he is Spirit.
The elements of divine supremacy are potentially
within him. Partaking of the Father's nature he
has but to be loyal to this divine relationship through
love and faith, to have all the latent possibilities of his
being brought to complete fruition under the immediate inspiration and guidance of the Father's love
and wisdom.

The demonstration of this we have in the living example of the Model Man and Beloved Son and Brother;
corroborated by the experience of thousands who have
sought to follow his example and instruction to the
full extent in which they have been faithful to these.
Yet we must again say that his teaching and example

have not been fully and faithfully followed by the
Church that bears his name, either in doctrine or
practice. Sectarianism, bigotry, intolerance, persecution and martyrdom for opinion's sake, which have
characterized its spirit since apostolic days, are anti-
Christ. The doctrine of vicarious atonement and substitution taught in his name for the gospel, is as
foreign to his gospel of the kingdom of God and as
opposed to its spirit and principle, as are the Eastern
doctrines of re-incarnation and the absolute supremacy
and inexorable character of the law of Karma.

The Supreme Message.—While immediate forgiveness and restoration were included and emphasized in
"the gospel of the kingdom," which applied to man on
the sensuous plane as well as to the spiritual man, the
supreme message was the promise of a new and higher
level of life. It was to be a life of divine illumination,
supremacy and perfection. This was to be reached
through another cycle of evolution within the sphere
of humanity itself, through which man was to be lifted
from the plane of the sensuous life to the supreme
level of the spiritual life. The means proposed for
this higher spiritual evolution of men was spiritual
regeneration. The principle of forgiveness and healing for sin and disease is one thing; the principle of
regeneration which lifts man through transformation
to another and higher level and order of life is another
and quite a different thing. The one delivers man
from the effects of sin and disease, the other saves him
from committing sin or falling into disease by lifting
him above their power.

Through regeneration is promised divine illumination, moral and physical perfection and all needful power of intellectual attainment and physical mastery. The clothing of the soul's faculties with intuition, and the extension of the power and sweep of their activity through illumination under divine guidance, opens the sure and direct pathway to the loftiest attainment possible to the soul, and the speediest realization of its supremacy over sensuous limitations and material conditions.

Gifts of the Spirit Defined.—"Concerning spiritual gifts, brethren, I would not have you ignorant. . . . For to one is given by the Spirit the word of wisdom; to another, the word of knowledge by the same Spirit; to another, faith by the same Spirit; to another, the gifts of healing by the same Spirit; to another, the working of miracles; to another, prophecy; to another, divers kind of tongues; to another, the interpretation of tongues: but all these worketh that one and self-same Spirit, dividing to every man severally as he will. . . . For by one Spirit are we all baptized into one body [brotherhood], whether we be Jews or Gentiles, whether we be bond or free; and have been all made to drink into one Spirit." These were the words of a philosophic seer, and a noble and consecrated Christian Hierophant, who had exemplified all these gifts of illumination in personal experience. Few readers of the New Testament, it would seem, have ever caught the full scope of this promise so remarkably fulfilled in Apostolic experience, much less sought in faith its fulfilment in their own experience; consequently the meagre results in the lives of professing Christians.

The Divine Sophia.—Here is the true Theosophy and occultism opened to the world through the pathway of the Spirit, by the Christ, who himself led the way, and in turn extends the help of his spiritual ministry unto all who truly seek to follow him. The "gifts of the Spirit" thus specifically defined by the great Apostle, are not given as the result of psychic culture, development of will-power and attainment of occult science, but as the result of being "made to drink into one Spirit," partaking of the one spiritual life; "gifts," or the spontaneous fruits of, and powers conferred by divine illumination. Here is promised, under the inspiration and final illumination of the one Spirit, an esoteric wisdom and spiritual understanding, with intuitive occult knowledge and powers of mastery, which certainly include all that is practical in what is hoped and sought for by the initiates of the Eastern occultism.

Through the Christ method this divine realization on earth is made possible to all who have come to years of discretion and the full sense of personal responsibility, and within the period of an ordinary lifetime.

The Final Contrast.—Christian Theosophy begins with the twofold recognition: first, of an immanent God of infinite wisdom, goodness and providence as the immediate Father of men; second, of the spiritual nature, divine sonship and brotherhood of man, and the possibility of full spiritual realization in the flesh through divine inspiration and illumination, accessible and free to all through love and loyalty to the Father.

Oriental Theosophy as presented by its Western interpreters, begins by ruling out all recognition of Deity as a Being of intelligence and will, to be known and communed with by man, or who has any active sympathy with, agency in, or providence over the affairs and conditions of men. It leaves man to confront alone a Godless universe and the irresponsible forces of Nature, and to struggle single-handed with the problem of destiny with no hope of sympathy or help from a divine Father and superintending providence, and makes many earthly incarnations a necessity to final emancipation and personal immortality in a spiritual existence. "It prefers believing that from eternity, retired within itself, the Spirit of Deity neither wills nor creates." These are the authoritative words of a prominent Western devotee and interpreter of the Eastern Theosophy. This it will be seen removes all basis of a moral law as the expression of a divine order or government, and leaves expediency as the only law and motive for the control of human conduct. It recognizes indeed a Spirit as distinct from the matter of the universe, but this only as an unconscious germinating principle and spontaneous energy, holding mysteriously within its original essence the germ of all possible development, and the first or controlling principles of Nature.

The Philosophy Involved.—Through the spontaneous union of Spirit (the active), and matter (the passive principle), the worlds were formed and life was born. Principles of life becoming individualized in this union as monads, became embodied in material forms, and thus began the structures of the organic world. By the union of principles and successive embodiments the original monads, as germs of higher possibilities, unfolded, and thus were brought forth through progressive development, under the law of evolution, the advancing structures and successive orders of the vegetable and animal kingdoms. The continued development of certain principles, through repeated incarnations, culminated at last in the human soul as an embodied self-conscious personality of intelligence and will, the first being in the universe to possess these attributes.

Through a sufficient number of incarnations on this and other planets, the soul in its unfolding life, ultimately exhausts the possibilities of matter and takes on more and more the ever expanding and developing qualities of Spirit which were latent in the original essence or cosmic germ of the universe. Having thus passed through the "septenary chain" of planetary worlds, the human soul attains at length to the high estate of the gods and becomes a divinity. These divinities are called "Planetary Spirits," and become ruling powers, which in turn preside over the formation of new worlds, and powerfully affect and hasten results in the evolution of life by the modifying influence of their combined wills.

These are the only gods possessing intelligence and will, recognized in the Oriental Occultism and Theosophy. It is claimed, also, that individuals who have passed through a sufficient number of incarnations to evolve the spiritual into ascendency over the material in themselves, may, under certain conditions, enter into communication with and receive help and instruction from these exalted intelligences. This high communion, however, is believed to be impossible to any until this evolution and ascendency is effected through repeated incarnations.

Asceticism and Yogi.—The practice of asceticism and " Yogi" are believed to intensify the process of purification in each incarnation, and thus hasten the evolution of the soul and lessen the number of physical incarnations by augmenting the power of the good or rising " Karma." The specific object of asceticism and mortification of the flesh, is to bring flesh, sense and personal desire into subjection to the intellectual principle, and develop will-power and self-control. The object of " Yogi"—a species of mental gymnastics—is the development of concentration and mind power, the control of the attention and the cultivation and exercise of the psychic powers of the sixth sense for the attainment of occult mastery.

To illustrate what these practices are supposed to effect after a proper season of faithful discipline, we will quote the words of a high official in the Theosophical Society. The " Yogi," he says, in the third stage " overcomes all the primary and subtle forces; that is to say, he vanquishes the nature spirits or elementals, resident in the four kingdoms of nature, and neither fire can burn, water drown, earth crush, nor poisonous

air suffocate his bodily frame. He is no longer dependent upon the limited powers of the five senses for
knowledge of surrounding nature; he has developed
spiritual hearing that makes the most distant and
most hidden sounds audible, a sight that sweeps the
area of the whole solar system, and penetrates the
most solid bodies along with the hypothetical ether of
modern science; he can make himself buoyant as
thistle-down, or as heavy as the giant rock; he can
subsist without food for inconceivably long periods,
and if he chooses can arrest the ordinary course of
nature and escape bodily death to an inconceivably
protracted age. Having learned the laws of the natural forces, the causes of phenomena and the sover-
eign capabilities of the human will, he may make miracles his playthings."

Such are the extravagant claims for the attainment
of the Mahatmas and Hierophants of the Eastern Theosophy, and such is the goal of aspiration for the
Chelas and Initiates. Remembering the poetical ex-
travagance and hyperbole of the Oriental speech, we
must not be too literal in the understanding of their
claims. But that their Adepts have attained most remarkable occult knowledge and power, and a high
degree of psychic development, there can be no question with those who are familiar with the evidence.
A full account of the "Yogi" practice and its results
will be given in the next volume of this series. The
attainment of God knowledge and the supreme wisdom is reached only through self-realization, and this
is wholly a matter of self-will and effort. Both the

possibility of a divine revelation and a revealing Spirit
are denied.

Deification of the Human Will.—In this philosophy the realization of self is the only realization of
God, and this is possible ultimately to all who will. Its
motto is, "There is no impossibility to him who wills."
Hence this doctrine is practically, and we may say
emphatically, the deification of human intelligence and
will.

What is Meant by Spirit.—Spirit and spirituality
as understood in this teaching, are not, we repeat, what
is meant by the same terms in the New Testament.
Here they have no moral quality. It is simply psychic
being and intelligence, as distinct from and in contrast
with flesh, sense and inert, insensate matter. The
ignoring of a Supreme Intelligence, divine order and
moral government render this position a necessity.
The whole doctrine is consistent with itself. It is a
logical outcome of its original premise, and illustrates
fully what was previously stated, that a man's
thoughts about God determine the character of his
thoughts about himself, or of man and his destiny;
and also his philosophy of Nature and life. Out of this
philosophy he must construct his ideal of attainment
and also the method and conditions of its realization.

Contrast the eternally hidden, unsympathetic and
unconscious Deity of this Theosophy, and the lone
struggle of man after realization it involves, with the
picture of "Our Father in heaven" and His perfect
providence and active sympathy and co-operation with
men as His children, in the Theosophy of Christ.

The Ideal of Attainment here presented, is simply the unfolding and perfecting of the personal intelligence and will through the soul's unaided effort. When the period of conscious struggle between the will, born of the unfolding life and intelligence of the soul, and the impulses born of the physical, begins, unless the individual concentrate his effort and develop his will power in the struggle, he may fail of the final mastery and sink under the contest into ultimate personal extinction. Rest in "Devachan," however (repose between the incarnations), and re-incarnation, give opportunity to recover and work out one's karma if he will. The suppression of the animal and the physical that the psychic and mental may find liberation and expression, calls for such rigid practice of asceticism and personal discipline, that few have the physical, mental and moral courage and hardihood to enter fully and perseveringly into it; hence the struggle must be prolonged through successive re-incarnations, until the rising karma is cleared and the final victory achieved, or the sinking karma ends in the final obliteration of personal consciousness.

Not Fatalism.—This is not a doctrine of fatality, for under it a man is allowed to work out his own salvation or final mastery, or, yielding, sink to oblivion if he choose. The way of his salvation is through the attainment of knowledge and the development of will-power; hence the attainment of knowledge and the power it confers is the supreme object and inspiration of his desire and effort. Under this inspiration his motive of self-denial and asceticism is like that of the miser, who denies himself present gratification and comfort that he may accumulate the gold upon which his heart is set. Possibly too, when the supreme knowledge and mastery is attained by the Adept, as in the case of the successful miser when the goal of his ambition is reached, he may have utterly killed out the very power of enjoyment in the use of his possessions that originally prompted the motive of acquisition.

The Higher Motive and Inspiration.—The Christian Theosophist recognizes the same freedom as well as necessity of personal effort in working out his own salvation; but he has the additional inspiration and comfort in the recognition and realization of the Father's Spirit and power working in and through his every effort, to will and to do of His good pleasure. And believing the Father's will to be infinite good-will, and His way the perfect way, he gladly and trustingly seeks to know and do His will, that he may become perfect as the Father is perfect, and be clothed upon with His character and share His righteousness. Hence, instead of the supreme knowledge of nature for the power of personal supremacy it gives, the perfection of character and spiritual wisdom attained through unity with the Father's Spirit, and the true power of mastery and service which these involve, constitute the supreme object and inspiration of desire and effort.

These distinctions are as essential to the proper understanding and appreciation of the philosphy, ideal and methods involved in the Oriental Theosophy, as they are to what is involved in the Theosophy of the Christ. The study of Oriental religions and philosophies can but be interesting and profitable to all who give it their attention. It will enable the unbiased and philosophic student of life and its marvellous possibilities to more fully appreciate the depth, richness and simplicity of the Christ ideal and method, and their more perfect adaptation to the conditions of the present life and civilization of our Western world, which sooner or later are destined to permeate and embrace the whole world in their own best genius and spirit. When the West is christianized, it will christianize the world; and the Christ will bring all men into fellowship with one another and with himself in the universal realization of At-one-ment with the Father. "And other sheep I have which are not of this fold; them also I must bring, and they shall hear my voice; and there shall be one fold, and one shepherd."

The following selections from high authorities in theosophical literature are presented as a more complete statement of the claims and essential principles and genius of the Eastern teaching. The first is from "Five Years in Theosophy," a standard work of the Theosophical Society.

"Theosophy is belief in Deity as the All, the source of all existence, the infinite that cannot be either comprehended or known, the universe alone revealing It, or, as some prefer, Him, thus giving a sex to that, to anthropomorphize which is blasphemy. True theosophy shrinks from brutal materialization; it prefers

believing that, from eternity retired within itself, the
Spirit of Deity neither wills nor creates; but from the
infinite effulgence everywhere going forth from the
great centre, that which produces all visible and invisible things is but a ray containing in itself the
generative and conceptive power, which in its turn
produces that which the Greeks called *Macrocosm*,
the Kabbalists *Tikkum* or Adam Kadman, the arche-
typal man, and the Aryans *Purusha*, the manifested
Brahm, or the Divine Male.   Theosophy believes also
in the *Anastasis,* or continued existence, and in trans-
migration (evolution) or a series of changes of the
personal ego, which can be defended and explained on
strict philosophical principles by making a distinction
between *Parámatmá* (transcendental, supreme Spirit)
and *Jivatma* (individual Spirit) of the V.edantius.

"To fully define Theosophy, we must consider it under
all its aspects.   The interior world has not been hidden
from all by impenetrable darkness.   By that higher
intuition acquired by *Theosophia,* or God-knowledge,
which carries the mind from the world of form into
that of formless spirit, man has been sometimes enabled, in every age and country, to perceive things in
the interior or invisible world.   Hence the 'Samadhi,'
or 'Dhyan Yog Samadhi,' of the Hindu ascetics; the
'Daimonionphoti,' or spiritual illumination of the Neo-
Platonists; the siderial confabulation of soul of the
Rosicrucians or Fire-philosophers; and even the ecstatic trance of mystics and of the modern mesmerists
and spiritualists, are identical in nature, though various as to manifestation."

"The search after man's divine 'self,' so often and
so erroneously interpreted as individual communion
with a personal God, was the object of every mystic;
and belief in its possibility seems to have been coeval
with the genesis of humanity, each people giving it
another name. Thus Plato and Plotinus call Noetic
work that which the Yogi and the Shrotriga term
Vidya. By reflection, self-knowledge and intellectual
discipline, the soul can be raised to the vision of eternal truth, goodness and beauty—that is to the *vision
of God*. This is the '*epoteia*,' said the Greeks. 'To
unite one's soul to the universal soul,' says Porphyry,
'requires but a perfectly pure mind.' 'Through self-
contemplation, perfect chastity, and purity of body,
we may approach nearer to It, and receive in that
state, true knowledge and wonderful insight.' 'The
soul in the human body can perform the greatest wonders by knowing the universal Spirit (or God) and
acquainting itself with the properties and qualities of
all things in the universe."

"Thus, while the Aryan mystic claimed for himself
the power of solving all the problems of life and death,
when he had once obtained the power of acting inde-
pendently of his body, through the *Atman*, 'self,' or
'soul;' and the old Greeks went in search of *Atma*, the
hidden one, or the God-soul of man, with the symboli-
cal mirror of the Thesmophorian mysteries; so the
spiritualists of to-day believe in the capacity of the
spirits, or the souls of the disembodied persons, to
communicate visibly and tangibly with those they
loved on earth. And all these, Aryan Yogis, Greek

philosophers, and modern spiritualists, affirm that possibility on the ground that the embodied soul and its never embodied spirit—the real self—are not separated from either the Universal Soul or other spirits by space, but merely by the differentiation of their qualities, as in the boundless expanse of the universe there can be no limitations. And that when this difference is once removed—according to the Greeks and Aryans by abstract contemplation, producing the temporary liberation of the imprisoned soul, and according to spiritualists through mediumship—such a union of embodied and disembodied spirits become possible."

"The Alexandrian Theosophists were divided into neophytes, initiates and masters, or hierophants; and their rules were copied from the ancient mysteries of Orpheus, who according to Herodotus, brought them from India. Ammonius obligated his disciples by oath not to divulge his *higher* doctrines, except to those who were proved thoroughly worthy and initiated, and who had learned to regard the gods, the angels, and the demons of other peoples, according to the esoteric *hyponia,* or under-meaning. 'The gods exist, but they are not what the hoi-polloi, the uneducated multitude, suppose them to be,' says Epicurus. 'He is not an atheist who denies the existence of the gods, whom the multitude worship, but he is such who fastens on these gods the opinion of the multitude.' In his turn Aristotle declares that of the divine essence pervading the whole world of nature, what are styled the *gods* are simply the first principles."

"Plotinus, the pupil of the God-taught Ammonius,

7

tells us, that the secret *gnosis* or the knowledge of
Theosophy, has three degrees—opinion, science, and
illumination. The means or instrument of the first
is sense, or perception; of the second, dialectics; of the
third, intuition. To the last reason is subordinate; it
is *absolute knowledge*, founded on the identification
of the mind with the object known. Theosophy is the
exact science of psychology, so to say; it stands in
relation to natural, uncultivated mediumship, as the
knowledge of a Tyndall stands to that of a school-boy
in physics. It develops in man a direct beholding;
that which Schelling denominates 'a realization of the
identity of subject and object in the individual;' so
that under the influence and knowledge of *hyponia*
man thinks divine thoughts, views all things as they
truly are, and, finally, becomes recipient of the soul of
the world. 'I, the imperfect, adore my own Perfect,'
says Emerson in his superb essay on the *Oversoul*.
Besides this psychological, or soul state, Theosophy
cultivated every branch of science and art. When
ignorant of the true meaning of the Esoteric divine
symbols of Nature, man is apt to miscalculate the
powers of his soul, and instead of communing spiritually and mentally with the higher celestial beings, the
good spirits (the gods of the theurgists of the Platonic
school), he will unconsciously call forth the evil, dark
powers which lurk around humanity, the undying,
grim creatures of human crimes and vices, and thus
fall from *theurgia* (white magic) into *goeta* (or black
magic, sorcery). Yet neither white nor black magic
are what popular superstition understands by the

terms. The possibility of raising spirits according to the key of Solomon, is the height of superstition and ignorance. Purity of deed and thought can alone raise us to an intercourse with the gods and attain for us the goal we desire. Alchemy, believed by so many to have been a spiritual philosophy as well as a physical science, belonged to the teachings of the theosophical school.

"It is a noticable fact that neither Zoroaster, Buddha, Orpheus, Confucious, Socrates, nor Ammonius Saccas, committed anything to writing. The reason is obvious. Theosophy is a double-edged weapon and unfit for the ignorant and the selfish. Like ancient philosophy it has its votaries among the moderns; but until late in our own days its disciples were few in numbers, and of the most various sects and opinions."

The following selections from Sinnett's "Esoteric Buddhism," will afford a glimpse of the deeper philosophy involved in the Eastern Theosophy as understood and interpreted by its Western devotees.

"The one eternal, imperishable thing in the universe which universal pralayus [states of repose alternating with corresponding periods of activity] themselves pass over without destroying. is that which may be regarded indifferently as space, duration, matter, or motion; not as something having these four attributes, but as something which *is* these four things at once, and always. And evolution takes its rise in the atomic polarity which motion engenders. In cosmogony the positive and the negative, or the active and passive, forces correspond to the male and female

principle. The spiritual efflux enters into the veil of
cosmic matter; the active is attracted by the passive
principle, and if we may here assist imagination by
having recourse to old occult symbology, the great
Nag, the serpent emblem of eternity, attracts its tail
to its mouth, forming thereby the cycle of eternity,
or rather cycles in eternity. The one and chief attribute of the universal spiritual principle, the unconscious but ever active life giver, is to expand and shed;
that of the universal material principle is to gather in
and fecundate. Unconscious and non-existing when
separate, they become consciousness and life when
brought together. The word Brahma comes from
the Sanskrit root *brih*, to expand, grow, or fructify,
esoteric cosmogony being but the vivifying expansive
force of nature in its eternal revolution. No one expression can have contributed more to mislead the
human mind in basic speculation concerning the origin
of things than the word "creation." Talk of creation
and we are continually butting against the facts. But
once realize that our planet and ourselves are no more
creations than an iceberg, but states of being for a
given time—that their present appearance, geological
and anthropological, are transitory and but a condition concomitant of that stage of evolution at which
they have arrived—and the way has been prepared for
correct thinking. Then we are enabled to see what is
meant by the one and only principle or element in the
universe, and by the treatment of that element as
androgynous; also by the proclamation of Hindoo
philosophy that all things are but *maya*, transitory

states, except the one element which rests during the mahapralayas only — the nights of Brahma. . . . It is no paradox to say that simply by reason of ignorance do ordinary theologians think they know so much about God.

"It is no exaggeration to say that the wondrously endowed representatives of occult science, whose mortal nature has been so far elevated and purified that their perceptions range over other worlds and other states of existence, and commune directly with beings as much greater than ordinary mankind as man is greater than the insects of the field—it is the mere truth, that they never occupy themselves at all with any conception remotely resembling the God of churches and creeds. Within the limits of the solar system, the mortal adept knows, of his own knowledge, that all things are accounted for by law, working on matter in its diverse forms, plus the guiding and modifying influence of the highest intelligences associated with the solar system, the Dhyan Chohans, the perfected humanity of the last preceding manvantara. These Dhyan Chohans, or planetary spirits, on whose nature it is almost fruitless to ponder until one can at least realize the nature of disembodied existence in his own case, impart to the reawakening world at the end of a planetary chain pralaya such impulses that evolution feels them throughout its whole progress. The limits of nature's great law restrain their action. They cannot say, let there be paradise throughout space, let all men be born supremely wise and good; they can only work through the principle of evolution,

and they cannot deny to any man who is to be in-
vested with the potentiality of developing himself into
a Dhyan Chohan the right to do evil if he prefers that
to good. Nor can they prevent evil, if done, from producing suffering. Objective life is the soil in which
the life germs are planted; spiritual existence (the
expression being used, remember, in contrast merely
to grossly material existence) is the flower to be ultimately obtained. But the human germ is something
more than a flower-seed; it has liberty of choice in regard to growing up or growing down, and it could not
be developed without such liberty being exercised.
This is the necessity of evil. But within the limits
that logical necessity prescribes, the Dhyan Chohan
impresses his conceptions upon the evolutionary tide,
and comprehends the origin of all that he beholds."

"The enormous areas of time and space in which our
solar system operates is explorable by the mortal
adepts of esoteric science. Within these limits they
know all that takes place and how it takes place, and
they know that everything is accounted for by the
constructive will of the collective host of the planetary
spirits, operating under the law of evolution that per-
vades all nature. They commune with these planetary spirits, and learn from them that the law of this
is the law of other solar systems as well, into the
regions of which the perceptive faculties of the planetary spirits can plunge, as the perceptive faculties of
the adepts themselves can plunge into the life of other
planets of this chain. The law of alternating activity
and repose is operating universally; for the whole

cosmos, even though at unthinkable intervals, pralaya must succeed manvantara, and manvantara pralaya.

"Will any one ask, To what end does this eternal succession work? It is better to confine the question to a single system, and ask, To what end does the original nebula arrange itself in planetary vortices of evolution, and develop worlds in which the universal spirit, reverberating through matter, produces form and life and those higher states of matter in which that which we call subjective or spiritual existence is provided for? Surely it is end enough to satisfy any reasonable mind that such sublimely perfected beings as the planetary spirits themselves come thus into existence, and live a conscious life of supreme knowledge and felicity through vistas of time which are equivalent to all we can imagine of eternity. Into this unutterable greatness every living thing has the opportunity of passing ultimately. The spirit which is in every animated form, and which has even worked up into them from forms we are generally in the habit of calling inanimate, will slowly but certainly progress onward until the working of its untiring influence in matter has evolved a human soul. It does not follow that the plants and animals around us have any principle evolved in them as yet, which will assume a human form in the course of the present manvantara; but though the course of an incomplete revolution may be suspended by a period of natural repose, it is not rendered abortive. Eventually every spiritual monad, itself a sinless, unconscious principle, will work through conscious forms on lower levels, until these, throwing off one after another higher and higher forms, will produce that in which the God-like consciousness may be fully evoked. Certainly it is not by reason of the grandeur of any human conceptions as to what would be adequate reason for the existence of the universe that such a consummation can appear an insufficient purpose, not even if the final destiny of the planetary spirit himself, after periods to which his development from the mineral forms of primeval world is but a childhood in the recollection of the man, is to merge his glorified individuality into that sum total of all consciousness, which esoteric metaphysics treat as absolute consciousness, which is non-consciousness. These paradoxical expressions are simply counters representing ideas that the human mind is not qualified to apprehend, and it is waste of time to haggle over them."

"That which antedates every manifestation of the universe, and would be beyond the limit of manifestation, if such limit could ever be found, is that which underlies the manifested universe within our own purview,—matter animated by motion, its parabrahm, or spirit. Matter, space, motion, and duration constitute one and the same eternal substance of the universe. There is nothing else eternal absolutely. That is the first state of matter, itself perfectly uncognizable by physical senses, which deal with manifested matter, another state altogether."

Selections from Oliphant's Scientific Religion bearing upon the practical results of the Eastern teaching.

"The test of the value and nature of an inspiration is to be found in the efficiency of the remedy it proposes to meet pressing human needs. Inspirations that do not pretend to grapple with the earth malady, and attack it at its root, lack the essential quality which is contained in the divine love for humanity, and which I propose to show later, was the one supreme animating principle of Christ, who was such an incarnation of divine inspiration as was never manifested upon the earth before or since, and who is now the radiative centre of the seen and the unseen worlds, which, enfolded one within the other, compose one system for the radiative influence of the highest forms of inspiration; and it will be found that all inspirations which ignore him as their source, through whatever channel they may come, degenerate into speculative theories as to the nature and composition of man, and the cosmogony of the universe, which have no direct bearing upon its present actual condition with a view to fundamentally changing it; but which attempt rather to solve, *ex cathedra*, such problems as the character of man's previous existence, his reincarnation, his progress through conditions, and final fate, than how to feed the hungry, clothe the naked, heal the sick, and infuse moral vitality into those who are spiritually dead to their obligations to God and their fellows.

"In order to prepare the will, the affections, and the intellect to be collectively the transmitting media of an inspiration which shall have a minute and practical bearing in this sense, their training and discipline

must have lain in the performance of minute and
practical details, controlled the while by an absorbing
desire to perform them as an act of worship to God,
and of benefit to the race. In the degree in which
this motive dominates all thought of self, whether in
the most sacred family affections, or in the ambitions
for spiritual progress of a personal character, will the
divine inspiration descend into these minute and practical details, and the human problem begin to find its
solution in the small everyday cares of life. The light
which shines in upon a man who is sitting under a bo-
tree with his eyes on his nose, or in a cave tapping a
gourd, is of a very different quality. It may unfold to
him the views of those in another state of existence
with whom he is in atomic *rapport*, about the seven
principles of which he is composed, and of the various
stages through which human beings, after leaving
this world, may pass before they return to it again,
and what they may have been in a previous state of
existence, but it gives him no hints as to social reconstruction in this one.

"By abstaining from eating meat, by always eating
alone, in order to avoid contagious magnetism, and by
various other corporal disciplines, he may attract
from his invisible associates into his organism such
powerful magnetic forces as to enable him to make
converts by hypnotic suggestion, or raise his body in
the air, or suspend his respiration for an indefinite
time; but so far from feeding others, as a rule, he
makes them feed him; so far from bearing their burdens, they bear his—in spite of his powers of levita-

tion; and the final result of more than three thousand
years of this kind of inspiration has been to crowd a
greater number of idle, useless monks, of ragged religious mendicants, and of revolting fakirs, upon a
given area of the world's surface, than can be found
in the same space in any other part of the world."

PART III.

THE GOSPEL OF THE KINGDOM OF GOD, OR THE
OPEN SECRET OF JESUS.

Now after that John was put in prison, Jesus came into Galilee preaching the gospel of the kingdom of God, and saying the time is fulfilled, and the kingdom of God is at hand: repent ye and believe the gospel (*Mark*, i. 14, 15).

Be not therefore anxious, saying What shall we eat? or, What shall we drink? or, Wherewithal shall we be clothed? For after all these things do the Gentiles seek; But seek ye first the kingdom of God, and his righteousness; and all these things shall be added unto you (*Matt.* vi. 31. 32, 33).

Enter ye in at the strait gate: for wide is the gate, and broad is the way, that leadeth to destruction, and many there be which go in thereat. Because strait is the gate, and narrow is the way, which leadeth unto life, and few there be that find it (*Matt.* vii. 13, 14).

And when he was demanded of the Pharisees, when the kingdom of God should come, he answered them and said, The kingdom of God cometh not with observation: Neither shall they say lo here! or lo there! for, behold, the kingdom of God is within you (*Luke*, vii. 20, 21).

Strive to enter in at the strait gate: for many I say unto you will seek to enter in, and shall not be able (*Luke*, xxiii. 24).

And Jesus looked round about, and said unto his disciples, How hardly shall they that have riches enter into the kingdom of God? And the disciples were astonished at his words. But Jesus answered again, and saith unto them, Children, how hard is it for them that trust in riches to enter into the kingdom of God? It is easier for a camel to go through the eye of a needle, than for a rich man to enter into the kingdom of God. And they were astonished out of measure, saying among themselves, Who then can be saved? And Jesus looking upon them saith, With man it is impossible, but not with God: for with God all things are possible (*Mark*, x. 23, 27).

The Kingdom of God.—The one supreme message of the Christ was, "The gospel of the kingdom of God." That gospel as announced by the angels at his birth was, "Good tidings of great joy which shall be to all people. For unto you is born this day in the city of David a Saviour which is Christ the Lord." This gospel was to bring "Glory to God in the highest, and on earth, peace, good-will toward men." It held, therefore, the promise of a new and diviner life for man on earth, in which the imperfections and evils that had hitherto marred his history, were to pass away forever in the realization of the kingdom of God and the final reign of millennial glory in truth and righteousness. This great change and transfiguration of humanity was to be effected through the advent and ministry of this new-born Messiah. "Thou shalt call his name Jesus: for he shall save his people from their sins," was the prophetic injunction of the heavenly messenger to his parents. To "save his people from their sins," is to prevent their sinning, by leading them to that perfect life which is above the possibility of departing from the right. This is a life of at-one-ment with God. This indeed was the work the prophets had declared the Christ would do for men. Hence the Christ came preaching the gospel of the kingdom

of God and saying, " The time is fulfilled and the kingdom of God is at hand; repent ye and believe the gospel."

Nature of the Christ Message.—As taught by him,
and illustrated in his own experience, this kingdom of
God was a new and divine order of life and society to
be established in the earth, in which the presence and
inspiration of the living God as the Father of men
were to be realized by all.

This higher level of personal and social life was to
be reached, as we shall see, through the evolution and
final embodiment in man of a higher attribute and
principle than had hitherto dominated the lives of
men. It was to be the higher evolution of man himself, through the working of the same law that had
carried the evolution of life through all the preceding
stages and crises of its development. Only in this
case man was to be an intelligent co-worker with the
law and share the responsibility of results, he being
the first in the ascending scale of existences qualified
to do so.

Every advancing step in the preceding stages of
the evolution of life, had been thus marked by the
springing forth and embodiment of a new and higher
principle or attribute of life than had hitherto been
manifest. It was thus that were established the various distinct types and advancing orders of vegetable
and animal life up to man, the crowning glory and
masterpiece of creation. All that differentiated and
distinguished man as an organic being from the highest type of animal life preceding him, was the evolu-

tion and embodiment in him of a higher attribute and principle of psychic being than was manifest in other animals. In accordance with the universal law, that the dominant and controlling attribute and principle of embodied life determines the character of the organism, the evolution and embodiment of the distinguishing and characteristic attributes of man brought forth the human brain and body to correspond with and express these functions. If, then, there was to be a distinct and still higher type and order of life into which man was to enter and share, as announced by the Christ, it could be reached only through the evolution and embodiment in man of another and still higher attribute and principle than had yet found organic expression in him. This would necessarily effect a change in the organic condition of brain and body to make them correspond with, and give spontaneous expression to the new and higher functions. As that next higher order and plane of life was to be of a spiritual and divine character, the embodiment of its characteristic attributes calls for the exercise of seership, intuition, and inspiration for divine communion and fellowship. This requires an organism suitable to and in condition for the spontaneous and reliable exercise of these high functions, and that is exactly what the evolution and embodiment of the higher attribute and principle of the spiritual life is to effect in man.

Man a Self-determining Power.—The distinguishing characteristic attributes which lifted man above the animal creation and made of him a distinct order of being, are those which constitute his rational and

8

moral nature. His other powers he holds in common
with the animal kingdom. The possession of a rational
and moral nature makes him a responsible and self-
determining being; hence the further evolution of life
in man depends upon his own voluntary choice and
personal co-operation. It was this self-determining
power to which the Christ appealed when he called
upon men to accept and act upon this gospel, which
held for them, through their own co-operation, the
promise of a divine and perfect life. Through this
higher evolution man was to be lifted to a plane of
realization as much transcending the highest level of
our common humanity as that transcends the highest
level of the animal kingdom. This indeed would be
necessary to constitute it a new, advanced and distinct kingdom of being.

The Basis and Law Epitomized.—We assume that
life, sensation, intelligence and moral quality are attributes or qualities of Spirit; that Spirit is the universal,
all-animating soul of Nature, the all-pervading and
all-encompassing Reality of Being; that Spirit is God:
Hence, that the operations of life in Nature are the
immediate manifestation of an immanent God and a
superintending Providence; that the universe is an
organism, and that life and all the higher attributes
that follow, are inherent in the constitution of things,
rooted in the Being of God: hence, that evolution, or
the unfolding of life from within, and the successive
embodiment of evolving attributes is the divine law
and method of creation; that the evolution of organic
life is marked by successive steps or waves of activity

culminating in cycles and marked by crises, each cycle effecting the complete embodiment of certain specific attributes or principles in organic function.

The first and simplest manifestation of life in active development, culminated in the establishment of the vegetable kingdom and its infinitely diversified forms of vegetable life. The specific principles of life which became embodied in vegetable structures, were growth, repair and reproduction. These are the characteristic principles of vegetable life, and constitute the essential functions of every vegetable organism. The next wave and higher cycle of development in the evolution of life, culminated in the animal kingdom and its diversified forms and phases of life. The principles first embodied in vegetable structures—growth, repair and reproduction—being necessary to all organisms, were re-embodied in the animal conjoined with the higher principles which characterize the animal life, viz., locomotion, sensation and instinct. These higher principles of life, requiring organs of a higher class and of a different texture for the expression of their functions, took on in their embodiment an organism to correspond with their nature and character. Hence, we say that the characteristic and dominant or controlling principles of embodied life determine, in all cases, the specific character of the organism in form and structure which must correspond with and express their functions, or the object of organism and embodiment is defeated.

Birth of Humanity.—Following the animal kingdom came the advanced wave of evolutionary activity culminating in the cycle of humanity. The principles of both vegetable and animal life, being needed also for the higher organism of man, were re-embodied in him in co-ordination with the higher characteristic principles of human life, which are reason, conscience and aspiration. Just as the vegetable and animal organisms corresponded with and spontaneously expressed the functions of their characteristic and controlling principles of life, so the addition of the higher attributes through their evolution and embodiment in man, extended the development of the brain and nervous system and transformed the entire animal organism to correspond with and represent these principles and express their functions. All the principles of life embodied in the preceding kingdoms are reproduced in man, in co-ordination with those higher characteristic attributes which differentiate him from and lift him above them, and make of him a distinct order of being. He is, therefore, a reproduction of all that has thus far been manifest in Nature, and is thus a child of Nature. Hence in the New Testament, he is called the "natural man"—the man of Nature.

The Ultimate of Evolution.—The principles which have thus far come forth in evolution and embodiment, were of necessity inherent and potential in the nature of things, which is the life of God in Nature. The evident object, therefore, of evolution through its successive and advancing cycles and stages of development, in each advancing stage of which a deeper and higher order of attributes was embodied, was to be the final embodiment of all the inherent attributes of the Spirit and life of God in one perfect organism, a divine incarnation, since the last embodiment gathered into itself all that had preceded it. Hence, if there are still attributes or principles in the Divine nature which have not yet been evolved and embodied in form on earth, the evolution and embodiment of the remaining higher principles must continue until this culmination is reached. This will bring the perfect type of organism and character representing a divine and perfect kingdom of organic life, in which the nature of God in all the attributes of His Being will be incarnated or fully reproduced in His children, the true order of the sons and daughters of God in the earth. This will involve another wave or cycle of evolutionary activity, lifting life to a level of embodiment as far above its present plane in man as this stands above the last preceding level in the animal. This will be but the fulfilment of all high prophecy, and the practical realization of the Christ ideal for man, and essentially the reproduction of his own attainment in universal experience.

The Practical Question.—In the light of inspired prophecy and the testimony of Nature, the practical question to be answered is: Are there yet latent principles of life to be evolved and embodied, and will this involve the bringing forth of a new and higher type of organism than the one which man now has? Let us take the last part of the question first. If we study the laws of form and symmetry, we find it impossible for the mind of man to conceive of or suggest a more perfect type of organism than is now his. Every attempt by poet or artist to improve on this—as in pictures of angels with wings—gives us a monstrosity. The human organism, it is true, is yet imperfect in its development and organic conditions. It is subject to disease, suffering and decay. It wears out and breaks down under the stress of excessive mental activity. Something is lacking in its composition for the realization of the ideal and desired perfection. Yet if perfected in its development and organic conditions, no higher type of organism seems possible, necessary or desirable.

When we turn to the study of the character and personality of the being that inhabits and uses this organism, we find him as imperfect and deficient in his development and the conditions of his inner life, as is the organism in which he is embodied. One is the exact counterpart and correspondence of the other. Something is yet lacking, and therefore needed, in the organic condition of the spiritual man to fill out and complete the symmetrical and perfect character. This deficient and higher co-ordinating principle is, then, still latent and awaiting evolution and embodiment in the life of man. It is that ultimate principle of the Deific life which controls the universe in wisdom and goodness, and maintains the balance of creation. This when evolved and embodied in man as the coördinating and controlling principle of his being, will bring soul and body to that degree of perfection that he will in very truth become the microcosm, in which all the principles of the Divine nature are embodied, and the perfections of the universe are reproduced and represented.

"Behold the Man."—Admitting the genuineness of the gospel story, the entire problem was solved in the Christ experience. The essential nature of God, he affirmed, was pure, unselfish love. "God," he said, "is Spirit," and the manifestation of life in Nature he pointed to as the immediate operation of the Divine activity: "If God so clothe the grass of the field," etc. Hence, as man is the product of the life of God in Nature, he recognized him as the immediate offspring of God. Yet he saw and specifically pointed out the one thing needed, and lacking to make men the perfect reproduction of the Father's nature, true children of God. This was the ultimate principle and essence of the Father's Spirit—divine love and absolute goodness. "Ye have heard that it hath been said, Thou shalt love thy neighbor, and hate thine enemy. But I say unto you, Love your enemies, bless them that curse you, do good to them that hate you, and pray for them which despitefully use you, and persecute you; That ye may be the children of your Father which is in heaven: for he maketh his sun to rise on the evil and on the good, and sendeth rain on the just and on the unjust." He is kind to the unthankful and the evil. "Be ye therefore perfect, even as your Father which is in heaven is perfect."

This principle of divine love had been evolved and embodied in the life of Jesus and brought his being to symmetry and perfection in soul and body; perfecting the organism without changing the type. This made him the complete reproduction and incarnation of the Divine nature in human form. The Divine ideal and purpose in creation was fulfilled in this perfect Son, "Son of man" and "Son of God." This divine realization was reached by him, according to the record, through his personal co-operation with the Father's Spirit in his life. Pure unselfish divine love becoming the animating and controlling principle of his life, he could understand the Father's nature and dwell and walk in sympathy, communion and fellowship with His Spirit. Dwelling in oneness of life with the Father, he spake and wrought under the immediate conscious inspiration and power of the Divine wisdom and goodness: "For he taught as one having authority," and, "his word was with power."

The Christ stands before the world, then, the representative and model man, the actualized ideal of the Father for His children, as shadowed forth in both Nature and inspired prophecy. Through his own attainment as a Brother of men, the Christ opened the door of this divine possibility and demonstrated the way of its attainment for all. "Love is the fulfilling of the law." By recognizing the Fatherhood and love of God, and seeking the personal realization of that love through unity with Him in the Spirit, as His child, we come under the immediate inspiration and leading of His Spirit, and through loyalty to that leading, the love of the Father is awakened and unfolded in the soul, and the entire being is held under its regenerating power until the transformation is complete, and the permanent incarnation is effected. Love is the divine and only co-ordinating principle which brings and gives perfection. Its evolution and embodiment in the individual and the race will thus transfigure humanity and enthrone perfection in the earth, because it will bring the tabernacle of God with men.

The Open Secret of Jesus.—The real secret of that new "gospel of the kingdom of God," opened fully to the world for the first time in the teaching and example of the Christ, and which was so difficult for the world to receive at the time of and since his advent, was the higher spiritual evolution and transformation of man through regeneration. This open secret of the Christ stands exactly where he left it; and whether it be the first or twentieth century from his advent and testimony, men will never enter into its life and realize its transforming power until its true nature is perceived and acted upon. The mass of men, even those who bear the christian name, are practically no nearer the realization of that higher life of the gospel promise, than was the noble Rabbi who sought the quiet and familiar interview with the Master which the night afforded, that he might more fully learn of this new doctrine of the kingdom he was preaching. The words of the Christ to this seeking soul apply with equal necessity and authority to the best of men, the world over. "Verily, verily, I say unto thee, except a man be born again, he cannot see the kingdom of God." . . . "Except a man be born from above," "born of the Spirit" "he cannot enter into the kingdom of God."

The nature of this new birth and of the transformation of man through spiritual regeneration, is as much of a mystery and as far from being understood in its true significance by the theologians of to-day, as with Nicodemus at that memorable interview. The mass of people professing to be followers of the Christ, preachers and laymen alike, are no more living the regenerate and millennial life promised in his gospel, than are the people of the world. This is not, however, because they do not desire nor seek it, but because they have not yet caught the secret, and do not seek aright. "For many, I say unto you, will seek to enter in and shall not be able." "Because strait is the gate, and narrow is the way which leadeth unto life, and few there be that find it," were the prophetic words of the Master. The teachers have been blind leaders of the blind, and together have fallen into the ditch of misdirection and failure. The pagan tares of error, misconception, and perversion which sprang up with the pure wheat of gospel planting, have grown with the gospel and vitiated so far the teaching, as to prevent the full reception of the original gospel and its power by men. The paganized corruption in the dogma of vicarious atonement and substitution, has for nearly eighteen centuries blocked the pathway and choked the growth of the original gospel of the Christ. This has been the most serious obstacle in the way of true spiritual realization to earnest souls, because it has been so authoritatively and dogmatically insisted upon as the veritable gospel itself.

The Law of Attainment.—The attainment and realization of a new type and spiritual order of life is possible, we repeat, only through the evolution and embodiment or incarnation of a new, distinct and higher principle of spiritual life than has hitherto controlled the lives of men—the principle of pure, unselfish love. The unfolding and final incarnation of this higher and ultimate attribute of spiritual life, as the controlling principle and co-ordinating power of the personality, will of necessity change the character of the entire man and make of him quite another order of being, as illustrated in its great Exemplar. Nothing less than this would be regeneration. Regeneration involves the complete reconstruction and transformation of man after the pattern of a, to him, new ideal, the divine ideal of the perfect spiritual life, under the controlling principle and working law of that life, which, we repeat, is pure, unselfish love. It is the transformation of what Paul calls the "natural man" represented in Adam—the Adamic order—into the "spiritual man" represented in the Christ, the long-prophesied order of the sons of God.

This higher spiritual order of life actualized in the Christ, and announced by him as open and possible to all men, he called "the kingdom of God," because in its attainment men were to come into a realized oneness of life with God, in love, communion and fellowship. It was, indeed, to be the realization in universal experience of the Fatherhood and perfect providence of God, and the Brotherhood and spiritual supremacy of men, through the unfolding of the love and goodness of the Father in the lives of His children, binding them in one unbroken fellowship of love and sympathy. It is but the fulfilment of all millennial prophecy, as of the vision of the beloved disciple on the Isle of Patmos in which he " Heard a great voice out of heaven saying, Behold the tabernacle of God is with men, and he will dwell with them and they shall be his people, and God himself will be with them, and be their God.   And God shall wipe away all tears from their eyes; and there shall be no more death, neither sorrow, nor crying, neither shall there be any more pain: for the former things have passed away."

The life here foreseen in prophetic vision, in which sin and disease, sorrow, pain, and death itself, are to be banished forever in the realization of life in God, and man enthroned in the mastery over all his environments, is certainly a type, order and condition of life, as much transcending our present humanity as this transcends the level of the animal life. This divine and perfect life for man on earth was certainly prophesied as coming through the advent and ministry of the Christ. It was also as certainly promised by the Christ in his gospel of the kingdom of God, through regeneration. The Christ himself, according to the record, practically attained and lived this life, to which his immediate disciples in the face of persecution and martyrdom bore witness; and indeed, to a remarkable degree they reproduced the same in their own experience according to the Master's promise. The Christ also affirmed in the most positive manner that whosoever believed on him, that is, accepted and acted in faith upon his promise, should do the works he did and even greater. But how shall men accept and act upon his gospel without accepting him as a living example of human possibility?

The Blinding Power of Tradition.—How hard, indeed, it was at the time, and still is, for men to enter into the spiritual understanding and grasp the full significance and promise of this open gospel of the Christ. The dominant ideals and traditional bias which shape and limit the thoughts of men, are the practical standards by which they interpret what they see and hear. It was inevitable perhaps that the Christ, lifting up as he did an entirely new and revolutionary ideal of life and experience to be attained by men, should be misapprehended and misinterpreted at and since his advent. This he foresaw and prophesied in his parable of the tares. In this prophecy also he announced the time as coming when there should be a separation between the tares and the wheat, and the work of true realization begin. This would be the end of that generation, or the then and still existing order, and the beginning of the regenerate life in universal experience. It was this crisis foretold by the Master, doubtless, that planted in the Apostolic mind the impression of a second coming of the Christ, which in a true sense it practically will be, but not in the literal way in which it has been conceived by men.

The Master himself announced the manner of his full appearing, in the general waking up of the world to the true understanding and power of his gospel. "And this gospel of the kingdom shall be preached in all the world, for a witness unto all nations; and then shall the end come. . . . Then if any man shall say

unto you, lo, here is Christ, or there; believe it not.
For there shall arise false Christs, and false prophets,
and shall show great signs and wonders; insomuch
that, if it were possible, they shall deceive the very
elect. Behold I have told you before. Wherefore if
they shall say unto you, Behold he is in the desert;
go not forth: behold he is in the secret chamber; believe it not. For as the lightning cometh out of the
east and shineth even unto the west; so shall the
coming of the son of man be." The second coming of
Christ is thus symbolized by himself as the dawning
of a new day and the shining of its light over all the
earth. It is the awakening of the world at length to
the recognition of the glad message of his gospel, the
"good tidings of great joy which shall be to all people." The "second advent" is not, therefore, to be
in any personal appearing or special incarnations.
Against all such expectation or claim, he especially
warned his followers. "Take heed that no man deceive you. For many shall come in my name, saying,
I am Christ; and shall deceive many." That new day
is to come as a universally illuminating Spirit in the
souls of men through their own awakening to its visi-
tation. As the light which kindleth in the east, and on
the wings of the morning envelopeth the uttermost
parts of the earth, even so shall the final coming of
the Son of man be. The seed of the first planting has
been growing among the briars, weeds and thistles of
human creed and dogma, and the story of the Christ
has been told to many peoples, and the earth has been
enriched and greatly blest by its silent power in spite

of the errors with which it has been encumbered. All this was inevitable, which the Christ foresaw, and with infinite tenderness and patience he bides his time. He knows that " he shall see of the travail of his soul and shall be satisfied."

The Planting and the Reaping.—"Another parable put he forth unto them, saying, The kingdom of heaven is likened unto a man which sowed good seed in his field: But while men slept, his enemy came and sowed tares among the wheat, and went his way. But when the blade was sprung up, and brought forth fruit, then appeared the tares also. [An exact picture of the beginning of speculative doctrine in the Apostolic church.] So the servants of the householder came and said unto him, Sir, didst not thou sow good seed in thy field? from whence then hath it tares? He said unto them, An enemy hath done this. The servants said unto him, Wilt thou that we go and gather them up? But he said Nay; lest while ye gather up the tares, ye root up also the wheat with them. Let both grow together until the harvest; and in the time of the harvest I will say to the reapers, Gather ye together first the tares, and bind them in bundles to burn them: but gather the wheat into my barn."

It was with the utmost difficulty that the little band of chosen disciples upon whom the Lord Christ concentrated his effort, were at length inducted, in any marked degree, into the deeper understanding and corresponding realization of the regenerating power of his gospel. Their experience was sufficiently deep

and mighty, however, to insure the planting of that
gospel in the earth, and to insure the final spread of
the gospel story throughout the world. Nevertheless
it was unavoidable that not only the Christ, but the
Apostolic experience also should be grossly misunderstood and misinterpreted by after generations. Nor
is it strange that centuries should roll by before the
world should awaken to the true message of that gospel. May we not hope that the days of waiting are
nearly over, and that the harvest time is at hand and
even now upon us? That the reapers are already in
the field under the Master's orders, "gathering up the
tares and binding them in bundles to burn them," and
that we may soon have the unmixed wheat for the
true bread of life for which the world is waiting?
What is this great shaking in the creeds and traditions of men to-day, both religious and social, but the
work of separation in the hands of his messengers,
rooting out and binding up the tares of false doctrine
to be burned in the fire of destructive criticism, that
the pure wheat may be gathered into the granary of
the Lord for the feeding of his flock?

A Life Not a Creed Demanded.—So long as men expect to find salvation in this or that form of doctrine
and worship, so long as their thought of salvation is
to escape the hell and secure the heaven of another
world, by some official work wrought in their behalf by
another, they are feeding and depending on pagan
tares and the chaff of superstition, and not on the
wheat and faith of Christ's gospel. He held up and
offered a life to be believed in and sought after now,

to be attained and lived in this world; not a creed to be accepted as a condition of salvation in another world. The present looking for an external coming of the Christ in outward personality and form, instead of an inward presence in the mighty power of his spirit in the souls of his followers, is as far from the truth as was the looking of the Jews of old for his first advent. And it may be to-day as of old, that in his coming he will be sooner recognized outside the Church that bears his name than in it. "And when he was demanded of the Pharisees, when the kingdom of God should come, he answered them and said, The kingdom of God cometh not with observation: Neither shall they say lo here! or, lo there! for behold the kingdom of God is within you."

The Jews believing themselves to be the chosen people of God, were at that time looking for the re-establishment of the throne of David through a coming Messiah who would "restore the kingdom to Israel," and sitting upon that throne extend its supremacy "over all the kingdoms of the world and the glory of them." Hence, when this new prophet proclaimed the kingdom of God as at hand, they could entertain no other thought of a coming kingdom than the realization of this long-cherished hope, in the light of which they had interpreted all the millennial prophecies. When, therefore, the true Messiah was actually present among them and in the real sense fulfilling "the law and the prophets," their eyes were so "holden" by traditional bias that they did not and could not recognize him. Are not the most of those who to-day

9

look for his second appearing repeating the same folly? This hereditary Jewish ideal and hope, for generations instilled into the minds of their children, proved one of the greatest obstacles in the minds of the disciples themselves in the way of their grasping the spiritual character of the kingdom which the Master was preaching. This was strikingly manifest by the confession of two of them after the crucifixion and burial of the Master, when as they mournfully talked on their way to Emmaus, the risen Lord himself joined them and asked: "What manner of communications are these that ye have one to another, as ye walk and are sad? . . . And they said unto him, concerning Jesus of Nazareth, which was a prophet mighty in deed and word before God and all the people: And how the chief priests and our rulers delivered him to be condemned to death, and have crucified him. But *we* trusted that it had been he which should have redeemed Israel."

And, again, after his resurrection and he was seen of all the disciples, save mistaken Judas, we read: "When they therefore were come together, they asked of him, saying, Lord wilt thou at this time restore again the kingdom to Israel?" We read the story of his familiar intercourse with his disciples, see the character of his faithful teaching and his tender patience with their stupidity, and wonder how they could have been so blind to the spiritual nature of that teaching. Yet his disciples to-day, equally honest and spiritually blind, are repeating the same stupidity in making the real word of Christ of little or none effect

by their traditions, in accepting for authoritative doctrine the speculations of the Fathers.

The Christ Himself Tempted.—This traditional
teaching and hereditary bias embraced even the Master, and was evidently the source of one of the great
temptations he had to meet and overcome. We read
that after his spiritual anointing and permanent illumination at Jordan, he "was led by the Spirit into
the wilderness" to be tempted, or tried and tested, before entering upon his work as the Christ or Messiah.
With the exaltation of his whole being through his
complete illumination, came the realization of the
transcendent power and insight of the new life, and
the assurance also that he was to do the work of the
long expected Messiah. With the opening to his
prophetic vision of the great work to be wrought in
and for the world, which he was sent not to condemn
but to save, this hereditary impression concerning the
nature of that work naturally arose in his mind to
bias and shape in some degree his new forming purposes and plans. The great historic leaders of his
people — he was born a Jew — had been both kings
and prophets, and under the supposed inspiration of
Jehovah had led their armies to conquest and victory. "He that was to come," was to be anointed
with wisdom and power above all others, and lead his
people to final victory and universal supremacy, "and
of his kingdom there should be no end." In the full
assurance of his Messiahship and the sense of power
and leadership it conferred, he could but feel that this
dream of his people could now be realized, and the

kingdoms of this world and the glory of them be theirs
and his by the consecration of this power and insight
to that end. This was the temptation of the race
spirit of his people, voiced in his soul through the bias
of hereditary impression and traditional teaching,
under the supposed sanction of divine authority, which,
everywhere and in all ages and peoples, is blindly
yielded to tradition. But the principle and spirit of a
new, broader, and higher life had opened its light and
power in his soul. The heavens had been opened unto
him in a beatific vision of the realized life of love and
brotherhood in celestial societies. The spirit of that
heavenly life had descended upon him as an abiding
ideal and living inspiration. Under his divine illumination a new conception of God and of His kingdom
had opened in his consciousness. God was revealed
to him as the Father of mankind, not of the Jews
alone. He saw all men as His childern who received
equal consideration and care at His hands; that Jews
and Gentiles, saints and sinners, were equally precious
as the subjects of His love and providence. He saw
that love and loyalty in the hearts of men toward
the All-Father and each other constituted the true
Israel, as well as the true kingdom of God to be
enthroned in the world and realized on earth as in
heaven. Hence, the real work of the Messiah was
seen in this higher light, to be the leading of men to
the realization of their divine sonship and the kingdom
of God through love and loyalty to God as their
Father and man as their brother. The coming kingdom of God was to be, therefore, a spiritual not a

political kingdom, and was to embrace all nations in the unity and equality of love and brotherhood. In the new illumination God was seen to be purely spiritual, universal and impersonal in His Being; and hence, His relations with and government over men were of a purely moral and spiritual character. Men under these relations to the Divine Government as children of God, were to be regarded and dealt with from the standpoint of their spiritual nature and moral character, irrespective of nationality, creed or social position.

The Spiritual Victory.—With this new conception of God and of man, and of the true kingdom of God in the world, the spiritual understanding of the law and the prophets was opened to his soul, and the magnitude and burden of his great work broke upon him. Before this higher vision of the kingdom of God in the spiritualization of humanity through love and loyalty to the All-Father, the narrow and selfish ideal of his people faded out, and the temptation of his hereditary bias was put under his feet. The vision of Humanity as a Brotherhood under the realized Fatherhood, love and providence of God, became to his soul the all-comprehensive reality into which he was to lead men, through the awakening of their love and faith. This was the real work to which he was anointed; and when all personal considerations were put behind him, in his entire and holy consecration to the work, he was prepared to " Return in the power of the Spirit into Galilee preaching the gospel of the kingdom of God, and saying, The time is fulfilled and the kingdom of God is at hand."

Having himself risen through divine illumination into the full realization of this kingdom, and the power of its new life, he could testify of it "as one having authority." "And they were astonished at his doctrine: for his word was with power." "And when he was come into his own country, he taught them in their synagogue, insomuch that they were astonished, and said, Whence hath this man this wisdom, and all these mighty works? Is not this the carpenter's son? Is not his mother called Mary? And his brethren, James, and Joses, and Simon, and Judas? And his sisters, are they not all with us? Whence then hath this man all these things?" Thus came the Christ proclaiming and opening a new and higher life to man, and demonstrating its possibility, practicability and divine character in his own experience before the world.

Another Order of Being.—Men in all the centuries since the advent of the Christ, in contemplating his marvelous life and works, and the divine perfection of his character and teaching, have said: Surely this was another order of being; he must have been an incarnated divinity. And this indeed was true. He was another order of being—a divine incarnation. He was a practical example and an embodied representative of that higher kingdom of life he was preaching, as open and possible to all men. While he bore our common humanity, he was something more than that humanity, just as the common man is an animal and something more. Man, as we have said, embodies every attribute and function of the animal, but

superadded to and overruling this animal nature are
the higher characteristic attributes of humanity. It
was the embodiment of these higher attributes with,
and their transforming power over the animal nature
and organism, that differentiated man from the animal in character, form and structure, and gave him an
organism to correspond with and represent the new
and higher order of being. He became the incarnation of a higher controlling and co-ordinating principle
than dominated the animal life and organism. So with
the Christ; while he possessed all that constitutes our
common nature, and was "tempted in all points like
as we are," he had, in addition thereto, brought forth
to full organic embodiment in his being the higher
controlling and co-ordinating principle of the spiritual
life, which is latent in all men. The transforming
power of this supreme attribute and principle of
spiritual life had thus lifted him to that higher plane
of realization, through its evolution and embodiment,
and inaugurated the new order and kingdom of life
which he truthfully announced as the kingdom of
God. As he had risen to this divine realization from
the level of our common humanity, through the evolution and regenerating power of a divine principle and
energy latent in all men, he had opened and demonstrated a like possibility for all.

Basis of the Higher Realization.—In this conception "God is Spirit," and His universal presence is the
immediate life of Nature. Man is the culmination and
ultimate of life in Nature, therefore the immediate
offspring of God. As such he holds potentially within

his being the engermed attributes of God. Hence, as
these attributes are evolved and come to organic embodiment in the individual life, the nature and character of a true son of God, the reproduction of the
Father's nature and character, is the inevitable result. In his present stage of development man does
not exhibit this perfect God-like nature and character,
yet there is universal aspiration and yearning for it.
This would be impossible but for the latent power of
its attainment. As there is no higher type of organism possible on the physical plane, it follows that the
principle needed for the perfection of the soul and the
corresponding perfection of the organism is latent in
the essential life of the organism itself, awaiting evolution and embodiment.

The one thing lacking, then, for the perfection of the
nature and character of man, is that which constitutes
the glory and perfection of the Divine nature, which,
according to the life and testimony of the Christ, who
lived to realize the most fully the Father's nature
and Spirit, is Love, infinite and changeless. When
this central principle of the Divine nature, latent in
man, is awakened and brought to organic expression
as the controlling principle of the personal life, it will
bring that life to perfection and clothe it with divinity,
because it will be a divine incarnation. It will do for
all men precisely what it did for Jesus; it will lift
them to the level of the Christ-life. On that divine
plane, as with the Master, intelligence will be manifest
in unerring intuition and wisdom; love in goodness
and perfection of character; and life in perfection of

organism and supremacy of power. Man will be perfect as the child of God, even as God is perfect as the Father of men.

Organism Included.—The unfolding of this higher principle in the soul will, in its embodiment, through its co-ordinating and transforming power, effect of necessity a corresponding perfection of organism as its instrument of outward expression. Organism can have no other possible object than the embodiment and external expression of the specific controlling attributes of its indwelling life. Through this universal law, each type of organism strictly represents corresponding specific types of life and character, from plant and animal to man. Each individual organism reflects the characteristic quality and state of its own embodied life. The present organism of man exactly represents the attributes of humanity on the plane of life to which he has risen; he could not, therefore, rise to a higher plane through the evolution and embodiment of a still nobler and diviner attribute, without a corresponding transformation of organism to constitute that embodiment.

As the offspring of God these possibilities are engermed in the latent spiritual life of man, but until they are evolved and brought to fruition in his experience, he cannot come to the realization of his spiritual nature and divine sonship. There is no true sonship, human or divine, without the complete reproduction of the essential nature and character of the parent in the offspring. From first to last, the ideal, promise and teaching of the Christ were based upon his recognition of the divine sonship, inherent spiritual nature, and corresponding possibilities of man.

Immediate Realization.—The one peculiarity which most distinguished the teaching of the Christ from that of all other great teachers who had caught glimpses of and prophesied man's higher possibilities, was the emphasis he placed upon the certainty of their immediate actualization in the earthly experience of all who should grasp the ideal with faith, and fulfil the conditions. "The time is fulfilied," he said, "and the kingdom of God is at hand," or within reach of all. This certainty of immediate possible realization was based upon his knowledge of the law of regeneration and the realization of its transforming power in his own life. What it had done for him, he affirmed it would do for all. Few indeed under his preaching seemed to grasp, fully, either the ideal or the law of attainment opened in his teaching and still preserved to us in the gospel narratives. These seemed to have been almost wholly lost to the world when the Apostles went to their rest. The bias of rooted traditions, and the materialistic tendency of the sensuous understanding, blinded the minds of men and led to an inevitable perversion and misinterpretation of the great Teacher's words. The kingdom of God which he taught for actualization in this world, men transferred in their conception to another world; and the conditions of its attainment were correspondingly conceived to mean an arbitrary and official scheme of salvation, in utter antagonism with the spirit, ideal and promise, which his words, as preserved to us, convey to the enlightened and unbiased mind of to-day.

Perversion Provided Against.—Foreseeing the misconception and perversion of his teaching—so fitly and clearly depicted in the prophetic parable of the tares—he preserved from utter destruction the supreme ideal, by framing it securely in that model prayer, which, while prayer is needed will remain the model for all men. "Our Father which art in heaven, Hallowed be thy name. Thy kingdom come. Thy will be done in earth as it is in heaven." It will be observed that in this perfect prayer given by the Master himself, there is not one petition concerning the after-life, either to be preserved from its hell or secured to its heaven. Were such salvation the object of our life work here, this could not have been left out of a model prayer. It would have been the central petition and especially emphasized. On the contrary, there is no hint of such a necessity, and the emphasis is placed upon the fulfilment of the kingdom of God and His righteousness in the universal experience of man on earth as it is in heaven. The ideal for which men were to labor and to pray, was the attainment of the perfect life in the realization of the Fatherhood of God and the Brotherhood of man on earth. Then follows the prayer for daily necessities, divine guidance amid temptations, deliverance from evil, and for such forgiveness of our sins as we mete to those who have sinned against us. In this brief all-comprehensive and inclusive prayer, everything for which men need to pray in this world while seeking and working for the attainment of the ideal life, is expressed, and all these are made incidental and secondary to that supreme object.

This prayer was given to his disciples as a model, in response to their request that he teach them how to pray. As such, being translated into every language of earth, it will hold this supreme ideal of the Lord Christ, in all its original purity and simplicity, until the nations shall at length awaken to receive and act upon its divine message. The Master not only emphasized the possibility and privilege of immediate entrance into the kingdom of God, and the attainment of the perfect life in the flesh in a single earthly experience (no re-incarnation necessary), but he specifically warned against making future conditions any consideration for present action. "Take, therefore, no thought for the morrow, for the morrow shall take thought for the things of itself. Sufficient unto the day is the evil thereof." Enter into oneness of life with the Father now and you will be at one with Him wherever you may go; and this is heaven. Fill the present with its highest possibilities, and the future will provide for itself.

No Future to Man.—Strictly speaking there is no future to the life of man. It is one eternal NOW; and it is his only work to bring that now to its highest possible perfection. This is the best preparation for any possible future. It is the only time man will ever have. It is the one arc of an eternal cycle of career into which he has entered, and the present realization of that particular point of the journey depends upon faithfulness to the highest light of the hour. In being true to that light, he will secure the expansion and unfolding of his being in the eternal present, and will learn that he is what he is, by virtue of what he does. While man is what he is by virtue of what he does, this will be determined largely by the ideal and faith he holds concerning his possibilities, duties and privileges. Hence the importance of holding the perfect ideal and a corresponding faith. "Therefore, whosoever heareth these sayings of mine, and doeth them, I will liken him unto a wise man, which built his house upon a rock: And the rain descended, and the floods came, and the winds blew, and beat upon that house, and it fell not: for it was founded upon a rock."

God as absolute Being, and man as His child existing only in His life and love, under the most vital relations, and protected by the sheltering arms of His perfect providence, are supreme facts or supreme fancies. They may be facts notwithstanding the unconsciousness of man concerning them. The majority of men are daily walking blindly in the presence of the most stupendous facts of vital importance to their well being. If then the message of the Christ was the manifested word of the living God and Father of all, man may be awakened to the realization of this divine relation with the Father and His kingdom, and enter consciously into its power and beatitude of experience.

The Inner Light.—"God is light and in him is no darkness at all." The pure life of God which animates and sustains the whole creation, is the inmost life and light of the soul. Hence, when the soul opens inwardly to the consciousness of its life in God, the personal life is deepened and expanded, the soul comes under the immediate inspiration of the Father's Spirit, and its powers of vision, comprehension and mastery are correspondingly quickened and enlarged. As man unfolds from within in the light and power of the spiritual life, he is enabled to perceive external things from a higher plane of vision in that light, and thus acquire corresponding mastery over them. He thus comes under the guidance of divine wisdom in his contact and dealing with all matters of the external world.

Divine inspiration and guidance is a free gift, and the privilege of every loyal soul. All who are faithful and obedient to it will be led to full illumination, and the attainment of the divine and perfect life in the flesh. It must be remembered, in this seeking of the higher life, that God and His kingdom are ever within; but as the soul opens interiorly and unfolds in divine communion and fellowship, it also rises in its transcendency and power over its external environments— over all that is external to itself.

The Pathway to Wisdom and Power.—All experience as well as inspired teaching has shown that divine wisdom and power can be attained only through the unfolding of divine love and goodness in the soul. If supreme power is sought as an end, and wisdom is sought for the power it is supposed to confer, it is practically an effort to enthrone self in the place of God. Pure, unselfish love, sympathy and goodness constitute the life of God and the spirit and law of His kingdom. Man can become a true son of God only as the Spirit of the Father unfolds in his soul, and becomes the animating and controlling spirit of his own life. This casts out all thought of self and greed of power. Nevertheless, with the death of self the soul becomes correspondingly crowned with the Fathers' wisdom and power.

Nature of Divine Love.—The love of God for His creation is impartial and impersonal, because universal. All beings and things of which we can conceive are the creation, consequently the objects of His love. Nothing was made in vain. He must, therefore, care with infinite justice and impartial sympathy for all the works of His hands; and to Him they are good. He thus loves, cares and provides for man as His child, for what He designs him to be; and there can be no change in Him toward man, whatever attitude man may take toward Him. "God is no respecter of persons," and nothing that He has made can to Him be "common or unclean." When, therefore, the love of God is awakened in the heart of man as His child, and the inexpressible sense of his divine sonship thrills his being, he is lifted out of self into the unself, and like a child in the warm and secure embrace of parental affection, knows and desires nothing but the fulfilment of the Father's will and purpose in his life. Coming into unity with and under the inspiration of the Father's Spirit, he begins to feel toward men and things as God feels toward them. The spirit of condemnation and judgment melts away, and a deep and abiding sense of universal love, compassion and charity takes its place. He learns to love and forgive his enemies. He comes to see men and things for what they are in the purpose of the Father, and if they have fallen out of their true position, he feels toward them a compassionate desire to help them to return.

Such were the feelings of the Christ for the world in its misdirections and carnality, as he gave himself in self-sacrificing efforts for its spiritual awakening and emancipation. When scorned and rejected by those who should have been the first to respond to his divine message—the leaders at Jerusalem—it was this spirit which wept in burning tears of commiseration and pity over the blind but beloved city; and when at last put to the shameful death of the cross, at the instigation of the people he had sought to bless, he still prayed for his murderers: "Father forgive them, for they know not what they do."

Mission of the Christ.—It was the work of the Christ to set specifically before the world the ideal of a perfect life for man in the flesh, and by precept and example to fasten it upon the attention and plant it in the heart of universal humanity. It devolved upon him then not only to open to men the law and condition of its attainment, but to practically demonstrate its possibility by its actualization in his own experience; and not only this, but to awaken interest and faith by an impressive example of its legitimate fruits in works of beneficence and power. He did not hesitate, however, to emphasize the difficulty that lay in the way of really entering upon the path and work of present attainment. He saw that many would gladly enough accept the gospel promise of a new and transcendent life, if they could still hold on to the things of flesh and sense in which self is centered. He saw the tenacity with which men would cling to the sensuous life, and their dependence upon the external, especially the desire for wealth and the advantages and pleasures that riches are supposed to secure. The impressive earnestness of his words on these points is clearly indicated in the passages at the head of this paper. The disciples themselves, for about three years under his daily ministry, were loath to accept the necessity of self-denial, so absolutely essential to the work of regeneration. Almost to the last they sought for prominence and position in the new kingdom which they persistently hoped and expected the Master to set up in the external. But this could not be. The nature of the kingdom and its new life were incompatible with the spirit of self. Its very realization was to be in rising out of the life of self into the life of divine love and sympathy. It was in dying to the selfish spirit and awaking to the spirit of divine sonship and brotherhood.

No Call for Asceticism.—Christ did not call upon man to leave the world and neglect its legitimate industries and become a recluse or anchorite, in order to reach the spiritual and perfect life to which he directed and led him. Neither did he require him to ignore in any sense the things of the outward life as such. " Your heavenly Father knoweth that ye have need of all these things." He simply urged that they should not live in and for these things, whereby they came into bondage to them, but to live in and for the higher things of the Spirit, those things that
10

pertain to the kingdom of God, and let the things
of the sensuous life become secondary and subordinate
to the spiritual and its divine communion and fellowship. "Seek ye first the kingdom of God and his
righteousness and all these things shall be added unto
you." This was practically saying that the realization of the spiritual life through loyalty to its righteous law, was the best and only true preparation for
the perfect and successful life in the world; because it
would lift man to a plane of attainment and power
that would give the perfect mastery of this world and
enable him to command the things he needed.

With the opening of the spiritual life in man comes
the dawning of the vision of God, and the beginning of
His kingdom in the doing of His will. Then comes
the glad recognition of the Father's compassionate
Spirit and providence, which hold all souls in all worlds
in the secure embrace of a quenchless and boundless
love and care, waiting in infinite tenderness and patience the opening of the door in the hearts of His
children, to become manifest and real to each and all.

The Opened Heavens.—We read of the Master that,
at his baptism by John in the Jordan, "Straightway
coming up out of the water," and praying, "the
heavens were opened unto him, and the Spirit descended and abode upon him." This opening of the
spiritual heavens unto Jesus, and the descent of the
Spirit as an abiding or permanent illumination in his
soul at this crisis of his life, is itself the evidence that
he had not before had the perfect illumination. It is
evidence also that in reaching this culminating crisis

through which he entered into his full illumination, he had been obliged to contend with the same limitations of the sensuous life that encompass our common humanity. The inspired Apostle to the Gentiles affirmed that "He was tempted in all points like as we are." Soon after entering upon his ministry, his possession of the inner vision of true seership became strikingly manifest in his interview with the woman of Samaria, whose history and the most secret acts of whose life he read at a glance; as she affirmed, he "told me all things that ever I did." Also with Nathanael, the guileless Israelite, brought to him by Philip, whom he also read, and had previously seen by the inner sight, under a distant fig tree before Philip had called him. At the expression of surprise by Nathanael at this exhibition of occult vision, " Jesus answered and said unto him, Because I said unto thee, I saw thee under the fig tree, believest thou ? thou shalt see greater things than these. . . . Verily, verily, I say unto you, Hereafter ye shall see heaven open, and the angels of God ascending and descending upon the Son of man."

In the gospel narratives of the Christ life, the evidence of his occult seership is continually shown; but it has seemed to excite no surprise, because the story has been read, in the main, under the traditional impression that he was a supernatural being, a god veiled in human flesh, and such powers were to be expected. This ungrounded superstition will sooner or later die out; then will be seen and realized in all its divine suggestiveness and power the real lesson of the Christ life as a divinely illuminated humanity—"the way, the truth, and the life," or Example for all men. Allowing him to have been, as believed by many, an incarnated Divinity, even then he came under the limitations of our humanity, and the exercise of all his powers was in and through the organism of a strictly human brain and body. Thus even were demonstrated the possibilities of the human organism under divine influence and illumination—all that is claimed under the interpretation here set forth. This conclusion is fully substantiated by the Master's own words. "Verily, verily, I say unto you, He that believeth on me, the works that I do shall he do also; and greater works than these shall he do because I go unto the Father." Thus in the most unequivocal manner he assured his followers that his highest experience was attainable by any man through faith in him as an Example, and the strict following of that Example. "He that followeth me shall not walk in darkness, but shall have the light of life." It is only as an example of our own possibilities, and of the divinely appointed way of attainment, that we are called upon in his gospel to accept and follow him. He had, as we have seen, the organic limitations of our common humanity to meet and overcome, through co-operation with divine influence which is open and free to all. This was, indeed, the simple message of his gospel.

The words of Jesus to Nathanael imply that after the heavens were opened unto him, angelic ministry and communion were a continuous experience. This was what Nathanael was to see with the dawning of

the spiritual vision, which Jesus prophesied would
come to him also. "Ye shall see heaven open," implying that from his full illumination it remained
"open" to him, "and the angels of God ascending and
descending upon the Son of man." This was further
evidenced by his words on a subsequent occasion when
he assured his disciples that by prayer to the Father
he could immediately summon to his aid, if needed,
"more than twelve legions of angels." When we consider the power over material conditions exerted by
the angel in the deliverance of Peter, and afterward
of both John and Peter, from a guarded Roman
prison, summoned by the prayers of their friends, we
can imagine something of the possibility resting with
legions of angels when summoned by the prayer and
faith of a Christ. From his struggle with temptation
in the wilderness to the dark hours of Gethsemane,
"angels ministered unto him and strengthened him."
If then, the opening of the spiritual life in the soul of
Jesus, through unity with the Father's Spirit, opened
the heavens unto him, and made angelic communion
and ministry a common experience, it must do essentially the same for all his faithful followers, as it did
in Apostolic experience after their illumination.

Worlds Unseen by Outward Eyes.—He who sup-
poses that the physical universe embraces all the substantial worlds of sentient being and organized activity there are, has but the faintest conception of the
arcana of substance and being. Within and behind
the veil of materiality and sense, vastly transcending
the sphere of sensuous observation and experience,

there is, indeed, a spiritual universe resplendent with spheres of celestial beauty and incomprehensible magnitude, of which the physical universe is but a vague and shadowy reflection and correspondence. This inner universe of eternal and indescribable realities, with its infinite gradations of interiorly ascending and expanding spheres, peopled by corresponding ranks of glorified beings, is a substantial universe, in the sense that each interior sphere within sphere is literally constituted of corresponding ethereal or spiritualized substance. The heavenly societies of celestial realms have actual place and environment, corresponding with their interior states or degrees of attainment in holiness, wisdom and power. Individual existence and personal consciousness would be inconceivable without this.

Infinite Gradations of Substance.—In the last analysis there is doubtless but one substance, yet that substance must be subject to infinite gradations of etherealization and refinement, for the embodiment and external expression of corresponding interior states of spiritual being and consciousness. The conscious existence and voluntary activity of individual life would be as impossible without individual embodiment in an organism, as without an external environment for those activities. There is, therefore, of necessity the corresponding substance appropriate to such embodiment. Hence "There is a spiritual body," as "there is a natural body." "Howbeit that was not first which is spiritual, but that which is natural; and afterward that which is spiritual." For the activity

of embodied spiritual beings there is the same necessity, we repeat, for external environment, a world of
forms objective to the organic personality, on a plane
of etherealization corresponding to the degree of spiritual attainment or the development of the interior life.
For these worlds within worlds in infinite gradations
of ascending orders, there is, then, the appropriate
substance in its corresponding degree of spiritualization. In a Divine Economy the law of demand and
supply is universal and inevitable. The progressive
and indestructible nature of man as a child of the infinite God, renders this system of unfolding life through
infinite gradations of spheres a necessity. Without
this, the career of an endless and progressive being
would be impossible. Without progress, or continually advancing stages of attainment, an eternal existence to a being like man would become monotonous
and unbearable. If God is infinite Being and man is
the child of God, as taught by the Christ, he is the
engermed embodiment of infinite and eternal possibilities. This fundamental postulate of Christian Theosophy accepted, then essentially what is here suggested
and vastly more follows of necessity. Every fact in
Nature, when fairly considered, is in harmony with
this conception; and every analogy drawn from the
history of organic life in its evolution from the moss
to man sustains it.

Matter and Spirit.—We need not here discuss the
profitless question whether matter and spirit are one.
They are differentiated one from the other to our present experience and consciousness, and therefore possi-

ble of being thus differentiated to all future experiences. That which we call matter now, is the analogue of that which will stand for objective substance forever. And that which we now call Spirit (mind, soul, etc.), that to which belong the attributes of intelligence, love, sympathy, aspiration and worship, is the analogue of that which will be Spirit, and will hold its supremacy over substance forever. A portion of this Spirit once individualized as an embodied soul, a self-conscious personality and child of God, will unfold and advance forever as an embodied personality, the capacity of the organism unfolding with the growth of the spirit in personal life and consciousness.

Sustained by Analogy.—From the standpoint of purely sensuous observation and experience, we are obliged to recognize the gradations of substance from that condition which we call gross, inert matter, up to the thinking brain of man. The one substance of earthy matter composed of the elements of the mineral world is transformed first into the organic substance of the vegetable structure, then into the vastly higher and finer tissues of animal flesh, and again to the still more delicate tissues of the higher and more perfect organism of man. Every step in these marvelous transformations is a process of refinement, and practically of etherealization.

We see all this resulting from the evolution of life from lower to higher planes of embodiment in the physical world, each advancing type of organism taking on, through the corresponding transformation, the appropriate substance or the more etherealized condition of the one original substance derived from the mineral kingdom.

There is absolutely no authority from the standpoint of physical science for either affirming or supposing that the evolution of conscious being ceases, or that the gradations of substance stop at the physical organism or brain of man. On the contrary there is good reason to believe they do not, but that both the evolution of life and the etherealization and gradations of substance continue without end in the infinite and all-embracing sphere of the Divine Substantiality. The indestructibility of substance, the supremacy of life over substance, and the controlling power of intelligence and ideals with the yearning after immortality in the aspirations of embodied souls, demand them.

Primordial Substance Invisible.—We have incontestable evidence that the very matter which seems so solid and enduring to the senses was precipitated, so to speak, through gradual and successive steps of condensation, from a primordial condition of invisibility. There is, therefore, nothing in the constitution of matter known to us to militate in the least against the conception here presented, of its return by an upward process of gradual transformation and etherealization to invisibility again, even in the form of ethereal organisms. The entire analogy of creation, or the evolution of life and consciousness through ascending grades of organism in the physical world, points toward the transcending results here suggested. Indeed the whole cycle of materiality from the first con-

densation of ethereal substance from invisibility into
the condition known as matter, the formation of
worlds, and the culmination of all in the evolution of
life, ultimating in the self-conscious personality of
man, indicate that the birth of immortal beings was
the specific and only object of material worlds. As
already intimated, we are not left to inference and
the indications of analogy alone for evidence of the
truth of the essential claim involved. We have the
positive testimony of a higher observation and experience than the senses afford.

The Testimony of Seership.— Inspired teaching
affirms that, "There is a natural body and there is a
spiritual body." The renowned Apostle who made
this statement was an illuminated seer of spiritual
things. He claimed to have been intromitted into the
"third heaven," and saw and heard things unutterable
in the language of earth. The truth of his affirmation
concerning the existence of the spiritual body and the
transcendent realities of the after-life, is sustained and
corroborated by the accordant testimony of many
seers whose spiritual vision has been opened, and
whose testimonies have been wholly independent one
of the other. Some of these have given unmistakable
evidence of the truth of their inner experience in the
fact of meeting and conversing with recently departed
spirits, of whose decease both the seer and his immediate friends were wholly unaware. The account given
by the spirit to the seer, of the circumstances connected with and previous to his departure, being corroborated by subsequent investigation not only identi-

fied the personality of the departed, but confirmed the truth of the seer's experience. Many instances of apparent death followed by subsequent resuscitation have been attended with the same and other remarkable experiences, which attest the realities of life beyond the physical body, and the substantial character of both the spiritual body and the world it inhabits, when it has passed "within the vail." Thousands of death-bed experiences add impressive weight to this glad testimony of the deathless nature of man. In numberless cases as the physical powers wane in the parting hour, the spirit triumphantly asserts its supremacy, and the inner vision is opened to behold the joyful presence of attending spirits, often the beaming faces of departed loved ones, waiting to receive them with the glad embrace of undying love to the companionship and larger life of a better world.

Where the spiritual vision is not thus open before the suspension of the outward consciousness, the same experience awaits the soul on its entire emancipation from the body. Frequently in the mesmeric trance the inner vision has been opened to behold the scenes of the invisible world and converse with the departed, with many corroborating circumstances to confirm the truth of their experience.

An Important Revelation.—The universal testimony of these spiritual seers, is to the effect that the spirit body of the departed corresponds in every essential particular to the physical one they left, save in the ethereal nature of its substance. Exception is made also to deformities from physical injuries and congenital defects, which do not pertain to the spiritual body.

One significant and important fact has been brought to light in these post-mundane revelations and experiences, which it is well to specially emphasize. The ethereal nature of the spirit body makes it a complete and perfect expression of the character and quality of the personal life, so that the very motives and unspoken thoughts are mirrored upon the surface and externally revealed. The activities of the inward life produce vibrations upon the all-pervading spiritual atmosphere, which appears as an aura emanating from and surrounding the person of each spirit. This aura of necessity bears the impress of the real character and moral status of the individual, and is, therefore, light or dark, beautiful or repellant, according to the character of the individual. No deception is there possible; all shams and pretence are gone forever. The inward states, through radiation, become practically the outward garment of the person, to be known and read of all with whom he associates.

Degrees of Inward Perception.—As there are different gradations and spheres of life and attainment in the spirit world, so there are corresponding degrees of perception in the different seers whose psychic vision has been opened to that world. Some are only opened to what may properly be called the natural plane in the spiritual world; that is, the sphere peopled by those who still live and act from the plane of the sensuous life. It must be confessed that vast numbers of our race have not yet risen through spiritual birth and regeneration to the plane of the spiritual man. These are furnishing continual recruits to the ranks of those who still linger on the corresponding plane in the home of the departed.

Some of our seers, however, have through the deeper ecstatic trance, been intromitted to the purely spiritual degree of the mind, the true spiritual consciousness temporarily awakened by the entire closing up for the time of the senses, and outward life—and thus opened to communion with the more interior regions of the celestial heavens. These, like the great Apostle, have witnessed and experienced scenes and things of unutterable glory and beatitude, as real to their exalted state of perception and experience as anything which mortal eyes reveal to outward sense. These beatific experiences are so vastly above and beyond anything corresponding therewith in the natural world, as to baffle every attempt at description.

An Important Lesson.—These exceptional experiences of seership reveal and establish a fact of the greatest importance and interest to every aspiring soul: it is that the personal life of every one, whether conscious of the fact or not, is in conjunction with the corresponding plane of life in the world of spirits, in which we all exist even now by virtue of our interior organism, though held to the outward world by the physical body. Hence the unfolding of our spiritual nature and life here will lift us into conjunction with corresponding planes of heavenly life and influence, and with the opening of the divine life within comes the opening also of the door of conscious communion

and fellowship with heavenly societies, who are one
with the ascended Christ in the ministry of heaven to
earth.   With full spiritual illumination all the psychic
powers awake to spontaneous activity, as illustrated
in the Master.   The mental faculties, taking on an
intuitive action, are lifted above the limitations and
drudgery of the sensuous plane.

Many instances of seership have been the unsought
and spontaneous experience of some of the most saintly
souls of religious history.   Many striking illustrations
are given in both the Old and New Testaments.   The
testimony of these interior, exalted and heavenly experiences is worthy the most serious attention and
study of all who would learn of man's higher nature
and possibilities.   The seership which opens the soul of
man in the body to independent converse with angelic
beings, is legitimate, normal and exalting in its character and influence.   We have a striking and beautiful illustration of this in the experience of our great
Exemplar and his three favored disciples on the
mount of transfiguration.   We have in that example,
also, an equally suggestive and instructive illustration
of the true conditions of such high communion and
exalted experience.   We read that "Jesus taketh with
him Peter, and James, and John, and leadeth them up
into a high mountain apart by themselves to pray.
And as he prayed the fashion of his countenance was
altered and he was transfigured before them.   And
his face did shine as the sun, and his raiment was
white and glistering; And, behold there appeared
unto them two men which were Moses and Elias: who

appeared in glory, and were talking with Jesus. But Peter and they that were with him were heavy with sleep; and when they were fully awake, they saw his glory and the two men that stood with him."

External Conditions.—As a preliminary and necessary condition of this high experience, they sought the solitude and silence apart from the bustling stir and hum of the outward life, where the attention could be wholly yielded up to a season of divine communion and heavenly converse, without danger of interruption from external diversion. This they found in the stillness of night and the hush and quiet of a lofty mountain retreat.

Opening of the Door.—When the proper external conditions were thus established, the first step was prayer, in which the soul opens itself to communion with and inspiration and teaching from the Divine. He led "them up into a high mountain apart by themselves to pray." The sole object of the retirement was prayer, to seek full and undisturbed communion with God the All-Father. For this to be perfect there must be full entrance into the spiritual degree of the mind, which in turn requires complete withdrawal from the external, and the stilling of self, that the divine voice may be heard and the revelation be complete. "When thou prayest, enter into thy closet [the inner sanctuary] and when thou hast shut thy door, [the door of outward sense] pray to thy Father which is in secret; and thy Father which seeth in secret shall reward thee openly." In thus withdrawing from the external and concentrating the whole attention

upon the divine within, in full and trusting desire for
communion with God as child with parent, the spiritual degree of the mind is opened and the inbreathing
of the divine, the kindling touch of the Father's love
and wisdom are unmistakably realized. This uplifts
the soul to the serene heights of spiritual vision and
understanding, and the needed revelation is perfect.
If angelic ministry and communion are needed, they
will immediately open to the soul thus prepared to
receive them, as with the Master and his three disciples on the mount.

Seership Normal to the Spiritual Man.— To one
who has attained to the spiritual life in the flesh, the
regenerate life of the spiritual man, this is as simple
and easy an act, as is the corresponding concentration
of the attention and absorption of the mind in any
special interest and activity of the sensuous life by the
natural man. But to the unregenerate or unspiritual-
ized, it is something yet to be attained. This very
process, however, or attitude and effort of the soul
persisted in, is the direct and certain way of attainment. There will come to every honest effort in this
direction some degree of inspiration and inward leading. If this is sacredly cherished and strictly followed,
the work of regeneration, involving corresponding
transformation of organism, begins. As the spiritual
life unfolds under the divine inspiration and leading,
the soul enters consciously deeper and deeper into the
realization of the spiritual life, and rises correspondingly above the plane and limitations of the sensuous
life and understanding. Sooner or later this will lift

the seeker into the full freedom, power, and inward
vision of the spiritual man, the final illumination and
gifts of the Spirit, as illustrated by the Master, and to
a high degree in Apostolic experience.

While this divine attainment is unquestionably
within reach of all, some will have more to overcome than others; yet none need despair who truly
desire it. It is the birthright of all, since in his
spiritual nature, every man has a divine as well as
human parentage and heredity. The recognition
of this in desire, faith and consecrated effort for its
realization is all that is required of any soul. The
transforming power thus evoked is of God, whose unchanging love and providence for His children are
eternally and unalterably pledged to this result.
Until the organism is prepared through the opening
and unfolding of the spiritual life under divine influence, for full illumination and the exercise of normal
seership, no one can enter into the full spiritual degree
of the mind except by the abnormal process of the
ecstatic trance, in which all the avenues of sense to the
outer world are locked in profound repose. The mind
thus disentangled from the influence of sensuous impressions, and inwardly awakened, may often be lifted
to the mount of vision. This, as before remarked, has
sometimes occurred in mesmeric experiments, and also
in the spontaneous trances referred to above. This
was evidently the condition of the three disciples on the
mount with Jesus; for we read that "Peter and they
that were with him were heavy with sleep: and when
they were fully awake [inwardly or in the trance state]
11

they saw his glory and the men that stood with him."
When the trance and the vision were to end, the Master himself restored them to outer consciousness by
his word and touch. "And Jesus came and touched
them, and said, Arise, and be not afraid. And suddenly, when they had lifted up their eyes and looked
round about, they saw no man any more, save Jesus
only with themselves." Those who have had experience
with the genuine spiritual trance, will recognize the
accuracy and faithfulness of the picture here sketched
by the evangelists. "As they came down from the
mountain, Jesus charged them to tell no man of the
vision." These words of Jesus imply that what they
had seen was not with the external sight, but the inner
and higher spiritual vision.

Nature of the Transfiguration.—There is always
some degree of external transfiguration in the heavenly glow and radiance which beams from the countenance of the rapt ecstatic, and sometimes this is exceedingly striking and impressive. This must have
been true and transcendently striking and impressive
with the countenance of Jesus during that season of
special spiritual exaltation; but to the vision of the
disciples his "raiment" also, "was white as the light,
and glistering." This is positive evidence that the
vision was spiritual and not physical, as the raiment
could not be transfigured with light to the physical
sight. With their opened spiritual vision they saw
him as they did Moses and Elias—a spirit. They saw
him robed in light, the pure white light of his own
spiritualized being.

The act of entering into the purely spiritual state and holding this high communion, was normal to Jesus, and easily effected through the subordination of the outward to the inward spiritual sense, by the simple act of abstraction and introversion, or the transfer of attention and desire from the outward to the inward life, without the entire suspension and closing of the external. But with the disciples, in whom the spiritual life had not yet been fully opened, trance was a necessity to spiritual vision and high communion; and the touch and assuring words of the Master were also needed for their immediate restoration to outward consciousness. Let it be remembered that regeneration or the full unfolding of the spiritual life, transforms and perfects the organism as an instrument for the exercise of the spiritual gifts, and through the permanent illumination it secures awakens all the psychic powers of the soul into spontaneous activity as needed. This is a condition of normal seership and occult power that may be wisely and safely desired and sought by all.

Dangers of Mediumship.—Intercourse with the spirit world, and communion with the departed—who are often made the guardian angels of their loved ones here—is, under proper conditions, not only possible and legitimate, but certainly very comforting to those who mourn the apparent loss of the departed. But the ordinary phases of mediumship are not the normal and legitimate way of seeking this communion. The normal exercise of spiritual clairvoyance, clairaudience and the psychometric sense, is the only re-

liable and legitimate method of seeking direct converse with the departed, or attendant spirits. All
other methods are unreliable through the liability
of imposition from deceiving spirits, even through the
purely mechanical methods, allowing all that is claimed
for them.   But aside from this, the trance of mediumship under the controlling influence of spirits is abnormal and illegitimate, and fraught with great risk and
danger to the subject thereof.   To yield our will or
organisms to the control of the will of others, and become a mere automaton for their intelligence and opinions, is destructive of our individuality and personal
character.   Personality and will are the most precious
and sacred trusts, committed to us for cultivation, perfection and proper exercise, and cannot be yielded up
to the control of another's will and intelligence without the violation of these trusts and obligations.

The Giver of this divine birthright will not encroach
one hair's breadth upon the liberty he has thus bestowed; neither will any human spirit, whether in or
out of the body, who is at one with Him.   Both the
practice and results of such control are abnormal and
unsatisfying. It is first attained by the breaking down
and overcoming of the individuality and will, by an influence external to the personality.   This is exact reverse of the divine process of reaching true and permanent illumination through the unfolding of the spiritual life from within. This by bringing out the divine
element in man gives nobility and strength to the
individuality and character, and clothes the will with a
power of resistance to evil and a corresponding power

for good which partakes of omnipotence itself. The subjection of the consciousness and will to the dominance of another personality, whether in the body or out, however intelligent and honorable the operator may be regarded in a given case, cannot be practised without weakening the will and thus prove demoralizing to the individuality and personal character of the subject. The danger lies in the fact that it cannot be followed without rendering the subject negative, and increasing his susceptibility to any and every psychic influence, good or bad, with which for the time he may be in contact. And while there is so much that is perverting in the present condition of life and influence in the world, to say nothing of the possibly corrupting influence from the lower circles of the spirit world, the danger referred to need only be mentioned to become fully apparent.

The power and influence thus obtained by men or spirits over others may not in many cases be abused and turned to bad account, but this is no excuse for seeking or desiring it. It certainly opens the door of danger and liability to such abuse, and gives no assurance that the subject will not fall under malign influences through his psychic susceptibility thus intensified. Is not this, in fact, the very source of a large part of the corruption, fraud and immorality which has disgraced the spiritualistic movement, to the regret of the pure and true who are interested in it, and the popular disgust of the general public, and of many who might otherwise be interested in its investigation? Experiment has demonstrated the fact that all the psychic powers of the sixth sense, including clairvoyance, clairaudience and psychometry, can be fully unfolded and exercised by the subject himself without the loss of identity, or the subjection of the will and personality to another's control. This form of psychic culture strengthens and develops individuality of character and will, and gives the subject perfect control over his own organism and sensations.*

Mediumship not Spirituality.—It will be seen from the above that the cultivation and practice of every phase of mediumship which depends upon "spirit control" is abnormal and injurious to the medium. It is neither regenerative nor spiritualizing, but rather degenerating and demoralizing to the subject; it opens the world more fully to the corrupting and degrading influence of disorderly spirits. The sooner these facts are recognized by "spiritualists," and all desiring a true and uplifting communion with the departed, the better it will be for the cause of a true spiritualism. The sooner they turn from their vain seeking of the promised gifts of the Spirit, through the mistaken gateway of mediumship, to the true source of illumination through the divine inmost of their own souls, the sooner will they find a true and soul satisfying angelic communion, fraught with divine blessings unmixed with danger. Instead of seeking the materialization of the spirits to the senses, let them rather seek the spiritualization of their own

* For a full and lucid exposition of the psychic powers, their cultivation and training, see Author's work, "The Way, the Truth and the Life."

being through divine inspiration and communion, and
they will soon be lifted to the perfect life of spiritual
supremacy and illumination in the open vision of the
Spirit. No other evidence of the immortal life will be
needed, and power will thus be given to work for the
corresponding elevation and emancipation of all souls
in the depths of ignorance and spiritual darkness
either in or out of the body. When the same time
and earnest effort are given to the true work of spiritual realization and divine illumination that is now
given to the cultivation of mediumship and the pursuit
of phenomenal spiritualism, there will come results
into the lives of the seekers infinitely more satisfying,
exalting and inspiring than is possible to mediumship,
in its least objectionable phase.

The inevitable tendency of phenomenal spiritualism
and external manifestations is to absorb the attention
in the phenomena, and thus divert from all thought
and effort after inward spiritual development and
divine realization. Seek first the knowledge of God
and the realization of divine sonship and brotherhood,
through personal communion with and inspiration
from the Father, and the certainty of immortality and
the possibility of a divine career for all men is settled
forever. Dwelling and walking in unity with the
Father in all things will secure all needed angelic
ministry and communion. Can we not trust the wisdom and goodness of the Father in this as in other
matters? When desire for angelic communion holds
the first place in the mind and heart, unity and fellowship with the Father become a secondary considera-

tion if they do not fade out completely from serious
thought and desire. The attempt to make spiritualism a religion, or to make spirit intercourse and
communion in any sense a basis of religion, will ever
prove a failure. The only possible basis for true religion — and there can be but one true religion — is
union and communion with God as the Father of
men; and the realization of this, as it always has,
will secure in its true and subordinate place, angelic
ministry and communion, with the sense of the great
Brotherhood of souls in every world and sphere of the
Father's boundless kingdom.

The Spiritual Life not Opened by Death.—Since
spirituality comes only from the unfolding of the spiritual life, the mere passing to and existence in the world
of spirits does not lift man to the plane of the spiritual
life nor open to him its treasures. A man out of the
physical body may be no more spiritual than in it.
There may be just as hard-headed materialists, agnostics, atheists and dreamy pantheists there as here,
since that world is as objective and external to them
as this world is to us. Men rise spiritually in the
ranks of being only as they unfold inwardly in the
divine life and consciousness. God is not found in externals nor through any exoteric search or intellectual
effort. God is Spirit and His kingdom is within. All
that is external pertains to form and the outward life,
and is but the shadow of the real, the spiritual and
divine. God and His kingdom are not found in the
shadow but in the substance. "The kingdom of God
cometh not with observation: Neither shall they say,

Lo here! or, lo there! for, behold, the kingdom of God is within you."

Spiritual birth and regeneration is a necessity to every soul, here or there, before it can have the true vision of God and rise to the plane of the spiritual man. Death, or the passing from the physical to the spirit world, does not change man's relation to God, nor the attitude of the All-Father toward His children; His mercy, forgiveness and loving kindness endure forever. All worlds are His and His providence is perfect in every sphere. Death, or the dying to one world and waking to another, is as simple a matter as falling asleep at night and waking in the morning. It neither suspends the necessity of spiritual regeneration, nor ends the opportunity and privilege. The dogma that probation or opportunity ends with the death of the body is a fiction of theology, and a libel on the changeless character and quenchless love of the Father. The opening up and unfolding of spiritual life in the soul is the only door and pathway to the kingdom of God, the only entrance into the more interior and exalted spheres of the celestial heavens.

The soul of the natural man on passing to the world of spirits, will remain on the plane of the natural life and be held in the sphere of self-love forever, unless he voluntarily seeks the kingdom of God in the realization of spiritual life in personal experience. And what is more serious still, he who persistently resists the call of the Spirit, which is heard in every soul and speaks in every earnest appeal and through every providence of life, is in danger of moral deterioration

and the delusions of the selfish spirit—however much
he may unfold in intellectual power—and all the more
for increased pride of intellect and self-worship. This
law applies equally to life here or there, for in the development of intelligence, man may unfold in subtlety
and wickedness as well as in wisdom and goodness.

Nothing Arbitrary in the Divine Economy.—In
this necessity of the "strait gate" and "narrow way"
of spiritual birth and regeneration as the only means
of rising from the plane of the natural to that of the
spiritual man, there is nothing arbitrary nor severe.
It is the same kind of necessity that requires physical
birth into the sensuous life, and growth from infancy
to manhood for the primary development and discipline of the natural man. The wisdom and beneficence
of the Father are revealed in this necessity, in that He
has thus opened a way whereby man as His child may
and must become a co-worker and participant with
Him in the work of destiny. The door and pathway
are open equally to all, and the invitation and help is
proffered with equal fulness and freedom to all.
Hence, by perfect co-operation with the Father the
perfect life on earth or in the spheres may be attained
by all. The earthly life and experience, therefore, will
not be complete, nor the purpose of the Father be fulfilled in them, until the kingdom of God in the perfect
life is realized on earth as it is in heaven.

Man an Inspirational Being.—Man, as we have
said, is distinguished from the animal by the possession of a rational, moral and aspirational nature, while
he has conjoined thereto all the animal qualities and

functions. The aspirational power necessarily involves a corresponding inspirational capacity. This is his noblest specific power for self-improvement and elevation, since his aspirations open him to inspiration from the centre and sphere of life and activity, upon which his aspirations are focussed. It may also become a means of degradation as well as elevation, according to the character of the ideal upon which the desires are centred. The character and development of man are determined largely by his dominant ideals and desires. When therefore the Christ ideal of the kingdom of God and its perfect life of divine communion and fellowship, or walking with God in the flesh, have been set before the mind as the supreme object of desire, they become the goal of aspiration, or prayer and effort. When this attitude of soul is fully established, man is opened to permanent inspiration from the sphere of the Divine, under which he is led into realized oneness of life with God which brings the full and abiding illumination.

The Natural and the Spiritual Man.--The natural man in the primary consciousness of his sensuous life is the child of Nature from whom he received his physical organism and heredity. On this plane of consciousness he realizes only his relations to and dependence upon the natural world for his existence and sustenance. The spiritual man, or man awakened to the consciousness of his deeper spiritual nature and relations, is the child of God, from whom he received his permanent spiritual identity and indestructible organism as a divine heredity. In this deeper nature

he inherits and holds potentially the qualities and
attributes of the Father's Being, which insure him an
immortal destiny and the possibilities of a divine
career. In this birth of the spiritual consciousness
man awakens to a realizing sense of his divine sonship,
and in all things his vital relation to and dependence
upon the Father. As the natural man was generated
on the plane and under the law of the sensuous life,
so he must be regenerated from the plane and under
the law of the spiritual life, before he can rise to the
higher level of the spiritual man and actualize his
divine sonship and brotherhood in experience.

The highest level of consciousness reached by the
natural man is attained through the senses, by the
evolution or unfolding of the intellectual and moral
powers in their relation to the physical world. The
highest intellectual attainment possible to this plane,
gives no power to apprehend the spiritual nature and
Being of God, nor any true understanding of spiritual
things. Hence the multiplicity of conflicting opinions
concerning them, on the plane of the sensuous understanding, which, in the New Testament, is called the
"carnal mind." The creeds and theologies of the
world are mostly the products of the sensuous understanding, as only the natural man would construct a
creed and make its acceptance by others a condition
of salvation. The Master set no such example. The
controlling principle and law of life in the natural
man is *self*. The controlling principle and law of life
in the spiritual man is *love*. The one desires to rule;
the other to serve. "Hereby know we the spirit of

truth, and the spirit of error." Spiritual things can be understood only through spiritual experience and illumination, from the unfolding of the spiritual nature and life. The elevation of man from the plane of the sensuous life to that of the spiritual can, therefore, be effected only through the awakening and evolution of the spiritual life in the soul under the quickening touch and inspiration of the Father's Spirit.

Divine, unselfish love being the essence and law of the spiritual life, its evolution in man exalts, transforms and co-ordinates all his powers of soul and body under its spirit, and lifts him to its own divine plane of spontaneous freedom, righteousness and power of service. Regeneration is thus seen to be the higher spiritual evolution of humanity, and Divine love the regenerating power.

Organic Changes Involved in Regeneration.—The opening of the spiritual life in man, and the higher activity of the soul's powers under its supreme law of love, quickened and carried forward by the immediate inspiration of the Father's Spirit, effects corresponding changes as before intimated, in the organic conditions of the brain and nerve centres as the physical instruments of these activities. This important truth needs further emphasis.

Why should there be organism at all? Because life is manifest in specific form and expression only in and through organism. We know absolutely nothing of life in active manifestation only as it is embodied and expressed in organic structures, each structure representing in form and texture the characteristic and

controlling principle of the embodied life. "God giveth it a body as it hath pleased him, and to every seed
its own body." Hence unless the organism in form,
texture and quality, exactly corresponded with and
correctly expressed the controlling principle and characteristic attributes of the embodied life, the very
object of organism would be defeated. The stalk of
barley differs from that of the wheat, and both of
these from the corn and other grains growing side by
side from the same soil and under like conditions,
simply because the principle of life engermed in each
differing seed unfolds and becomes the life of the
stalk, and determines the character of the structure
in which it is embodied and expressed. This is the
supreme law of organism, and will bear frequent statement because of its importance.

Under this law is manifest the absolute power of
life over the material it uses in the construction, reconstruction and repair of organisms, converting it into
any kind and quality of substance or tissue required.
Vegetable life thus lifts mineral substance to its own
level, and converts it into the kind and quality of
vegetable texture that shall be identified with and
represent the specific form of life embodied in any
given structure. The same is true of animals and man
in the transformation of substances used as food, so
that every organism on any plane of life is identified
with and correctly represents the essential character
and quality of the life it embodies. Hence, when the
soul of man is fully opened to the spiritual life and becomes imbued with its higher principle of unselfish love,

the external organism comes under the higher vital chemistry of the spiritual life and law, which transforms or reconstructs the body into a perfect organic expression of its own divine quality and character. The brain is the organ of the mind, the physical seat or centre of action for all the conscious powers of the soul. It is also the co-ordinating centre of all the vital and mechanical activities of the body, so that all the vital centres of the brain are specifically related to, and connected with, corresponding vital portions of the dependent organism. Hence, as the brain is the throne and centre of the soul's powers, and at the same time the co-ordinating and controlling centre of the entire organism, the physical body, as a whole, is both the organic instrument and physical temple of the soul during its connection with the outward world. The brain being the throne room and centre of power, as is the brain so will be the body, and as is the soul so will be both brain and body.

In accordance with this controlling law of organism, the human brain and body must and do correspond with and essentially represent the character and quality of the soul's life, the differences in the organisms of men corresponding exactly with their differing characteristics in these respects. As the higher attributes unfold and become prominent, the body takes on refinement to correspond with the change. If the animal come into undue prominence and activity, the body takes on grossness and expresses animality. When therefore the spiritual nature and its supreme attribute of divine love unfold and come to their rightful supremacy, the physical organism will become the complete incarnation and expression of that nature, "the Word made flesh."

As is the soul, so will be the brain and body; and when love becomes the animating life of the soul, the principle of love in activity will so open the life to the divine influx, that the soul's powers will be held under the immediate inspiration of divine wisdom and goodness against error and sin, and the body kept secure in that life against the power of poison and disease. The one involves the other. "They shall take up serpents; and if they drink any deadly thing it shall not hurt them; they shall lay hands on the sick and they shall recover."

It should be emphasized continually in mind and thought, that the transformation to be effected embraces the entire man—body as well as soul. It seems needful to press this point, because it has been so entirely overlooked in the traditional teaching. The potent influence of decided mental impressions over the vital processes, and the limiting power of imperfect ideals over both thought and effort, add to this necessity. This all-inclusive transformation, for which perfect faith is required, is the gospel promise; and, as we have seen, a physiological and organic necessity of spiritual regeneration. The physical body is to be lifted as much above the power of poison and the possibility of disease, as the soul is raised above the power of temptation and the possibility of sinning.

The Ideal Man of the Gospel.—The unmistakable ideal held up by the Christ for the attainment of men in the present life, was the perfect manhood of a true son of God, in which the divine perfections of the Father's nature and character were to be reproduced and represented. This, however, he especially emphasized as impossible to man by his own unaided effort, yet possible to all through divine help which the impartial Father freely gives to all true seekers. No power less than the quickening touch and inspiration of the Father's Spirit, can awaken and bring to fruition the germs of divine attribute and power latent in the soul of man. The divine provision and regenerating power are absolute and perfect, awaiting only the desire, faith and co-operation of man. This co-operation is the supreme and only necessity. The ideal, invitation and promise are of God, and the infinite and changeless love of the Father is pledged to their fulfillment through the co-operation of His children. The rapidity and thoroughness of the transformation and realization will depend in great degree upon the personal devotion to the ideal in thought and desire, the firmness and energy of the faith, and the corresponding closeness of the walk with God in humble dependence, communion and trust.

Nature of the New and Higher Life.—The personal realization of that divine relationship which binds man to God in the love and loyalty of child to Parent, and the divine communion and inspiration thus secured, constitutes the new and spiritual life. The growth and development of this life is in the deepening and unfolding of that love and inspiration, through a living, vital contact and unbroken commun-

12

ion with the Father's Spirit. The realization of divine sonship and the faith it awakens, are possible only through love in the heart for God as a Father. The child of an earthly father may have a full recognition of his relation, but unless he have a genuine love in his heart for the father, he has no true appreciation or realizing sense of this tender and sacred tie of kinship. So man may have an intellectual conception of his relation to God, but until the heart is open to a genuine love for the Father, a passionate desire for an intimate and unbroken communion and fellowship with His Spirit, he has no true realization of this exalted and holy relationship. Love to God can be awakened in the human heart only through a realizing sense of His Fatherhood, and of His tender and supreme love for us as His children. "We love Him because He first loved us." It is the privilege of each soul to feel that he is as precious to the Father as through he were the only child.

The awakening of love to God through a realizing sense of His Fatherhood and love to us, and of the perfect security and indestructibility of the individual life in Him, constitutes the true spiritual birth. It is the opening of the life of love in the soul under the melting touch of the Father's Spirit, in response to the heart's supreme desire. The quickening and unfolding of the faculties and powers of the soul under the inspiration of this divine life, and the corresponding transformation of body, is the work of regeneration. The constant love and loyalty of the heart toward the Father is necessary for the perfect growth of His love and wisdom in us, since He can give Himself to us only through love, and this to be effectual must be mutual. If our love grow cold and cease, we close the door of entrance against His love, and regeneration stops at that point; and unless the soul return immediately in love and penitence, moral degeneration begins. Self-love, pride and ambition bring in their delusions and insanities to take the place of divine inspiration and guidance. Hence the necessity of the narrow way of loyalty to the Father in the constant and unswerving love and faith of the heart. With this, regeneration goes forward under the continuous inspiration of the Father's Spirit, until the transformation is complete. The level of the Christ-life is then reached, and the power of temptation and sin over the soul and of poison and disease over the body, and all danger of either moral or physical degeneration are gone forever. The prince of this world cometh and findeth nothing in him. He has attained to and dwells in the perfect life.

The Prophecy of Evolution, one with The Christ Ideal.—The prophetic testimony of evolution in Nature and in man points, as we have seen, unmistakably to the final realization of this Christ ideal and promise of the perfect life, in the universal experience of mankind. Since evolution is but the coming forth and embodiment of spiritual principles in external organism, and their specialization in organic function, the ultimate of this process can be nothing less than the final embodiment of all the attributes of divinity in a perfect and permanent incarnation. As every

new and advanced embodiment is but the type and
starting of an entire order or family, the evolution of
one man to the level of such an incarnation is but the
beginning of an experience which, through an understanding of this law and principle, shall ultimately
come to the entire race.

Allowing therefore, the genuineness of the Christ
experience, his example will sooner or later be understood and followed and his experience essentially reproduced in all. Thus will his claim of being "The
Way, the Truth and the Life," for all men be established in the practical experience of the race. As organism is but the incarnation of specific attributes or
principles of life in organic function, the final incarnation of all the Divine attributes will give not only the
perfect character in personality, but the perfect organism as well. The individualization and embodiment of such a personality and character would be
impossible without their perfect expression in organism. The processes of evolution will be incomplete
until both of these ends are accomplished; the one involves the other. Recognizing life in Nature as the
manifestation of an immanent God and a Divine providence, and evolution as His law and method in creation, then the promise of evolution, or of God in Nature
and man, is a divine incarnation, or the reproduction
of Himself in the bringing forth of the final order of
His true sons and daughters in the earth.

Thus the Old Testament millennial prophecies, the
Christ ideal and promise, the apocalyptic vision of the
beloved Disciple, and the promise of evolution, all

point to and prophesy the one ultimate result, the divine and perfect life in the universal experience of mankind. Evolution thus not only involves the ideal and promise of the gospel of Christ, but is itself the law of their fulfilment. It is the "Word" and law of God, as the universal Father in both Nature and the Gospel, and both are one in Him. The study of evolution in connection with the moral law of human responsibility, throws a flood of light upon the Christ doctrine of regeneration, and demonstrates its divine origin and also its necessity in the nature of things.

Human Responsibility.—The processes of evolution below man and culminating in him, were largely if not wholly spontaneous and automatic. When man appeared, however (a god in embryo), holding in his life as the embodied offspring of God the engermed attributes of the Father's nature, he was necessarily endowed with self-will, or a self-directing and self-determining power. At first in his primary and savage state, this power as well as his observing and inventive faculties had to be urged into activity by his physical necessities, necessity being "the mother of invention." When these powers became sufficiently developed through the exercise thus secured, the mere love of invention as well as of the exercise of power thus awakened became an additional incentive and powerful motive to further activity and development.

The same was true of the primary development of the intellectual and moral powers. Knowledge was a necessity to the understanding and improvement of the evironment, and removal of causes of suffering.

The pursuit of knowledge under this spur of necessity developed the intellect of man, and enabled him to improve his condition and enlarge the sphere of his life. This added to his growing love of knowledge for its own sake, carried forward his intellectual development, and opened to him the ever-widening fields of science, philosophy and invention.

The Moral Sense.—The accumulation of possessions developed the sense of personal rights and this with the instinctive attachments of family ties and kinship, and finally of tribal relations, rendered necessary some form of common law and standard of ethics. This in turn deepened the sense of personal responsibility, and thus was started the career of moral development corresponding with the intellectual and social advancement. Man has thus risen from a state of savage animalism to a high degree of civilization, through the evolution of his intellectual and moral powers on the external plane under the law of the sensuous life, which is self. This law was a necessity to the primary awakening and development of the human powers, by which alone man can be lifted from the ignorance and darkness of the infant and savage state to an intellectual and moral consciousness. This gives the sense of personal responsibility and establishes the recognition and the necessity of obedience. Until this is established man is not prepared for the higher freedom of the spiritual life, in which, under the motives and inspirations of truth and righteousness, he becomes a law unto himself. For this higher spiritual evolution of man, the evolution and final embodiment of the

divine attribute of love, which will crown the soul
with intuition, wisdom and a new power of mastery,
and evolve thereby the true civilization, it is left for
him to respond to divine suggestion and invitation
and become a co-worker with God. These suggestions
and invitations are and ever have been abundant in
the striking indications of Nature and Providence;
and especially in the inspirations of seers and prophets,
and finally in the full "Word made flesh" in the "Beloved Son."

The Law of the Perfect Life.—"Ye therefore shall
be perfect as your Father in heaven is perfect." To
be a true child of God and become perfect as He is
perfect, man must become the incarnation of the spirit
of love which is the Essence of the Father's nature
and the law of His kingdom. In proportion then as it
is unfolded in man he comes under the inspiring
motive of the divine life, which prompts to unselfish
and impartial service.

To be at-one with God in His righteousness, is to
be in unity with Him in the spirit of love and service.
There is no other basis of unity with the Father, nor
with the Christ His loyal Son and our divine and loyal
Brother. "And this is life eternal, that they might
know thee the only true God, and Jesus Christ, whom
thou hast sent." To know God as Father through
love from the heart as His child, is the only real
knowledge of God, and the only way He can be known;
and to know Christ thus as our Brother is the only
true knowledge of the Christ, and the only way in
which he can become the Christ to us. To know

Christ as the Son of God and the Brother of men is to understand the nature and possibilities of our own divine sonship and brotherhood.

Only through the inspiring motive of love can we be absolutely loyal to God in our relation to Him as His child, or loyal to man in our relation to him as brother, which alone will secure perfection to the individual and social life of man on earth or in the spheres. Love then is the law of the perfect life and so the perfect and perfecting law of life. "Love is the fulfilling of the law."

Theory and Fact.—This is true and beautiful in theory, but can it be made absolutely and unequalifiedly true in experience, will be the practical question of many who will read these pages. Do I, can I love my enemy, one who hates me and despitefully uses and persecutes me? or even my neighbor as myself? No! to the natural man this is impossible. He is living on the plane and under the law of the sensuous life, and the law of that life is *self*. He must be born again, born from above, born of the Spirit, and lifted by its regenerating and transforming power to the higher plane of the spiritual life, the law of which is Love. "Verily, verily, I say unto thee," "Ye must be born again." "That which is born of the flesh is flesh; and that which is born of the Spirit is spirit."

"Then said one unto him, Lord, are there few that be saved? And he said unto them, Strive to enter in at the strait gate: for many I say unto you, will seek to enter in and shall not be able. Because strait is the gate and narrow is the way that leadeth unto life and few there be that find it." In view of the difficulties so apparent, the question was raised, Who then can be saved? To which the Master replied, "With man it is impossible, but not with God: for with God all things are possible." "Fear not, little flock; for it is your Father's good pleasure to give you the kingdom."

On one occasion, when explaining to his disciples the true principle and spirit of prayer, he gave them a parable illustrating and enforcing the necessity of importunity, or a persistent determination, based on a sense of imperious need that will not yield one jot of seeking, until the need is supplied, and the thing desired is attained, which implies faith at the outset, that the persistent effort will be successful: then added, "Ask and it shall be given you; seek and ye shall find; knock and it shall be opened unto you. For every one that [thus] asketh receiveth; and he that seeketh findeth; and to him that knocketh it shall be opened. If a son shall ask bread of any of you that is a father, will he give him a stone? or if he ask a fish will he for a fish give him a serpent? or if he shall ask an egg, will he offer him a scorpion? If ye then being evil know how to give good gifts unto your children; how much more shall your heavenly Father give the Holy Spirit to them that ask him."

PART IV.

INSPIRATION AND DIVINE ILLUMINATION: THEIR
SPECIFIC NATURE AND DISTINGUISHING CHAR-
ACTERISTICS.

I will instruct thee and teach thee in the way which thou shalt go: I will guide thee with mine eye (*Ps.* xxxii. 8).

There is a spirit in man and the inspiration of the Almighty giveth them understanding (*Job,* xxxii. 8).

These things have I spoken unto you being yet present with you. But the Comforter which is the Holy Spirit, whom the Father will send in my name, he shall teach you all things, and bring all things to your remembrance whatsoever I have said unto you (*John,* xiv. 25, 26).

I have yet many things to say unto you, but ye cannot bear them now. Howbeit when he, the Spirit of truth, is come, he shall guide you into all truth, . . . and he will show you things to come (*John,* xvi. 12, 13).

WHAT IS INSPIRATION?

The Fact of Inspiration.—We have said that man is an aspirational and therefore an inspirational being. In the nature and constitution of things there can be no normal demand without its appropriate and certain supply. Every legitimate desire is an innate or constitutional demand which implies both the reality of the thing desired and the power of its attainment and appropriation. The relation between desire and the good desired is vital and organic in the nature of things, which makes the supply and gratification not only legitimate, but under proper conditions inevitable.

Aspiration is an eager desire and innate longing after unattained good, which implies a normal demand, for which there is, therefore, the legitimate and certain supply. The relation between the soul and the higher state or condition desired being vital, its realization is not only possible and legitimate, but under proper conditions certain. Just as expiration or breathing out from the lungs, is followed in living bodies by fresh inspiration or inbreathing from the atmosphere; so aspiration, which is a breathing out of a vital want, or true prayer, opens the soul to an immediate influx, inbreathing or inspiration of life and power from spiritual centres of supply, which, in due time, brings the full realization of the state desired.

Under the universal law of demand and supply it will be seen then, that the power of aspiration involves the power of a corresponding inspiration. This necessarily uplifts and expands the soul's life, and leads to ultimate realization, or final unity and identification with the state and condition desired. This is the foundation of all real progress in the life of man. Aspiration is true prayer, since "Prayer is the soul's sincere desire, uttered or unexpressed," and all true prayer is practically answered. The spiritual experiences of mankind, previously considered, demonstrate beyond all question the fact that in all ages men have aspired after and received inspiration from a sphere of life and intelligence above the level of their own realization, by which they have been led and lifted from lower to higher conditions. It remains for us to consider more specifically the laws and conditions as well as the nature and sources of inspiration.

Nature and Basis of Inspiration.—In the physical world the attraction of gravitation binds atom to atom and world to world in one complete system of relations which involve unceasing action and reaction, in which each exerts its specific influence upon the others according to its magnitude and density, and is correspondingly reacted upon by them. In the interaction of sun and planets the central orb exerts its specific influence upon each individual particle of matter on the subordinate planets of its system, and in turn, the tiniest grain of sand upon each globe exerts its proportionate power of attraction, or influence and reaction upon the sun.

This principle is none the less true in the realm of mind and the world of souls. There is a corresponding law of psychic attraction and repulsion which holds the world of souls in an equally inevitable network of relations, interdependence and interaction, in which each soul influences all other souls with whom it comes into psychic relations, and they in turn influence it. Each person is thus a subject of psychic influence from his associations, as well as a living centre of radiating influence upon others. As material bodies exert an influence in proportion to their magnitude and density, so do living, thinking beings exert an influence according to the measure of their personality and activity. This law is as universal and spontaneous in the world of mind as is gravitation in the realm of matter, whether man is conscious of the fact or not. The personal influence is none the less potent for being silent and unrecognized. It should be remembered that the most potent forces of the world are always silent.

There is this difference, however, between inanimate bodies and living souls: In self-conscious and self-determinate beings the measure of personal influence is modified by the varying dominant mental and emotional states. Under the stimulus of intensified mental and emotional activity, it is correspondingly augmented; and in the opposite state of inactivity and dormant mental and emotional life it is proportionally lessened. Again, the influence which each exerts upon others, tends to awaken in them either a corresponding activity in sympathy with the influence that called it forth, or in opposition to and reaction against it. In either case the reaction is returned upon the centre of influence from which it was awakened.

The Power Thus Conferred.—Man thus affects in greater or less degree, for good or ill, all within the circle of his influence, and especially those with whom he holds specific relations. The character of the influence which he exerts will be determined by the character of his dominant mental states; that is, whether his feelings and desires are charged with good or ill, love or hatred, a spirit of self-seeking, or of sympathy and service. Hence the importance of cultivating a spirit of good-will and the development of a harmonious character, that the personal influence be exerted only for good. This is quite as essential to the personal interest of the individual as to those upon whom his influence is exerted; since the reaction awakened by his influence is returned upon himself. What adds special cogency and importance to this suggestion, is the unavoidable fact that the influence of each one affects in greater or less degree many; so that the reaction of the many is returned upon the one. Hence the great truth emphasized by the Apostle, "Whatsoever a man sows that shall he also reap," and, we may add, with increase, "some thirty, some sixty and some a hundred fold." If he sow to the wind he will reap the whirlwind; but if he sow love and good-will into the lives of men, blessings will be returned to him many fold.

Mental Alchemy.—Since man may cultivate his powers and learn to control or determine his mental and emotional states, he may by an understanding of this law, make himself a power for good, as in ignorance of it he may be a power for harm. In seeking the good of others, man really finds the most potent means of his own exaltation. There is a mental alchemy, so to speak, based upon the working of this law, which holds a tremendous potency for good or ill little dreamed of by the mass of men, though recognized by some. This is the true basis of healing physical diseases by a strictly mental process often blindly applied under the name of "Mind-Cure," "Metaphysical Healing," "Christian Science Treatment," etc. It is also the basis of the "White Magic" and "Black Magic" of the East, where this law in some of its phases is more thoroughly studied and understood than with us.

Measures of Inspirational Capacity.—Under this law the measure of a man's inspirational capacity will be determined by the degree of his impressibility. That is, he receives continually into his being influences that awaken in greater or less degree activities corresponding with the influence that called them forth, and which modify in some measure his own spontaneous impulses, and thus affect the development of his character.

This psychic impressibility is susceptible of an indefinite normal cultivation, development and intelligent direction, and may thus be made the mightiest means for the exaltation and perfection of man. Through it, as we shall show, he may make himself the recipient of the divinest influences and ministry of heaven. This impressibility, like all the gifts of God, is designed to

bless, but may be perverted and turned to unmeasured
harm.   For it is equally susceptible of abnormal development and perverted use, by which its possessor is
brought under the molding and corrupting influence
of malign and dangerous powers.   By it he may be
plunged into the lowest depths of mental slavery and
imbecility, moral depravity, obsession or insanity.

The richest, choicest gifts of heaven when perverted
become the most blighting curses.   History is full of
illustrations of this truth; and to shut our eyes to its
recognition and attempt to ignore its lesson is a dangerous and suicidal policy.   The only insurance against
any and all possible harm is a thorough knowledge
and understanding of the laws of being, and an intelligent co-operation with the will and purpose of the divine wisdom and goodness in them.   This alone will
secure perfect immunity from danger in any direction;
while ignore-ance, especially of this central law of our
being, is the greatest enemy of man and hindrance to
his progress.   It is through a knowledge of this law
and the normal cultivation and proper direction of
this impressibility, that man may place himself under
the immediate inspiration and guidance of the divine
wisdom and goodness and attain, in due time, full and
perfect illumination and mastery.   In the working of
this law we have the nature and basis of inspiration;
and it requires no argument to show that there are
various phases and degrees of inspiration, and that all
inspiration is not of a divine and uplifting character.

A Choice of Inspiration.—All men are to some
degree subjects of inspiration, and the kind of inspira-

tion they shall have depends upon themselves. The nature of a man's inspiration will ever be determined by the character of his personal aspirations or dominant desires. This law of influence is, as we have said, spontaneous and universal, and man thus practically determines by his aspirations, or desires, the character of the inspiration he receives, or the influence by which he is to be affected, modified, and to a greater or less degree molded for good or ill. One involves the other. Aspiration is a yearning after the divine and heavenly, or that which is above present realization; and opens man to the inspiration and ministration of the same. Desires, however, may be from abnormal and perverted conditions, and centered upon that which is beneath a true manhood. The gratification of such desires, and the influences to which they subject man, can but degrade him to lower depths of sensuous slavery and moral debasement. All aspirations are desires; but all desires are not aspirations. As a psychic being and a subject of influence, man necessarily opens himself more or less to the influence of that circle or sphere of life and association on which his aspirations or dominant desires are centered. By a knowledge of this law he will be enabled wisely to select his associations, or if forced into unfavorable associations by circumstances beyond his control he will be on his guard, and fortified against their perverting influence. Some are temperamentally more sensitive to and conscious of psychic influence than others; yet the mass of mankind are thus led and held to certain lines of thought and experience by the powerful influence of association

and environment. A few exceptionally strong and
decided individualities rise in psychic power and influence above their environment, and instead of being
molded by prevailing ideals and traditions, originate
new ideals and standards, and become themselves
positive centres of influence and inspiration to mold
others and lift communities and even nations to higher
levels of thought and life. The mass of men, however,
are largely the creatures of circumstance and environment, and insensibly the subjects of the subtle
psychic influences generated in the sphere and circle of
life with which they are associated. It is thus that the
fictitious authority of tradition and popular opinion
exert such a tremendous influence over the many.
Nevertheless the specific quality of the influence that
most affects each individual, is determined by the
character of his own dominant desires, and the particular centre upon which they are fixed.

Knowledge Here Gives Power.—As the law of heredity was designed to advance and lift each generation
above the preceding one, and not to entail a tendency
to vice, disease or crime, by which it may sink below,
so this law of psychic impressibility and influence was
designed to exalt man and lift him ultimately to the
realization of his divinest possibilities, not to enslave
and hold him in bondage to false standards and de-
basing influences. It is only through ignorance that
man becomes the slave of either; and a practical understanding of the law puts into his hands the key
to his own emancipation and ultimate perfection. This
psychic impressibility, we repeat and emphasize, is

susceptible of systematic cultivation and intelligent direction, so that a man may learn to open himself to and draw to himself, any quality of inspiration desired; and at the same time close himself to and fortify himself against any influence undesired.

By this practical understanding and application of the laws and conditions of inspirational development and spiritual education, man may lift himself out of subjection to unfavorable association and environment, and become a positive centre of influence and power for good in the emancipation and elevation of others. We say man may thus lift and elevate himself; we should rather say that man thus takes hold of a power which lifts, transforms and perfects his being. This inspirational capacity possessed by all, and which can be indefinitely increased, may thus become and will yet be made, the most efficient means of personal elevation and improvement, as well as of general emancipation and development. It is our purpose here, to show that there is no man, however low he may have fallen in bondage to enslaving influences, or however strongly he may be bound and held in the chains of sensuality and vice, but still has the inherent ability to lay hold of this emancipating and saving power, and that a knowledge of the law we are here enforcing, will enable him to practically use this ability.

Every man, we have said, has a human heredity and a divine heredity. Only the human can become perverted and enslaved. The divine heredity, man's divine inmost, is the pure spirit which can never be perverted nor corrupted. In the lowest depths of perverted and depraved humanity this remains the pure divinity, and its voice which is never wholly silent, is forever the changeless and incorruptible Word of God speaking in the soul of man. Through this divine, indestructible and incorruptible centre of his being, he will forever have the ability to lay hold on God and join himself with the forces of divinity. When the human has spent all its substance in riotous dissipation, and fallen to its lowest depths, the man as the child of God may still, as in the parable, come to his true self and remember his Father, and with this memory return to the Father, and what the result will be is sufficiently told by the Master in the parable of the prodigal.

Said the great Apostle, who clearly understood and defined this law, "Be not overcome of evil, but overcome evil with good." And again, "Finally, my brethren, be strong in the Lord, and in the power of his might. Put on the whole armour of God, that ye may be able to stand against the wiles of the devil. For we wrestle not against flesh and blood, but against principalities, against powers, against the rulers of the darkness of this world, against spiritual wickedness in high places. Wherefore take unto you the whole armour of God, that ye may be able to withstand in the evil day, and having done all, to stand. Stand, therefore, having your loins girt about with truth, and having on the breastplate of righteousness; and your feet shod with the preparation of the gospel of peace; Above all taking the shield of faith, wherewith ye shall be able to quench all the fiery darts of

the wicked. And take the helmet of salvation, and
the sword of the Spirit, which is the word of God."

The Threefold Character of Inspiration. — To
make the practical application of this great law of inspiration simple, direct and specific, it will be necessary to refer again to the threefold nature of man
and his corresponding relations to the threefold universe to which he belongs, and of which he is a living
vital and organic part, and, indeed, of which he is a
reproduction in miniature—a microcosm. First, to
the external and material world with which he is related through the physical senses, and by which he
has acquired his sense-consciousness. Second, to the
inner occult or soul-world—the soul of things as well
as of men—with which he is, as a living psychic personality and social being, related through the great
law of the unity and solidarity of life, out of which
spring the relations and interactions between individuals and things, already noticed. It is through this
relationship that man has acquired his soul-consciousness, or the indestructible sense of personal identity
and responsibility in relation to other personalities and
things. This relation being twofold — external and
internal—the soul-consciousness when fully developed
comes to embrace both. That is to say, all animate
things have an outward form and an inner soul life
and identity, which gives configuration and character
to the form. Man as a fully-established, self-conscious
psychic and social being, has an external and an internal plane of relationship and activity toward men
and things, through which he attains to this twofold

consciousness. By a process of normal introversion previously referred to, the activity of the external senses is turned inward and opened upon the psychic plane where the five senses in this higher action combine on their mental side to form what is called the sixth or psychometric sense. This higher psychic sense is spontaneously active in the experience of many, and may be profitably cultivated in all.*

Third, to the sphere of the Divine, within, behind and above the changing world of form and phenomena; and still deeper, within, behind and above the soul-world, or sphere of personalities and things, the realm of the Impersonal, Universal and Absolute, the region of pure Spirit and governing principles, the kingdom of God in which alone His Being and presence can be fully realized. To this sphere of the Divine, man is related through his own divine inmost or spiritual nature as the offspring of God. When the recognition of this sphere and man's normal and vital relation with it is full and decided, and the entire and undivided attention of the soul in aspiration and faith is turned within and centred upon God in earnest and determined seeking for the realization of His presence, through the yearning love of the child for the Father, the spiritual or God-sense is opened, and direct communion with and inspiration from the Divine is realized. The God-consciousness becomes thus perma-

---

* For a full description of the psychic development and training, and for the specific exposition of the threefold constitution and relationship of man, see the Author's book, "The Way, The Truth and the Life."

nently established in the realization of divine sonship and the inexpressible felicity of its love, which brings him into unity with the Father, and the brethren.

Man through this deeper, inmost and spiritual nature, which is the last to come to the recognition and realization of personal consciousness, is more fully and vitally, because permanently and indestructibly, related to and rooted in God than he is to the external system of things we call Nature, and of which he is so pre-eminently conscious. Accordingly, when this deeper spiritual consciousness is opened, and established in the full sense of his Divine relationship, he is lifted forever above the limitations of the sense-sphere and the bondage to sensuous impressions, and enthroned in spiritual supremacy over all his relations to external things. In this threefold nature and relationship of man, we have three clearly defined and distinct spheres to which he is specifically related, and from which he may draw and receive direct inspiration. Both the sense-sphere and the soul-sphere are external to himself, and inspirations from them are consequently from without; while the Divine and purely Spiritual, or God sphere is within yet above the soul, as it is within and above the soul-world and all things. Hence Divine Inspiration is in no sense from without man, but through his own divine inmost from within, yet above the plane of his spiritual consciousness, which involves an indestructible sense of dependence upon the Divine as well as a differentiated personal consciousness.

The Specific Application.—By keeping this three-fold nature and relationship of man in mind, the prac-

tical application of this great law of inspiration becomes simple, direct and specific. Since aspirations or
dominant desires determine practically the source and
character of the inspiration, it will readily be seen that
if the desires are centred wholly in the sense sphere,
the inspirations and molding influences will be of a
sensuous character. This will tend to hold man in
subjection to the sense-consciousness and its limitations, and is liable to perversion and he through it to
corresponding degeneration.

If he centre his aspiration and desires upon the
higher planes of intellectual and social activity, and
put forth corresponding effort for their realization, he
opens himself to the inspirations and molding influences
which flow from that sphere of life, and focalizes them
upon himself. He thus becomes strengthened, uplifted
and more rapidly unfolded by them to higher levels of
personal life, and helped to attain the goal of his desire. In like manner if he centre his attention and
desires upon the psychic side of his relation to men
and things, he opens through introversion the inner
and psychometric sense and penetration, which brings
him into conscious sympathetic contact with the inner
life, character and condition of persons or things to
which the attention is specifically directed, and reads
them like an open book, independent of external contact. If he push his psychic powers in their development in this direction, he will find open communication
with people of the inner world, the home of the departed.

All this we repeat, and especially emphasize, may be

attained through a normal development, without the induction of the trance, loss of external consciousness or any abnormal experience whatsoever. In the very process of the normal development of the psychic powers, and the practice of psychometry, the individuality and personal character, instead of being weakened as in the abnormal mediumship of " spirit control," is strengthened and made self-asserting and vigorous. This is effected through the attainment of perfect control over personal desire, physical sensation and the animal impulses which this training necessitates. The perfect development and normal exercise of the psychic powers, especially the higher phases of psychometry, are impossible without this control. Fortunately this is secured by the very process of normal introversion and psychic training (see " The Way, The Truth and The Life "). For this attainment time and persevering, systematic effort are needed, as for the mastery of any art or science; but with these comes a corresponding inspiration and help to the seeker from the very sphere of attainment to which he aspires. This he draws by his own persistent concentration of desire or prayer, and consecrated effort.

If, however, his supreme aspiration and heart's desire are centred upon the realization of the presence of God in the soul, in communion with and guidance from Him, and he hold himself in faith to this divine centre, he will presently come under the immediate conscious inspiration and guidance of the Father's Spirit, and be thereby open to the direct influence of all holy ministration and Heavenly fellowship. This brings forth and establishes the divine in man and gives him the spontaneous mastery of all lower and subordinate spheres and influences. He thus becomes a focalizing centre of divine inspiration and power within himself, which puts him in a positive attitude and relation of good toward all that is external to him. Since this divine realization is the evident object of man's being, as the child of God, the opening of his life and consciousness to the immediate inspiration and guidance of the Father's wisdom and goodness should be the first and supreme aim and effort of his life.

The Two Methods Contrasted.—We have said that the successful development and exercise of the psychic powers require the control of the attention, and the perfect mastery of personal desire, physical sensation and the impulses of the animal nature. To secure this mastery as a condition of psychic development, thousands have retired from the world to lead the life of an anchorite in gloomy forests, deserts and caves, and have given themselves to extreme austerities of asceticism and mortification of the flesh. That some have thus attained this mastery by their own unaided effort, and with it a high degree of psychic vision and occult power, is not denied; but when attained they have not yet reached spiritual illumination, nor what in the New Testament is called, "The Gifts of the Spirit." These do not call for asceticism nor the life of a recluse, but they send man more fully into the world a lover and helper of his kind.

Spiritual illumination is found only in and through the realization of the presence of God in the inward life, in conscious communion with and inspiration from Him as Father with child. The realization of this as the first step, lifts man at once from his thralldom to flesh, sense and materiality, into the freedom and power of the spiritual life. This opens the intuition and psychometric penetration and power, and brings spontaneous activity to all needed psychic powers, which thus awakened under spiritual illumination, become the permanent and reliable " Gifts of the Spirit." They are the legitimate expression of a regenerated life, a life at one with the Father and under the immediate inspiration of His omniscient wisdom and absolute goodness. This is the spiritual way of attainment, the method of the Christ, who bids us "Seek first the kingdom of God and His righteousness, and all these things shall be added unto you." Seeking first divine inspiration and guidance we have the immediate help of the Father's Spirit and power. To ignore this and attempt to climb up to heaven some other way, or to attain the perfect life by human effort alone is the Oriental method.

There is, however, as we have elsewhere shown, a method of normal development and training of the psychic powers that does not require the austerities of Eastern asceticism. It is difficult, however, in the whirl and intense activity of our western life, to secure the attention and persevering effort necessary for the successful achievement of the desired results. The spiritual way of attainment is the only immedi-

ate, direct and certain method which is open to and
will secure success to all. Since the advent and
achievement of the Christ, as we hope to show, immediate regeneration and spiritual illumination are
possible to all. Since man is of necessity subject to
some kind of inspiration, and is molded in greater or
less degree by it, it behooves him to select the source
from which the molding influences shall come. This
power of choice is in his own hands, and when enlightened why should he not at once put himself under
the immediate influence of the highest, the Divine and
Absolute, since this gives him the mastery of all?

The realization of life in God, and of God in the life,
the realization of oneness of nature, spirit and purpose
with the Father, is the only condition of the perfect
life; and this is possible only through the opening of
the soul by aspiration or prayer to the immediate inspiration and guidance of His Spirit. This leads to
illumination, and illumination brings divine realization,
which is thus within reach of all who truly desire it
and are ready to lay down all else for this "pearl of
great price." "The time is fulfilled, and the kingdom
of God is at hand; repent ye and believe the gospel"
is the standing message of the Christ.

A Universal Mistake.—The naturalist seeks communion with God in and through Nature, and studies
Nature to the end of looking "through Nature up to
Nature's God." The modern spiritualist seeks communion with the world of spirits under the impression
that God communes with man and inspires him only
through heavenly messengers, or the "ministry of

angels." Both are vitally mistaken. Nature does not stand between the soul and God, neither do angels, spirits, men nor books. God is nearer to the soul than Nature or angels. "In Him we live, move, and have our being." To become awakened to the realization of this fundamental truth, and enter into immediate, conscious communion and fellowship with Him as our heavenly Father is the supreme necessity of our being.

There is communion with and inspiration from Nature that is lofty and grand, as the poet and scientist truly know. There is also communion of souls, and, if you please, "communion of saints"; and there is inspiration that is quickening and exalting in its influence and power, from association with superior intelligences and characters, whether clothed in garments of flesh, or as heavenly visitants from the unseen world; but this is not communion with nor inspiration from God. These are all external to the human soul as an individual; while God is interior and cannot be found in and through externals. Man must be at one with God in his own being before he can be at one with Him in other beings or in Nature. And when he is at one with the Father in personal communion and fellowship, he is not dependent upon communication from Him through that which is external to himself.

The promise is that "None shall have occasion to say, Know the Lord: for all shall know me from the least of them unto the greatest of them saith the Lord." When man is at one with the Father in his own being he is at one with himself, and with all beings and things, because he dwells and walks with

God in all his relations and experiences in them. The sooner this great underlying truth is recognized and acted upon by all seekers after God and the perfect life, the better it will be; for until this first important step is taken, no advance can be made toward that divine realization for which devout souls have sought in all the ages.

The Perfect Life Begun.—A shining host of royal souls have found this divine realization, and dwelt and walked serenely in its high and holy fellowship and communion. At the head of these illuminated sons of God stands the Divine Galilean, "the Man of Nazareth." Whether fact or legend, the picture of that transcendent life which the gospel narratives hold for us, stands pre-eminently above all the ideals which the world has had, and the words which his biographers accord to him are pregnant with a wisdom and insight found in no other Teacher. The sympathetic and unbiased study of these broken and imperfect records, brings an inevitable conviction to the mind of the reality of the life and character there portrayed. "Never man spake like this man," because he spake from an altitude of experience and insight attained by no other soul on earth. Let us not, then, fear or hesitate to follow Him who reached the divinest realization our world has known, and who from the summit of that experience and higher wisdom assures us that all who truly follow him shall share in this divine attainment.

The Law of Inspiration.—We have said that the influence we exert over others, whether consciously or unconsciously, is charged with the dominant states of

our own mentality, and tends to awaken and call
forth corresponding activities in them. Antagonism
awakens resentment and calls forth antagonism, hatred
breeds ill-will, fear awakens fear, and discord brings
inharmony; while love, charity and sympathy quell
discordant elements, allay the troubled waters of inharmony and perverted activities, subdue hatred, ill-
will and lust, and awaken and call forth the nobler
attributes. Again, we have said that whatever activity we awaken in others, the influence of that action
reacts upon ourselves many fold; so that if we sow
to the wind we reap the whirlwind; but if we sow to
the Spirit we reap the life which endures and brings
forth the undying fruits of the Spirit, some thirty,
some sixty and some a hundred-fold. This law of personal influence need only be stated to be recognized,
since it finds its corroboration in universal experience.

A Principle of Transcendent Importance.—There
is one principle involved in this law which we must
especially emphasize because of its importance, since
it holds the sure promise of the ultimate and final redemption of the human race, and which was the basis
of all millennial prophecy. It is this: Love is stronger
and more enduring than hate, and Good than evil.
Love and goodness are eternal, infinite, absolute. They
are the very nature and Spirit of God, therefore divine
and omnipotent. Evil being but the perversion of
good has a beginning and must have an end. It is
held to the sphere of perverted human activities and
this sphere has its limitations. While humanity in its
present condition of life and development is easily
14

thrown out of balance, tempted and perverted, when
that life is regenerated and a soul under divine influence is led into unity of life and spirit with God, it is
lifted above the power of temptation, and held against
the possibility of disturbance or harm from any influence whatsoever. The deadliest shafts of calumny,
hatred and malignity can awaken no resentment, irri-
tation nor ill-will in a soul centred in Love and unity
with the Father. The most irritating thrusts from
enmity, malice, envy, spite, or any form of persecution,
can call forth from such a soul nothing but compassionate charity, sympathy and kindness, returning
love for hatred, blessing for cursing, and divinest service and ministration for persecution.

And further, as the regenerated soul unfolds more
and more in the life and Spirit of the Father, the deeper
and wider does its love, sympathy and ministration
enter into and embrace the heart and life of Humanity. Thus as the life enlarges in God the All-Father,
the more fully it opens itself to the needs and demands
of man, the brother. In this ever-deepening love and
sympathy it takes into itself the burdens, woes, sor-
rows and sufferings of mankind, and holding the torch
of wisdom, perceives the cause thereof, and goes out
in an ever-enlarging ministry of service for his salvation. Hence as the discords, antagonisms, animosities,
cruelties, perversions and depravities of the world roll
in upon the soul thus opened by love, all these discordant elements become, in that alembic of wisdom and
goodness, blended into harmony and distilled to sweet-
ness by the melting tenderness of a wise and loving

sympathy, and returned in heavenly blessing to the world.

Universal Redemption. — Love and goodness, we have said, are absolute and eternal; while evil is relative and limited in nature, extent and duration. When, therefore, love and goodness become incarnate in but one member of the human race, the positive, perfect and irresistible reaction of divinity is set up in the race life, and the ultimate redemption of the entire humanity is from that hour assured. The regenerate soul becoming the incarnation of the Divine nature, is not only raised to a condition absolutely above the power of temptation and the possibility of perversion, but is charged with a divine enthusiasm to work for universal redemption in the certainty of ultimate victory.

A Sure Basis for Millennial Prophecy. —There are four great fundamental facts upon which we may base a sure prophecy of the ultimate, complete redemption of the entire human race. First: the fact of the absoluteness, eternity and omnipotency of the Divine love and goodness. Second: the relative nature and limitation of evil as contingent upon the perversion and depravity of man. Third: that all souls whether in or out of the body are living centres of influence upon so much of the life of humanity as comes within the radius of its action; and Fourth: that any one soul in perfect unity with God has more power for good than have an army of depraved souls for harm. He cannot be overcome of evil but can overcome evil with good. One with God is a majority. "One thousand shall flee at the rebuke of one." One shall "chase a thousand and two put ten thousand to flight." With these facts in mind it will readily be seen that with the actual beginning of a regenerate humanity in but a single member of the race, he becomes the enthroned centre of the reactionary influence and power of omnipotent love in active and unceasing ministration for the salvation of all. This will inevitably effect the final overthrow of evil and the complete redemption of universal humanity from all perversions and depravities, and the ultimate enthronement of the perfect life in all.

The Opposite Principles Involved.—Since goodness once incarnated can never be overthrown, it follows that with the enlarging nucleus of regenerate life and its reactive influence, from increasing numbers of redeemed ones, the accumulation of overcoming and redemptive power in active service must increase in geometric ratio, while the perverting power of evil influence must correspondingly wane. On the present level of human life one perverted nature may for a time pervert others, and these in turn still others, and thus extend the circle and augment the power of depraving influence; but none of its victims can be degraded or depraved beyond the power of recall. On the other hand let one soul be lifted through regeneration out of that vicious circle into unity of life and spirit with the Father, he is then above the power of temptation and all perverting influences. The combined powers of evil and depravity can henceforth awaken and call forth nothing but compassionate love, sympathy and heavenly ministration.

Here is a point beyond which the contagion of evil
cannot go. In that presence it is shorn of its power,
and melts away under the reaction of the very love
and kindness it awakens and calls forth. Such a soul
is above resentment, disgust, or the possibility of turning away with coldness and indifference. Let the depravity of a world be turned to hatred and poured in
murderous venom upon such a life, and all the more
will it be bent on returning love for hatred, blessing
for cursing, and deeds of mercy and highest service
for persecution and abuse.

The Supreme Example.—We have at least one illus-
trious and victorious example of the truth of this, in
the spirit and conduct of the Christ. When betrayed
into the hands of his enemies, forsaken by his disciples, spat upon and contemptuously handled by a brutal
soldiery who were urged on by the maddening crowd
who were clamoring for his blood, a nation's scorn and
hatred turned in murderous fury upon his defenceless
head, and humiliation and indignity heaped upon him
by a felon's death, in that complete test of his divine
serenity and unruffled temper, from the deep and undisturbed tenderness, sympathy and overflowing love
of his compassionate heart, he could but pray for his
murderers, " Father, forgive them; for they know not
what they do." The spirit and power of depravity
could rise no higher and swell no further. They spent
their force and fury upon that enthroned centre of a
divine humanity and fell powerless at his feet, while
on that seething sea of perverted and distorted life,
he poured forth the oil of love and forgiveness, under

which it fell back upon itself shorn of its power and
deprived of its venom. From that hour to this his undying love and world-embracing sympathy, brooding
in a spirit of peace, charity and mercy over the human
race, has continued in active ministration the work of
redemption fully inaugurated in that hour of his supreme victory as the Prince of Peace and Saviour of his
race. He could not separate himself from the life of
the race if he would, and he would not if he could.
Hence the spirit of love, charity, forgiveness and healing, the Spirit of the Father incarnate in this royal
Son, still and forever loyal to his brethren, has from
that hour of triumph over evil, entered with its regenerating power deeper and deeper into the heart and
life of humanity, calming disturbed and depraved activities, subduing the fires of lust and sensuality, and
awakening love, charity and good-will among men,
until to-day, eighteen centuries since his advent, his
spirit and power are more fully manifest than ever
before.

He foresaw with clearness and certainty the final
result of that earthly victory, as announced in the
prophetic utterance, " And I, if I be lifted up from
the earth [the power of earthly conditions], will draw
all men unto me." The victory over hell and evil was
wrought for humanity in that hour, and the world's
attention was fastened upon it by the tragic nature
and circumstances of the struggle. Thus, too, his
leadership in the new and victorious life for men on
earth and in the spheres became established. Legions
of regenerated souls have risen under his ceaseless

spiritual ministry into fellowship with him, and the mighty and ever-swelling phalanx of the Spirit, one with him and the Father, return in the power of his name and spirit in this divine and heavenly ministry to hasten the fulfilment of that assuring prophecy which cannot fail—"And I, if I be lifted up from the earth, will draw all men unto me."

He was thus lifted up, and having seen "of the travail of his soul shall be satisfied." Humanity was anchored in divinity, and the final redemption of the entire race secured when he in his humanity was thus lifted into perfect unity and oneness with the Father's Spirit. The combined wickedness of the world cannot drag him down to its level, but he can and will lift the whole world unto himself. It needed but the triumph of one to open the door and secure the ultimate entrance of all. Under Providence he proved to be that one. On the inevitable working of this law were based all the millennial prophecies. Upon the advent of this long-prophesied Messiah the angels of God, foreseeing this result of his life and work, announced, "It is he that shall save his people from their sins," and broke forth in that glad song of rejoicing triumph, "Glory to God in the highest, and on earth peace, good-will among men."

The angelic song of coming victory shall yet be fully realized. The world shall be purified under his holy ministry and the millennial prophecies shall be fulfilled. The hells of the other world also shall be emptied and the eternal Fatherhood realized in the actualization of universal brotherhood on earth and in the spheres, through the triumph of that one loyal Son and Brother. "For since by man came death, by man came also the resurrection of the dead [resurrection from the state of death]. For as in Adam all die, even so in Christ shall all be made alive. But every man in his own order: Christ the first fruits; afterward they that are Christ's at his coming [those that respond to his spiritual ministry]. Then cometh the end, when he shall have delivered the kingdom to God, even the Father; when he shall have put down all rule, and all authority and power. For he must reign till he hath put all enemies under his feet. And the last enemy that shall be destroyed is death. . . . And when all things shall be subdued unto him, then shall the Son also himself be subject unto him that put all things under him, that God may be all in all." (1 *Cor.* xv. 21–28.)

Man Himself may Hasten the Time.—"To-day if ye will hear his voice harden not your hearts," is the message of inspired wisdom. We have said that through a knowledge of the law of inspiration man may open himself to or shut himself from the molding power of any influence he chooses; and in fact, he is unwittingly doing this very thing when ignorant of the law. In whatever direction, and on whatever centre of activity and influence his attention is turned and his interest and desires awakened, he inevitably opens himself to the molding power of the active influence proceeding therefrom. And whatever appeal or centre of interest he diverts his attention and desires from, by their absorption in other matters and perhaps opposing conditions and interests, he correspondingly closes himself to their specific influence.

We have said that if a man recognize his immediate relationship to the Divine, through his own inmost nature, and turn his whole attention and interest in supreme desire and faith on God within, in earnest prayer for divine communion and inspiration, he not only opens his soul to the realizing sense of the Divine presence and inspiration, but opens himself also to the active sympathy, interest and ministry of heaven. "I say unto you, that likewise joy shall be in heaven over one sinner that repenteth, more than over ninety and nine just persons, which need no repentance." The redeemed in heaven as on earth, the great and mighty Brotherhood of Spirit are one with Christ and the Father, in this living, active and unceasing interest in and spiritual ministry to the needy children of men, whether on earth or in the spheres—wherever spiritual darkness is.

Those who have lived and wrought and died on earth for man, still live and pursue their labors of love for him with ever increasing wisdom, sympathy and power. All these are one with the Christ, who, being first in the fulness of divine realization, leads the holy ministry of heaven in its work for universal redemption. Hence this divine ministry comes in his name, spirit and power. When he speaks for himself he includes all that are one with him in this work and fellowship of love and service. "Behold I stand at the door and knock." He has taken his stand to work for the spiritual awakening and redemption of humanity, and, like the Good Shepherd and Bishop of Souls that he is, he will not desert his post till the last wanderer is safe in the fold. All they that have the Spirit of Christ will follow him and enter into fellowship with him in his labor of love and mercy. "Now, if any man have not the Spirit of Christ he is none of his." "If any man hear my voice, and open the door, I will come in to him, and will sup with him, and he with me. To him that overcometh will I grant to sit with me in my throne, even as I also overcame, and am set down with my Father in his throne."

The ministry of Christ is the ministry of the Spirit, and embraces in its work and sympathy the whole humanity; it is directed to the spiritual awakening and redemption of the race as a whole. Like the sunlight and air, and all the ministrations of the Father's providence, it is universal and impersonal; it becomes special and personal only through the personal and specific co-operation of the individual. Each must and may make it as special to himself as if there were no other needy and dependent soul in existence. The resources of heaven are limitless, and are limited in their divine ministry to man only by the measure of his own personal co-operation. The power and work is of God, but man must voluntarily put himself in unity with the spirit and purpose of that work, to become personally a partaker of and participant in it. "Work out your own salvation with fear and trembling [sense of dependence]: for it is God which worketh in you both to will and to do of his good pleasure." "It is your Father's good pleasure to give you the kingdom." In so far as nations, communities or individuals have dropped self-interest to work for the general good, to that extent have they put themselves in unity with the spirit and purpose of the All-Father, and become co-workers with Him, and received His special blessing on their labors. They have thus opened themselves also to the special sympathy, ministry and co-operation of the unseen hosts enlisted in this work.

During the earthly ministry of the Christ, we read that "Angels ministered unto him and strengthened him." That ministry will never cease while the need of it remains. That ministry is one in him and he voices it to the world when he says practically: Humanity and I are one. Whatsoever ye shall do unto the least of one of these my brethen ye have done it unto me. I have entered into the life of the race, in my love, sympathy and service, and have made its needs, its interests and destiny one with my own. "I and the Father are one." I am one with man my brother and one with God our Father. When man responds to my ministry and spirit, he becomes reconciled and at one with God and man in me. Behold I stand at the door and knock; if any man hear my voice and open the door, I will come in to him, and will share with him and he with me. The entire end and aim of the ministry of heaven is the at-one-ment of man with God, his entrance into the kingdom of God in the realization of his own divine sonship and brotherhood in unity with the Spirit, purpose and providence of the Father. When man is at one with

God as true and loyal child with Parent, he is also at one with man in love, spirit and purpose, at one with himself and with all things in God. Being at one with God in himself, he is of necessity at one with Him in all things. And this is the call of Christ in the Spirit to mankind.

When therefore any man awakens to a sense of his divine sonship and possibilities in God, and rises out of self in the supreme desire to be at one with the Father's Spirit in his own being, and thus to know and fulfil the Father's will, he has heard the voice of Christ and opened the door to his special ministry and help. As he rises into the realization of oneness with the Father he finds himself not only one with Christ in the mighty Brotherhood of Spirit, but also bound in inseparable bands of sympathy with the brotherhood of flesh; nor will he let go his hold on this brotherhood of the unregenerate, until the last one is lifted into oneness with the great Brotherhood of Spirit in the realization of the kingdom of God.

The Threefold Gospel Message.—While the Christ proclamation of the Fatherhood of God and the Brotherhood of man may be readily accepted as an abstract proposition, and cherished even as a pleasant sentiment by all who believe in God and in humanity, the practical side of the Christ message is too easily and too generally overlooked and forgotten. The moral and physical perfection of man is the demand and promise of Christ's gospel. "Ye therefore shall be perfect as your Father in heaven is perfect." This cannot be too often repeated and emphasized. The perfect Fatherhood and providence of God, and the corresponding perfectibility of man as His child, are two parts of a beautiful ideal which the majority of people would gladly cherish and wish at least that it were true in experience. But the means provided for its realization is that part of the gospel message least thought of and least understood, yet it is the one vital part of the message. Of what value is a lofty ideal to us unless we also know and make use of the means for its realization? While the kingdom of God and its realization in a perfect life by man on earth were the ideal and the promise of Christ's teaching, the necessity of the New Birth and "walking with him in the regeneration," as the only means of the divine realization, were the real essence of the gospel, and that part which was most impressively emphasized by the Master. This is so humiliating to human pride, so opposed in its demands to the spirit of self in the natural man, that it is not welcomed, and so comes to be ignored, overlooked and forgotten. Men prefer trying to climb up to heaven and the higher realization some other way.

If it be asked why eighteen centuries of Christian teaching have failed to impress this supreme truth and its divine ideal of possible realization for man on earth, upon the minds and hearts of men, we can find but one answer—Spiritual things are spiritually discerned. The spiritual eyes of the teachers have not been open to perceive the full message of the gospel. They have neither caught nor taught this Christ ideal of the perfect life for man on earth. Accepting the ideal of the fathers they have been blinded

by tradition from beholding the divine ideal and promise which has clearly shone in radiant beauty during
all these centuries, from the gospel record. The ideal
and the promise are there, for all who have eyes to
see. The teachers have been "blind leaders of the
blind." Interpreting all things from the sensuous understanding, not having the spiritual vision which
penetrates behind the letter to the Spirit, they have
built up systems of theology on the letter of Scripture
which they have mistaken for the gospel, and have
taught the fictions of theological speculation in the
place of the gospel. They have imagined and taught
the fiction of a fallen race, an angry God and a hell
of endless torture, from which man is to be saved by
a scheme as barbaric and blasphemous as this conception. No soul whose spiritual vision was ever opened
to perceive and realize the loving Fatherhood of God,
and the supreme value and importance of the human
race and its destiny to Him as the offspring of His
love and the infinitely tender object of His providence
and care, as taught by the Christ, could for a moment
cherish this caricature of "Our Father in heaven."
Such teaching would necessarily prevent the recognition of the Christ ideal and promise of the sinless and
perfect life on earth, and so the motive for effort at
realization.

Concerning the New Birth.—The supreme necessity of the second birth, officially announced and emphasized by the Master as the only door of entrance
into the kingdom of God, renders it of unspeakable importance that all should have a clear apprehension of

its nature and character, and of what is really involved in the experience, since without it not a step of permanent advance can be taken in the realization of God.

When the Jewish Rabbi came to inquire of Jesus concerning the new doctrine of the kingdom of God which he was preaching, the divine Teacher answered, "Verily, verily, I say unto thee, except a man be born again, he cannot see the kingdom of God." As this seemed to puzzle the Rabbi, who evidently could think of birth only as applying to a physical body, or in a physical sense, asking, "How can a man be born when he is old? Can he enter a second time into his mother's womb and be born?" the Master added that the real man—who, in his thought and teaching was a spiritual being—must be twice born: first under material conditions and relations requiring a physical body; then under spiritual conditions and relations in that body. As a spiritual entity, brought forth to conscious personal existence under material conditions, he must first awaken to the consciousness of the outward world and his relations to things under which he is individualized and differentiated as a personality, which constitutes the first birth; afterward he must awaken to the consciousness of his deeper and permanent relations with the inner spiritual kingdom—the kingdom of God—to which he is indestructibly related by the spirituality of his being, which is the second birth. "Verily, verily, I say unto thee, except a man be born of water and of the Spirit he cannot enter into the kingdom of God." That water was here used as a symbol of the changeable, transitory and evanescent

character and conditions of life in the senses, is evident
from the words that follow, as a part of the statement,
"That which is born of the flesh is flesh; and that
which is born of the Spirit is spirit." The life of flesh
and sense is indeed transitory, changeable and mortal;
while the spiritual life is permanent, divine and indestructible. "Marvel not that I said unto thee, Ye
must be born again." All the fleshly activities and
the conscious experiences of the soul's life based upon
them, are born, or awakened and called forth by contact with the outer world through the senses; hence
these pertain only to the sensuous life and understanding. The senses belong to the flesh, and all the activities of body or mind awakened by impressions from
the outer world through them, are "born of the flesh"
and belong to the sphere of the sensuous life.

Spirit and spiritual things, all that pertain specifically to the kingdom of God, are not and cannot be
revealed to or discerned through the physical senses.
They are deeper and above the sphere of sensuous observation and experience. "The kingdom of God cometh not with observation." "The natural man receiveth not the things of the Spirit of God, . . . neither
can he know them because they are spiritually discerned." All those activities of the soul which are
awakened and called forth by active contact and conscious communion with the Divine Spirit, are "born of
the Spirit." They are spiritual in character and pertain to the spiritual life and kingdom of God—the
supremacy and reign of love, truth and righteousness
in all the relations of life and experience.

Birth Pertains to Soul or Conscious Being.—It is the birth of the soul to which the Scriptures refer, the body being but the physical instrument of the soul's activities. It is the inner spiritual organism which in its complete individualization and awakened activities constitutes the indestructible form and personality. "There is a natural body and there is a spiritual body." Until this understanding of man is embraced fairly in the thought, no progress will be made in the understanding of the New Testament teaching, since all its references to man are based upon this conception. He is treated as a moral and spiritual, not as a physical being. His body is always referred to as something that is his. He is not the physical body nor the physical body he. It is identified with him as something that belongs to him; but he is not in the same sense identified with it. "For we know that, if our earthly house of this tabernacle were dissolved, we have a building of God, a house not made with hands, eternal in the heavens. . . . For we that are in this tabernacle do groan, being burdened: not for that we would be unclothed, but clothed upon, that mortality might be swallowed up of life. Now he that hath wrought us for the selfsame thing is God, who also hath given unto us the earnest of the Spirit."

Children of the Kingdom Twice Born.—The great Apostle saw that life in the senses was but a rudimentary state of being, as a preparatory step to a higher realization in which it was to be clothed upon with the higher spiritual consciousness of being, and become "swallowed up of life." "For this corruptible must put on incorruption, and this mortal must put on immortality. So when this corruptible shall have put on incorruption, and this mortal shall have put on immortality, then shall be brought to pass the saying that is written, Death is swallowed up in victory." The Apostles had been born into the new and higher life of the Spirit, and were spiritually unfolding under its regenerating processes and transfiguring power; and so much of the divine life as they had thus experienced was to them the earnest of the Spirit, prophetic of the ultimate, complete transfiguration.

The very figure " birth," used by the Master, implies the radical change in the condition of being which it brings to every one who passes through it. It implies the birth into a new and entirely different order of life from that hitherto experienced. The tremendous possibilities it opens to man in the new life to which he is thus introduced—possibilities which are utterly beyond the reach of the natural man—stamp it with the supreme importance which the emphasis of the Master gave to the event, and to which a no less radical term could apply.

Physical Sense the Prototype of a Higher Spiritual Sense.—Should the five senses remain closed and inactive at physical birth, the innate powers of the soul would not be awakened into action, and there would be no consciousness of personal existence; the soul would not then be born into this world though the body were. It is the awakening of the soul to the consciousness of personal existence through the activity of its innate powers, first called forth by the stimulus of impressions from the outer world through the senses, which constitutes the first or primary birth referred to by the Master, as being " born of water," or " of the flesh." The yet higher awakening and activity of the soul's powers on the plane of the spiritual life, by the immediate inspiration from the sphere of the Divine Consciousness, through the deeper spiritual and God-sense, gives the spiritual consciousness of being and of divine sonship. This is being " born of the Spirit."

The physical body and the sensuous life are obviously a first necessity to the individualization of the human soul and its powers, and the establishment of a self-conscious personality in its differentiation from the Divine Being and consciousness, and in its relation to other personalities and things. This first and primary sphere of the self-conscious personality and its activities, in its relations with the outward world in which the intellectual, social and moral faculties are awakened, individualized and established in their primary functions, constitutes the life of what, in the New Testament, is called " the natural man." When this is fully established, however, " the time is fulfilled " for the soul to be awakened to the consciousness of its spiritual being as the offspring of God, and of its vital and immediate relations to the Father and His spiritual kingdom. The natural man in his consciousness of being dwells on the plane of physical existence within the sphere and under the dominion of the senses. The awakening of the consciousness to this sphere of relations is the primary or sensuous birth. The spiritual man dwells above the plane of the senses

and the limitations of sense perception, in the illumination, freedom and mastery of the spiritual life, to
which physical sensation and material conditions are
completely subordinated. The awakening of the consciousness to this higher sphere of relations is the
second or spiritual birth.

Not a Fallen State.—The plane of the sensuous life,
and the organic limitations of the "natural man"
were not regarded by the Christ as a fallen state, from
some pre-existent condition of holiness and perfection.
No allusion to such a conception is to be found in his
teaching. He referred to it as the first or primary
and legitimate stage in the evolution of the soul's consciousness, from which man was to rise by an orderly
process of awakening to the higher realization of his
spiritual being and relations. The very method of
his presenting his doctrine of the kingdom of God and
his call to its new life implies this. "The time is fulfilled and the kingdom of God is at hand." This was
practically saying that man as he is has had sufficient
experience on the plane of the sensuous life to have
his attention turned to the recognition of the higher
possibilities of his being, and seek the realization of the
spiritual life in the body, and rise to walk and dwell
in communion and fellowship with the Father. It
was his special mission to awaken man to the recognition of these higher possibilities by opening the doctrine to his understanding through precept and parable, and demonstrating its reality by a living example
in his own experience.

The second birth, which opens this new kingdom of

life, is the awakening of the soul to the consciousness
of its spiritual being as the child of God, and its immediate relationship to the Father, under a quickened
sense of the Father's love and providence, and giving
itself unreservedly to the inspiration and leading of
His Spirit. The earnest desire or prayer of the heart
for communion with the Father and the guidance of
His wisdom, is itself the opening of the God-sense and
the birth of the God-consciousness in the soul. The
soul's cry "O my Father, is Allah's answer, Here my
child." It is evident, therefore, that the primary development of self-consciousness and the soul's powers
through the discipline of experience in the school of
the senses, was a necessary step as a preliminary preparation for the higher education and experience in the
school of the Spirit. The first birth was a necessary
prelude to the second—"Except a man be born of
water *and* of the Spirit," etc.

**The New Birth Based upon the Divine Sonship of
Man.**—Whether the doctrine of the divine sonship of
man so specifically taught and emphasized by the
Christ and his great Apostle to the Gentiles be accepted or not, the Christ doctrine of the New Birth
can be correctly understood and interpreted only in
the light of this conception. The entire ethics of
Christ's teaching are based upon this supposed relation of man to God as child to Parent, and the corresponding relation of man to man as brethren of a
common family. No doctrine of the Lord Christ can
be correctly understood and applied, except in the light
of this conception as the fundamental basis of all his

teaching. The Fatherhood of God, the divine possibilities of man as his child, and the immediate and complete realization of this divine relationship in human life and society, was the central idea at the root of all his teaching and personal ministry. This means the actual reproduction or unfolding of the nature and attributes of the Father in the life and character of His children. It is "the Word made flesh" in universal experience, the divine attributes incarnate in the organic life of the sons and daughters of God on earth as in heaven. This in the teaching of Jesus was the end and object to be reached in the earthly experience of men, and the Second Birth was a means to and the first step in its realization. Whether this was a chimera of his thought or a divine reality possible to all, let his own transcendent life as an Exemplar and Model, and the corresponding experience of his Apostles who took him at his word, be the answer.

The necessity and nature of the Second Birth were based upon the recognized yet undeveloped and unrealized powers of the human soul as the immediate offspring of God. A moment's reflection will make this obvious. If indeed man is the child of God, he is, we repeat, a reproduction in embryo of the Father's nature and attributes. These are all latent or potential within him, as the very germ of his being, even as the full-grown oak is potential in the germ life of the acorn, and the powers of the man are latent in the embryonic life of the unborn infant. The various stages in the germination and development of the life of the tree or of man, are but the birth into organic and functional activity of powers and attributes that were latent in the spiritual germ of the tree and of man at the outset. There can be no power or quality of life in the full-grown tree that did not exist potentially in the seed-germ from which it sprang; neither can there be a power or attribute in the mature man that did not exist potentially in his life as an infant. Hence whatever power or attribute has been brought forth to organic expression in any one man, is necessarily latent and potential in the life of all men. Being latent in all, these powers may, under proper conditions, be evolved and brought to organic expression in all. This was the ideal and promise of the Christ message, and the spiritual birth and regeneration opened to us in his teaching were the law and means of this higher evolution.

Evolution of the Human Soul.—Individual existence, so far as we know, begins in embryonic conditions. The portion of Spirit which animates man, and from which all his powers and his consciousness are born, existed from eternity in God. It is the differentiation or specialization of the Spirit and life of God, in the faculties and powers of the soul under material conditions and organic limitations, which constitutes the progressive personality of man, capable of indefinite degrees of unfolding and development from within. The energy of life thus flowing forth from the exhaustless fountain of Spirit into embodied expression, molds the organism it takes on into an instrument suitable for such expression. The outward body is made universally to correspond in general character with the stage of evolution which the life and powers of the individual soul have reached. The spirit in man being so much of God the Father specialized in him, holds in his inmost life the engermed attributes of God, which in the true, normal development of his being, must ultimately come to expression in his life.

The Twofold Organism of Man.—The dual organism—physical and spiritual—in which the individual faculties and the personal consciousness are established and unfolded, is individualized and completed in organic conditions before physical birth and the beginning of self-conscious, personal life. "A body thou hast prepared for me." This dual organism is begotten, gestated and born into individual existence under strictly human parentage and conditions, with the bias of human heredity stamped upon it. The animating spirit, however, the inmost life, is a divine seed-germ of infinite possibilities deposited from the pure life of God, and potential with the essence of His Being. The spirit in every child born into the world is an immaculate conception—the immediate offspring of God.

The Twofold Heredity of Man.—Man, we repeat, has a twofold heredity, one human, the other Divine. His human heredity is external, transient and subject to change; his heredity from God is spiritual, changeless in character, divine and imperishable. The natural man is the man of the flesh, external and sensuous in his life and consciousness; the spiritual man when evolved is divine, dwelling on the interior and higher plane of the spiritual life and consciousness. And so it is written, "The first man Adam was made a living soul; the last Adam was made a quickening spirit. Howbeit that was not first which is spiritual, but that which is natural [pertaining to outward Nature]; and afterward that which is spiritual. The first man is of the earth, earthy: the second man is the Lord from heaven. As is the earthy, such are they also that are earthy: and as is the heavenly, such are they also that are heavenly. And as we have borne the image of the earthy, we shall also bear the image of the heavenly. . . . For this corruptible must put on incorruption and this mortal must put on immortality." The great Apostle having actualized in his own experience ·a high degree of the spiritual life, in view of the certainty of its possibility to all exclaimed in the lofty enthusiasm born of his experience, and the conviction of this certainty, " I am not ashamed of the gospel of Christ, for it is the power of God unto salvation to every one that believeth."

The Natural Man Prefigures the Spiritual.—We see the powers of the human soul beginning to manifest themselves in the dim and feeble consciousness of infancy, and watch their marvellous development through the unfolding stages of childhood, youth and adolescence to a full rounded and mature manhood. We know, therefore, that the marvellous powers of a fully developed manhood were potential or latent in the organism of the new-born infant, though no one could have predicated such stupendous results on so slender a promise. We know further, that all these wonderful possibilities of manhood were latent in the unconscious stages of his embryonic life.

Now if all these powers of the soul are brought to such a marvellous development in the life of the " natural man " on the plane and within the sphere of the physical senses, what shall we say of those higher possibilities of the divine nature yet latent, when the soul shall awaken to the realization of its spiritual being and divine heredity, and the spiritual man enters upon his career of development under the immediate inspiration and guidance of the Father ? We shall have a spiritual and divine manhood with the unfolded attributes of wisdom, goodness and power, as far above the level of man at his best, on the plane of the sensuous life and understanding, as he is above the level of the brute life that preceded him. In short, we shall have the reproduction of the Christ-life, as promised by himself and all millennial prophecy, in universal experience.

Jesus a Thorough Evolutionist.—The broadest conception and generalization of modern science concerning creation, or the bringing forth of life upon our planet, is expressed in the comprehensive term evolution, supposed to embrace all the processes involved in the inception and development of life. If we interpret this law of evolution as God's method in creation, we have essentially the philosophy of Nature to which Christ's doctrine of the divine sonship and infinite possibilities of man is the key; and which will sooner or later come to be recognized as such.

That Jesus clearly recognized evolution as the law of life and its development in Nature and man, is evident from his constant allusion to the processes of li.e

in Nature as the immediate manifestation or work of
the immanent God, and the lessons he drew therefrom
for his disciples to awaken and establish their faith
and trust in His immediate and perfect providence.
This conception is especially brought out in his efforts
to unfold to their understanding the laws and conditions of spiritual realization, which indeed were based
upon and embraced the principle of evolution. Take
his parable designed to illustrate the bringing forth of
the kingdom of God in the personal and social life of
man on earth. "And he said, So is the kingdom of
God, as if a man should cast seed into the ground;
and should sleep, and rise night and day, and the seed
should spring and grow up, he knoweth not how. For
the earth bringeth forth fruit of herself; first the blade,
then the ear, after that the full corn in the ear. But
when the fruit is brought forth, immediately he put-
teth in the sickle, because the harvest is come." Here
is a clear picture of the evolution of life from the seed-
germ to its ultimate development, applied in illustration of his great doctrine of the ultimate realization of
the kingdom of God in the earth.

In this illustration he recognizes the animating
principle of life in Nature, culminating in man as the
seed-germ of spiritual being which God the great Hus-
bandman deposited in the world of materiality, to bring
forth children unto Himself, man being the ultimate
product of that life. And the earth brought forth the
fruit thereof, "first the blade, then the ear, after that
the full corn in the ear." "The blade" in the parable
symbolizes the organic world before man; the primary

"ear," is the symbol of the "natural man" on the plane of the sensuous life and understanding; while " the full corn in the ear" most fitly and beautifully symbolizes the true spiritual manhood, or the complete spiritual life yet to be realized in the flesh. When this fruit of the Spirit on the tree of planetary life is all brought forth and perfected, the sickle will be put in; for the harvest will have come, and the earth will have finished its work in the production and perfection of humanity.

The Philosophy Involved.—While the Christ did not pose as a philosopher, still the comprehensive philosophy involved in his teaching is the real philosophy of life and will yet be universally recognized as such. We have in his teaching, First: the conception of life in Nature as the immediate expression of the immanent God. Second: the doctrine of man as the immediate offspring of God, because the direct product of the life of God in Nature, and to become perfect in the realization of being and character even as his Father in heaven is perfect; because, again, as the child of God, he must in the normal unfolding of his life bring forth or reproduce the nature and attributes of the Father in the functions of his being. Third: we have this parable, illustrating directly, the law of evolution as the law under and through which this higher realization is to be reached; and Fourth: his specific application of the principle involved in the two phases or cycles of human evolution, one culminating and terminating in the sensuous life of the natural man, the other taking him into another and higher cycle of evolution—regeneration—culminating in the perfect life of the spiritual man in the body, "the full corn in the ear."

In this conception the life of the soul is rooted in and flows direct from God, making each individual the child of God, and the embodiment, in embryo, of His indestructible life and attributes, and as such, the depository and seed-germ of infinite possibilities in a career of endless life and development. If man is thus born to a career of unending life and progress, it will be readily conceded that the germ of such a stupendous possibility must have been deposited from a source vastly deeper than human parentage. All that is permanent and eternal, capable of infinite unfolding and development, must have its origin and fountain in the infinite and divine. "Call no man father on earth; for one is your Father which is in heaven;" "and all ye are brethren."

A Key to the Problem of Life and Destiny.—The Christ was a seer in whose open vision the problem of human life and destiny had no unsolved mystery. The very existence of the embodied soul with its boundless possibilities as the child of the infinite Love and Wisdom, was to his mind its own reason for being, and the all-sufficient reason for the universe itself. The Universe was made for man who was brought forth through it as a child of the Eternal, to unfold and dwell forever in communion and fellowship with the Father, and find a sufficient and appropriate field for the development, exercise and enjoyment of all the

powers of his being. Man himself is the key to the
solution of the problem of being.

In these conceptions of the Master we catch a
glimpse of the limitless sweep of his thought of man's
nature and destiny; and also of the tremendous and
comprehensive grasp of the philosophy involved in his
conception of life and being.

If this fundamental conception of the Master concerning the divine sonship of man, and the unfolding
attributes of his being from within by a process of
evolution is kept in mind, there will be less difficulty
in apprehending what is really involved in the process
of spiritual birth and regeneration, through which man
is to rise from the plane of the natural and sensuous
life to the realization of the spiritual and divine.

"A Change of Heart."—As the personality and organism of the "natural man" are molded after the
pattern and under the inspirations and motives of the
sensuous life, whose ruling law is *self*, so the personality and organism of the spiritual man must be
molded after the divine ideal of a perfect man, and
under the inspirations and motives of the spiritual life
at one with the divine, whose law of life is *Love*—love
to God and love to man, based on the realization of
divine sonship and brotherhood. The regeneration of
man, or the evolution of the spiritual within him, can
be effected and carried forward under no other conditions. Man must of his own free will and choice, adopt
the Christ ideal of the spiritual and perfect life of a
child of God, and place himself under its perfect law
in unreserved consecration to its attainment, seeking

in confidence the inspiration, guidance and help of the Divine Spirit to which he thus inevitably opens himself. This positive and radical beginning must be made in the full determination to lay down at once and forever the old man, that the life of the new man may be taken up and fully realized.

Man cannot be governed by or act under two opposing motives at once. He cannot live the life of the natural and of the spiritual man at the same time. Thousands have failed in attempting this, not giving a full and entire consecration to the leading and inspiration of the Spirit. In most Christian effort there has not been an unreserved abandon to the ideal and law of the spiritual and perfect life. Unfortunately the ideal of the higher spiritual life and the standards of its possibilities have been measured and judged from the standards which have come from actual experience under the necessary limitations of the sensuous life, instead of taking the victorious example of the Christ as the true Model and representative of that life. The universal law of configuration and transfiguration of organism, corresponding with the dominant states or unfolding developments of the inward life, to which we have called special attention, has been entirely overlooked in this connection. Hence the ideal of the perfect life in both soul and body, presented by the Master as the goal of attainment through regeneration, has not been fully embraced in the popular conception of regeneration and the spiritual life. Men do not rise above the level of their own ideals, nor seek the attainment of that in which they have no faith: "According

to your faith be it done unto you," is the law of attainment and realization.

The first great difficulty in the way of entering seriously and radically upon the path of the new life, the
pathway of the Spirit, is perhaps the awakening and
establishing in the mind the true and perfect ideal of
attainment, and then the requisite faith in the ideal,
without which it is impossible to commit the soul in
perfect consecration and abandonment to its realization. This difficulty confronted the Master at every
step of his teaching. The supreme difficulty, however,
is in laying down *self*. "Except a man deny himself
and take up his cross daily and follow me he cannot
be my disciple." The laying down of self, seeking Divine guidance and following the leading of the Spirit,
is an absolute necessity and the first step. The motives and inspirations of the selfish, or of the spiritual
life, one or the other must rule; and these have vastly
different centres or springs of action. Out of the
heart are the issues, or motives and inspirations of
life, and the heart will be centred upon the treasures
or objects of one life or the other, hence one must be
yielded *wholly* to the other. "Ye cannot serve God
and mammon." No compromise between the two is
possible. "No man can serve two masters." Before
one can live the spiritual life, the realization of God
and the things of the Spirit must become the supreme
desire of the heart, for the heart will be where its
treasure—the things most desired, are, and where the
heart is there is the centre and spring of all motive
and action. Hence there must be an entire change of

basis in both motive and conduct. The centre of motive and action must be transferred from the ideals and ambitions of the sensuous and selfish life, to the ideal and ambition of the spiritual life; and this can be effected only by transferring the desires of the heart from one to the other.

So in the fullest and most literal sense, there must be an entire and radical change of heart before any soul can rise from the natural into the realization of the spiritual life. There must be not only the shutting of the eyes or sleeping to the things of flesh and sense, and awakening to the perception or recognition of "the things of the Spirit of God," but there must be dying to the things of the selfish life, and living to the things of the spiritual. This radical change of heart is the "new birth," the beginning of the new and spiritual life. Henceforth communion and fellowship with the Father in all experiences and under all circumstances is the supreme desire of the heart and the deep joy of the life. Under this ideal and motive the work of regeneration goes forward. The essence of the sensuous life is self-seeking, and its ruling law self-will. The essence of the spiritual life is unity with the Father in the ministry of service, and its ruling law the will and purpose of the Father in all things.

Walking With God in the World.—Entering into the realization of the spiritual life in the flesh does not take man out from the active life of the world, nor necessarily change his outward circumstances, occupation or relations with the world. He simply changes his attitude toward them in these relations and condi-

16

tions. He sees and walks with God in them, fulfilling
his duty toward them, but is not brought into subjection by them. He is in the world yet not of the world,
on the earth yet above the earth in the spiritual supremacy of his being as a child of the Eternal. The
things of the world and their allurements to the natural
man lose their power over him, because he seeks no
longer the treasures they hold. He is no longer their
servant but their master. Having attained the mastery of himself he is the master of his environments.
Being at one with the Father in all things, he holds
the supremacy over them by his unity with the Father
in them. The unity of his own life with God brings
reconciliation with the will of God in all things and all
experiences, and this brings good out of all. "All
things work together for good to them that love God."
Unity with the Father in will and purpose brings
unity with Him in truth and righteousness, because it
opens the soul to the illumination and guidance of His
wisdom, and the inspiration of His love.

This is the law and essence of all spiritual experience and permanent realization. To enter into this
unity of will and purpose with the Father, there must
be a deeply rooted conviction of and unshaken faith in
the absolute wisdom and goodness of God, and therefore of His work and will, and a supreme desire to be
in accord therewith. The heart's desire for the inspiration of the Father's love, guidance and wisdom,
that His will and purpose may be fulfilled in us, when
it becomes the permanent aspiration and prayer of
the daily life, is the one thing which unites the soul

with God in the reciprocal and unyielding embrace of Parental and filial love.

There is one other serious impediment in the way of a perfect understanding of the Christ doctrine of salvation which perhaps should be noticed in this connection, because while it remains the true Christ ideal will not be grasped, and the perfect effort will not be made. We refer to the false impressions which have been fastened upon the religious thought and consciousness of the Christian world by centuries of misinterpretations of Scripture based upon a false anthropology, or a fatal misconception of the nature of man and his relations. In nothing, perhaps, has this been more conspicuous or misleading, than in the understanding, or rather misunderstanding, of the symbolic story of the creation and fall of man, since this lies at the foundation of the popular theology of Christendom, and without which the doctrine of vicarious atonement could not have been invented. A brief consideration of this mystic parable, and of the understanding of man involved, may serve to suggest the true key to the interpretation of all Scripture. This key is the correct understanding of the nature of man to which they refer. Men first read their preconceptions into the Scriptures, then succeed in reading them from the Scriptures. If these preconceptions are correct they serve as true principles of interpretation, because truth is homogeneous; but if false, they lead men to wrest the Scriptures to their own destruction.

The Story of Eden and the Fall.—How any intelligent mind, with the faintest knowledge of the symbolic character of all oriental inspired writing and teaching, could possibly have taken the symbolic story of Eden as veritable, external history, and thus made its literal and sensuous rendering the basis of a system of theology and religious philosophy, passes comprehension. It would seem that the very figure of temptation by the serpent would have been sufficient to show the least spiritually minded the symbolic character of the entire narrative. That it was an inspired parable representing the profoundest truths of human experience there need be no question. It represented, therefore, inward spiritual experiences and moral states not external history, and must be so read and interpreted to be correctly understood.

The garden of Eden symbolizes in the parable the garden of the human soul in the innocence of childhood, Eden signifying innocence. It typifies the beginning of every human life, and thus we find the tragedy of the temptation and fall reproduced or actualized in universal experience. "And the Lord God planted a garden eastward in Eden." From the east or eastward springs the dawning light of each new day; so "eastward in Eden" symbolizes the dawning light of consciousness in the morning of each new life, in the innocence of childhood. "And the Lord God took the man, and put him into the garden of Eden, to dress it, and to keep it." By "the man" is here represented the awakened consciousness of personality and moral responsibility, as these constitute the distinguishing features of humanity. "To dress it"—the garden—was to cultivate and bring to fruition the co-ordinated powers of the soul in the development and clothing upon of a perfect character. "And to keep it" was to keep and maintain the innocence and purity of the soul's original and primary estate. "And the Lord God commanded the man" [made a law of his being], "saying, Of every tree of the garden thou mayest freely eat." As the garden symbolized the soul, the trees of the garden symbolize the faculties of the soul, every one of which was for use and to be freely exercised and enjoyed. "But of the tree of the knowledge of good and evil, thou shalt not eat of it: for in the day that thou eatest thereof thou shalt surely die." Mark, it was not every tree of the garden but one thou mayest freely eat, but "*every* tree of the garden." The eating of every tree, or the right use of every faculty, would bring the knowledge through experience only of good; while the wrong use of any faculty would bring the experience and thus the knowledge of evil. Hence the misuse of any faculty would be partaking of the tree of the knowledge of good *and* evil, bringing, of necessity, death to the state of innocence, and thus casting the soul out of Eden.

"Now the serpent was more subtile than any beast of the field which the Lord God had made." The serpent plainly enough symbolizes the animal nature in man, which, being linked and associated with the higher powers of humanity, takes on a subtlety of desire and invention, impossible to the beast. The woman in the parable symbolizes the heart or seat of desire and motive; while the man symbolizes the intellect or judgment. By the voice of the Lord God

walking in the garden and speaking to the pair, first
in their innocence warning them against transgression,
and afterward in their guilt pronouncing judgment on
their sin, is symbolized the monitions of the Spirit
through the conscience, approving of the right and
accusing of wrong. The great law of good and evil,
temptation and sin involved in the experiences symbolized in the parable of Eden, will be made clear by a
careful study of

The Function of the Animal in Man.—The law of
animal life is self-indulgence, and its organism is constructed with direct reference to the unrestrained
activity of all the impulses, appetites and propensities
of the animal nature, fear being the only restraining
influence. The human body on the contrary is constructed with reference to the higher activities of the
rational and moral powers under spiritual guidance, as
the physical instrument of the soul in these activities,
and not for the gratification of animal desire as such; it
cannot, therefore, be given over to unrestrained indulgence of animal propensity and impulse without injury.
The law of the human life is right and duty, not pleasure as an end. Man is under a moral government and
accountable to a moral law; hence his sense of right
and wrong, good and evil, and of personal obligation
or duty. As an intellectual and moral being under a
Divine Government, the true ideal of the personal life
is intellectual and spiritual achievement, the development of truth and virtue, the attainment of wisdom
and the perfection of character. When man comes to
esteem and love truth and duty above pleasure, he

will find his true and lasting enjoyment in the performance of duty.

The ideal life in the animal, if it could be formulated to his consciousness, would be pleasure *per se;* and his highest ideal of enjoyment would be the full gratification of desire in physical indulgence. In so far as this ideal and motive dominate the life of man, he is living under the law of the animal life and not the true life of humanity. The organism of the animal being in harmony with this law, such indulgence is compatible with health. As he has no higher nature demanding the conservation of energy on the lower plane for expenditure on the higher, as in the human, he has no moral sense or conscience to protest against this indulgence. Blind indulgence is his true and normal life. He is not subject to the moral law, and therefore has no protest. The house is not divided against itself.

Law of Animal Activity in Man.—The human body being the instrument of the soul's activities on the higher plane of the intellectual, social and moral life, there is a necessity for the conservation of energy in the animal activities—appetites and propensities—for expenditure in the legitimate and higher activities of the intellectual, industrial and social life. Hence the necessity to the life of man of a moral law and the restraining voice of conscience in the ineradicable sense of right and wrong; also of the guiding power of spiritual inspiration and wisdom. These are necessary to co-ordinate the functions of his complex being, and hold each to its legitimate sphere of activity, and thus carry him forward to the complete fulfilment of his grand and exalted destiny as a child of the Eternal Wisdom and Goodness. Experience has demonstrated that man cannot yield himself to the unrestrained indulgence of animal desire in the appetites and propensities without intellectual and moral debasement, social degradation and physical degeneration, involving disease and premature death. This is never true of animals but always of man. This fact is sufficient demonstration that the human organism was not designed as an instrument of mere animal indulgence and enjoyment, and that the animal functions were designed to serve, not to rule in the human economy.

Necessary to Nutrition and Reproduction.—The animal nature and functions in the life of man, are, we repeat, a necessity to the preservation of the physical body as an instrument of the soul during its earthly experience, and also to the perpetuation of the species. Without the animal nature in the human economy, the important functions of nutrition and reproduction would be utterly neglected and forgotten in the absorbing interest of the soul in other activities. The physical organism is so constructed that all its activities, including brain function from mental action, involve the consumption or waste of tissue. This in turn causes a demand for constant renewal for which the function of nutrition was established. This being a physical and animal function was brought to perfection in the animal kingdom before man appeared. Being essential to the existence and preservation of the physical body, the animal nature was reproduced in man for this purpose, or for the service of man in this capacity. Hence the periodic demand for food to renew the waste of the body furnishes vent to the spontaneous play of animal desire, which, knowing no law but indulgence for physical enjoyment, would make physical desire so vehement but for the restraining influence of the judgment and moral sense, that the human body would become a mere instrument of animal impulse and gratification. This shows that while the animal impulses cannot be utterly ignored and suppressed with impunity, they are nevertheless to be governed, controlled and guided by the higher judgment and spiritual intuitions. When the moral and spiritual intuitions are properly cultivated the soul will be led to govern wisely, and hold the animal functions to their legitimate and perfect service in the physical economy. But to the full extent to which the higher demands of the soul upon the body are sacrificed and compromised to the ends of animal indulgence, will be the prostitution of the human life to base and ignoble activities, the excess and perversion of the physical functions and the demoralization of true manhood.

Yet, as we have said, without the animal instinct or impulse for indulgence to emphasize the desire and earnestly press the demand for food, the actual necessities of the physical organism would be unheeded, because of the complete absorption of the attention in higher things. This would soon end in the wearing out and destruction of the instrument itself, cutting the soul off from its immediate connection with the

outward world, and the normal and needful experience
this was designed to give. The same is true of the
function of reproduction; were the animal impulses
entirely rooted out of man, the physical relation of the
sexes would be ignored and forgotten, and the perpetuation of the species would end.

Relation of the Spiritual to the Animal in Man.—
From what has been said, it will be seen that the animal in man could not be wholly dispensed with in
this life, without the destruction of his legitimate organic relations with the outward and physical world.
The animal nature is an absolute necessity to the
preservation, development and perfection of the physical body as an instrument of the soul in these outward
relations and activities, as well as for the perpetuation, physical development and perfection of the human race. And again, the normal development and
perfection of the physical organism is an equal necessity to the corresponding perfection of the inward and
permanent spiritual body, of which the physical is
practically the organic mold. The animal functions
and activities in their legitimate sphere are thus as
essential to the development and well-being of man in
this world as are the inspirations of the spiritual and
divine in their sphere; hence every attempt to root
them out is abnormal and suicidal. While divine inspiration and guidance are a necessity to the integrity
and development of the soul's life and powers, the animal functions are an equal necessity to the health and
development of the body as an instrument of the soul.
The interest of both the animal and spiritual in their

true relation are one in the soul, since the functions of both are a necessity to the integral development of the soul and its powers.

Which then should exert the dominant and controlling influence? To ask the question is to answer it. There is no room for doubt in the matter. For the animal activities to subserve their true function, they must be limited and held to their legitimate sphere of service in the human economy. Nothing but the full realization of spiritual inspiration and guidance in and through an illuminated moral sense and judgment will effect this result. This is needed also to guide the soul in the unfolding of its powers in the field of physical as well as of intellectual and spiritual achievement, and thus to lead man in the path of wisdom and the way of truth and righteousness, as illustrated in the life of the Master. Without divine inspiration and guidance, the soul is liable to fall into bondage to the animal, and become the slave of lust and depraved desires. From this nothing can rescue man but the re-awakening of the sense of his relationship and obligation to the Divine as a moral and spiritual being, and seeking divine help and healing in the forgiving love of the Father, and the regenerating and saving power of His Spirit. Since, then, the moral nature relates man to the moral law and order of a Divine Government, and the full development and activity of that nature is essential to a normal and well-balanced life, entire submission to and immediate inspiration from the Father's Spirit is the supreme and absolute necessity of his being.

The Real Source of Evil and Sin.—All the evils of humanity, its diseases, vices, crimes and miseries, in other words, human sin and its results, spring, as can easily be shown, from the excessive activities and perverted functions of the animal in man. This is the only fountain of selfishness, and out of it springs the law which dominates and rules the natural man, and which has thus far largely ruled the life of the race. The unfolding and supremacy of the spiritual life and its ruling law will reverse all this, and place man in his true relations with both the natural world and the kingdom of God. While the animal functions are needed to call the attention of man to his physical necessities and spur him to the needed activity in supplying them, both the physical desires and the activity they prompt should be under the perfect control and direction of a divinely enlightened judgment and moral sense. It is for want of this direction and control that men have plunged into excesses on the one hand, and into illegitimate and dishonest methods of obtaining the means of abnormal gratification on the other.

The true and normal life of man, therefore, can be realized only through the development and supremacy of the spiritual nature. This will not only save him from all sin and the power of temptation, but will bring the outward world also into co-ordinated harmony with his being. The perfect control of the animal and the physical in his own organism will give man the control of the conditions of life in both the animal and vegetable kingdoms, the perfect command of the animals, and also of his own immediate physical environments. The controlling of storms, and the prevention of great aërial disturbances, etc., will result from the full realization of his spiritual power. To many this statement will seem like the wild and extravagant dream of a disordered mentality, instead of the sober prophecy of a coming reality. Nevertheless we do not hesitate to affirm this to be among the normal attainments of the higher life for men on earth, promised in the gospel or Theosophy of the Christ.

The Basis of the Claim.—We read that the Master quelled the storm on Galilee by the supremacy of his spiritual being and the legitimate exercise of the power it conferred, and also so overruled the power of gravity in his own body as to walk upon the surface of the sea. Is this an unfounded legend or a fact of history? We accept it as a veritable fact, and as such, typical of the normal and legitimate power of humanity risen to the level of the Christ-life. Humanity is the head and brain, so to speak, of the organic world. When, then, the full life and power of the Spirit has become incarnate in that head, its reactive influence upon the world with which it is thus vitally related, will bring the conditions of that world into co-ordinated harmony with itself. If the Master single-handed in his supreme faith could perform the works he did, the combined faith and effort of any community of his true followers even before they have reached the level and supremacy of his perfect life, could readily break the power of a storm, drought, pestilence or any threatened calamity. And this act of united prayer and faith, intelligently performed through an under-

standing of the law, would be neither superstition nor
fanaticism, but a normal and worthy act of filial
obedience and trusting faith in the immanent God
and Father of men, and in His inspired teachers and
prophets. "Verily, verily, I say unto you, He that
believeth on me, the works that I do shall he do also;
and greater works than these shall he do, because I
go unto the Father. And whatsoever ye shall ask in
my name, that will I do, that the Father may be glorified in the Son. If ye shall ask anything in my name
I will do it." This is a possibility that has been actually verified by experience in many instances. The
Apostolic history is filled with them, followed by many
well authenticated instances in the succeeding centuries down to our own times. Some striking examples of recent date are related by President Mahan, of
Oberlin College, as occurring under his ministry.

It may be objected, that this would be a dangerous
power in the hands of men whose shortsightedness
might lead them to make a very unwise use of it.
This objection is met by the fact that the condition
under which the power is promised, is one of spiritual
enlightenment and divine leading in which man will
be wisely directed in its exercise. The secret of spiritual emancipation, attainment and power, the realization of life above the power of temptation and sin, and
the mastery of the outward world it involves, is the
complete subjection—not destruction—of the animal
in man, and the perfect co-ordination of its functions
with the nobler activities of the soul under spiritual
inspiration and divine guidance.

Specific Application in Nutrition.—The function of nutrition was established in the human economy for the sole purpose of maintaining the balance of physical waste and renewal, and sustaining the processes involved in the transformation of tissue in the mental and bodily activities. The animal enjoyment in eating and drinking—the process of supply—is incidental and secondary, and cannot be made the motive of indulgence without leading to excess and perversion. We should eat and drink to subserve the purposes of life, not live to the end of eating and drinking. This law and the principle involved are simple enough to be practically understood by all. In a normal, unperverted life the demands of the system for sustenance are comparatively light, and the food best adapted to meet the demand is plain and very simple. The more the intuitive and inspirational powers of the psychic and spiritual nature are cultivated and exercised, the less the energy expended and the less the friction and waste of tissue in mental activity, and so the lighter the demand and need of physical renewal. This has been demonstrated in the experience of thousands. The demands upon the vital economy are reduced to their minimum, while the complete conservation of energy on the plane of the animal and vital functions adds immensely to the accumulation of active working power on the plane of the mental and spiritual activities.

On the other hand, the more the true function of nutrition is lost sight of in the mere pleasure of indulgence, the more abnormal and perverted the appetite

is sure to become, and the *seeming* necessity for its
indulgence increased. This involves a waste of energy
in protecting the system against derangement and
disease, and in disposing of the unassimilated material
injurious in itself, unnecessarily taken into the system.
It diverts energy also from brain and mentality, crip-
ples their activities and sensualizes the man.

Is Flesh Eating a Necessity?—It is a significant
and suggestive fact that as the higher nature is cultivated and spirituality unfolds, the grosser, heavier and
especially the stimulating foods and drinks are abandoned, and the higher products of the vegetable kingdom adopted as the staple articles of diet, with only
such products of the animal kingdom as can be obtained without the taking of life. Thousands have
come, through the awakening of their intuitions and
spiritual nature, independent of any previous thought
or theory in the matter, to abhor the eating of flesh,
and shrink from the thought of taking life for the
purpose of food, as from a species of murder and can-
nibalism. It is the animal in man that calls for flesh
and the grosser and sensualizing forms of food; hence
as the animal becomes subordinated to the unfolding
spiritual life, manifested in quickened intuition and
spiritual inspiration, these are spontaneously abandoned for the more attractive food products of the
vegetable kingdom, that grow above the ground and
mature and ripen in the sunlight. Great intellectual
ability may exist with a strong animal nature which
revels in the consumption of flesh and the grosser stimulating and sensualizing forms of food; but these foods

are absolutely incompatible with spirituality. With the unfolding of the spiritual life, the dominance of animal desire in the physical is overruled and the animal activities sink into their legitimate sphere in the human economy, and the appetite becomes natural and simple, expressing only the normal demands of the system. It is the dominance of animal desire in the physical functions that clings to the grosser and stimulating food and drinks, the indulgence of which leads to over-feeding and the abnormal activities of all the animal propensities. In the lower, savage and animal stages of human development, animal food may be deemed a necessity, though the animal nearest man in form and structure, as with other of the most powerful and long-lived animals, eats no flesh. It is certain, however, that as the nobler attributes unfold, the grosser foods give place to a simpler dietary, and one in natural and spiritual accord with the more refined and elevated conditions of life. Is this not a sufficient hint for those who would rise out of animal conditions and attain the supremacy of spiritual life and power, to adopt the simple foods that do not pander to animal desire; and with these also correspondingly simple habits of life? Many chronic invalids have been restored to health and vigor by this means alone; while the attainment and untrammeled exercise of the spiritual gifts are impossible without it.

The Specific Law Formulated.—The law of human life may be simply defined as the conservation of energy in the animal activities for expenditure in the legitimate exercise of the higher powers under divine

17

inspiration and guidance, the animal impulses and desires to be controlled and wisely directed by a spiritually enlightened judgment and moral sense. The human body being constructed with direct reference to these higher activities will, through observance of this law, be found a perfect instrument in its adaptations to the legitimate work of life, and will not wear out nor fail in health and vigor during the years allotted to that work in the normal cycle of the earthly career. We do not believe that any man beginning with an average stock of vital stamina, who has conserved his energies in the animal functions, ever wore out or prematurely failed in health and strength in any legitimate occupation. The elasticity and recuperative power of life and vitality under these conditions are practically unlimited. A man who endures years of gluttony, drunkenness and the attending dissipations before he breaks down, as some do, would endure many more years of active and profitable labor if at the same time he observed the law here formulated.

If we would live at one with God, and enjoy His fellowship and communion, and be guided by His wisdom, we must follow that guidance in using the powers he has given us strictly to the ends for which they were bestowed and ordained. It is utter mockery to repeat the Lord's prayer, "Thy will be done on earth as it is in heaven," while we live in daily violation of this righteous law of our being—a law that the simplest can understand, and the weakest will receive power to observe if it be the sincere desire of his heart. "There hath no temptation taken you but such as is common to man: but God is faithful who will not suffer you to be tempted above that ye are able; but will with the temptation also make a way of escape." "Be not deceived; God is not mocked: for whatsoever a man soweth, that shall he also reap. For he that soweth to his flesh shall of the flesh reap corruption; but he that soweth to the Spirit shall of the Spirit reap life everlasting. And let us not be weary in well doing: for in due time we shall reap if we faint not." The sowing here spoken of by the Apostle refers to the motives and intents of the heart, the motives which prompt the activities of our being and the use we make of our powers in those activities, whether we sow to our flesh or to the Spirit. What then is

Sowing to the Spirit?—What indeed can it be but desiring and seeking the realization of God in our being as His children, through the fulfilment of His love and purpose in our existence, and His will in all our activities? The Spirit and purpose of God find expression in the normal exercises of each and every function of our being. When therefore we seek to know the real object of these functions and to exercise them only to that end, we are seeking to know and to do the Father's will and be at one with Him in these activities. We are sowing to the Spirit in them, and will reap the perfect and incorruptible life through them. On the other hand, to lose sight of the end in the use of the means, and forget the purpose of a function in the mere pleasure of indulgence, is to sow to the flesh, pervert the function and place ourselves in antagonism to the will of the Father in it. This persisted in will bring the certain result so graphically pictured in Apostolic language: "He that soweth to his flesh shall of the flesh reap corruption."

Object of the Earth Life.—The evident object of human existence in this world is threefold. First: the individualization of the soul and its permanent spiritual organism. Second: the primary development, education and discipline of its innate powers, first in their relation to the outward world in the school of the senses, then in their higher relation to the inward life and kingdom of God; and Third: the essential experience and discipline to be gained in acquiring the mastery of the sensuous life and the outward world through the development and supremacy of the spiritual nature, in unity with and under the inspiration and guidance of the Father. The necessity and promise of Divine teaching and guidance is the burden of both Hebrew and Christian Scripture, and cannot be too often referred to and emphasized in our thought, because it is, perhaps, the one privilege least recognized and resorted to by man, and the one necessity least realized by him. "I will instruct thee and teach thee in the way which thou shalt go: I will guide thee with mine eye." "But the Comforter, which is the Holy Spirit," "even the Spirit of truth which proceedeth from the Father," "he shall teach you all things, and " "will guide you into all truth," "bring all things to your remembrance, whatsoever I have said unto you " "and he will show you things to come."

The physical body and its senses were provided, therefore, as the suitable organic instrument and means to this end, and are thus to be regarded and made the servant, never the master of the soul. Man is not a body with a soul to care for and save, but a living soul and a spiritual being, with a body to use while acquiring his primary earthly education and discipline in the integral development of his powers, and their adjustment to both the outer objective or phenomenal world, and the inner spiritual realm or kingdom of God.

Key to the Parable.—In this analysis of the function and relations of the animal nature in the human economy, we have the key to the true doctrine of the temptation and fall of man symbolized in the parable of Eden. In it also we find the true basis of the Christ doctrine of the necessity for the birth and evolution of the spiritual man through the regeneration of the natural man. The primary or natural man (child of Nature) represented in Adam, though born in innocence—Eden—is subject to temptation and liable to fall into sin. As a child of God he is endowed with a moral nature through which, if he listen, he will hear the silent but revealing Word of the Spirit, and through its "*still*, small voice," heard only in the silence—stillness of sense—will receive divine guidance. The animal functions, uncontrolled by the moral nature under spiritual leading tend to excessive indulgence and perverted action. This when yielded to constitutes sin, and brings disaster into the life.

The rational and moral powers are subject to the

law of growth and development through healthful exercise, and require cultivation to this end. This healthful exercise, as we have shown, is possible only through the dominance and leading of the spiritual; since without this the forces are all expended in sensuous activities which divert attention and effort from the legitimate work of life, blunt the moral sense, drown the voice of the Spirit and bring the soul into bondage to flesh and sense. This is the fallen state and a most assuredly depraved condition, from which nothing can rescue the soul but the re-enthronement of the spiritual nature in its rightful supremacy, through the return of the soul itself in repentance and faith to the immediate inspiration and redemptive power of the Father's love.

Not an Inherited State.—Man, however, is not born a fallen being. Every child is born in Eden, and hears the authoritative "voice of the LORD God" speaking in and through the moral sense, as surely as he hears the seductive voice of the tempter in the enticements of animal desire and physical sense. The rational and moral powers with the spiritual life in which they are rooted, and through which they have access to and inspiration from God, have their beginning as such with man, and, therefore, start at their minimum of expression and power. The animal life, on the other hand, which culminates in man, was brought to full development in the animal kingdom before the kingly nature of man in his infancy appeared. It is for this reason that the natural man begins his conscious existence with a perfected animal life as his natural inheritance; while his spiritual inheritance, the spiritual life—in which the rational and moral powers are rooted, and from which they derive their divine possibility of an infinite development—is at its minimum of engermed activity, and needs another cycle of evolution to bring it to complete embodiment in organized expression. Nevertheless the animal nature when properly restrained and directed is not perverted and will not pervert the life, but remains a needful and true servant of the soul. Hence its tendency, when uncontrolled, to excessive indulgence and perverted activity, is not strong enough in the innocence of childhood before the unperverted instincts have been corrupted by depraved associations, to drown the divine voice which, in the engermed spiritual life, is a sure spiritual instinct, and becomes in the unfolding of that life a divine and unerring INTUITION.

For the spiritual nature to hold the supremacy and exert its rightful restraining and directive power over the animal activities, it must unfold with the development of the rational and moral powers through obedience of the soul to its divine leading. When this leading is not strictly followed from childhood the soul comes more and more under the dominance of the animal nature, and the bondage of sensuous impressions, until fully submerged in the sphere and activities of the sensuous and selfish life. This constitutes the state or condition typified by the wandering sheep and the prodigal son in those striking parables of Jesus, and which theologians call the fallen state. Since this has been and still remains so widespread and universal

we have abundant illustration of the urgent necessity
of immediate regeneration in the complete evolution
of the spiritual life in all whose attention and interest
can be awakened to it.

May Begin With Childhood.—The Lord Christ took
young children in his arms and blessed them saying,
"Suffer little children to come unto me, and forbid
them not; for of such is the kingdom of God." This
was practically saying that the kingdom of God or the
divine nature and life were implanted or engermed in
the innocency of childhood, or, in the normal supremacy
of the spiritual nature before its righteous law has
been consciously violated in the life of the child. By
retaining this innocency, and unfolding the soul's
powers under the supremacy and ideal of the spiritual
life, the spiritual man will be fully evolved and the
kingdom of God brought forth and established in the
earth life, as in heaven. This work can begin and be
carried forward in adult life in no other way. "Verily
I say unto you, Whosoever shall not receive the kingdom of God as a little child, he shall not enter therein."
We must return to the innocency of entire obedience
to the law of the spiritual life before it can unfold and
come to complete embodiment in us. The perfect
evolution of the spiritual life involves and effects, as
elsewhere shown, the regeneration or transformation
of both the psychic being and physical organism. It
should be remembered that there is the same necessity
for the transformation and change of the physical organism as an instrument for the expression of the
higher powers of the spiritual man, that there is for

the evolution of the spiritual life and power in the psychic being. Regeneration effects this organic transformation.

That children can be brought to Christ, that is, to embrace the Christ ideal of the perfect life through obedience to the inward voice, we have the authority of the Christ. They may be brought to understand that they are spiritual beings and children of God, and that the whisperings of duty are Divine monitions and of infinitely more importance to be heeded than all other desires can possibly be. If this is done before the child-life is led astray by corrupting associations and the enticement of sense, and thus helped and kept in obedience to the law of truth and purity, the outward man and the inward life will unfold together, the outward man being moulded after the pattern of the inward life, its perfect correspondence and expression. The Christ nature would unfold normally in such a life as it did in the child Jesus—the pattern of all normal childhood and youth, as well as of a true spiritual manhood. There would be divine inspiration and leading from earliest life, though permanent illumination would not come until later as with the Christ himself. The development of certain organic conditions of brain and body are a necessity to this illumination, and this development will correspond with the progressive steps involved in the evolution of the higher soul powers. While the successful beginning of the spiritual evolution is the possibility of all childhood, there is, we repeat, no certainty of its realization until we have a regenerated parentage, and children are begotten and brought forth under the perfected parental conditions of the spiritual life. From the plane of a regenerate humanity parents living in the realization of their own divine inheritance will not only transmit a rich endowment of the spiritual nature, but will have the inspiration and ability to impress upon their children from the dawn of intelligence a full sense of their immediate relation to God as His children, and of His guiding voice and helping power in their souls and inward life.

Immediate and Permanent Results.—In the offspring of the spiritual man the higher nature, under parental training, will hold its rightful supremacy from infancy. The human heredity will have the active dominance of spirituality and upward tendency stamped upon it instead of animality and perverted tendency. From this will follow an entire reversal in the order of human life and society resulting in the immediate and complete fulfilment of millennial prophecy. The natural man in the order of Adam will be replaced by the spiritual man in the order of Christ. The children of the spiritual man will not have to struggle against such odds with temptation as confront those of the sensuous man. Like the Christ child they will grow and wax strong in spirit, filled with wisdom (spiritual intuition) and the grace of God will be upon them.

The child of the natural man begins with the maximum of animal life and activity and the minimum of spiritual. The fully regenerated life will reverse this and give the child of the spiritual man the maxi-

mum of spiritual and moral power with the minimum
of animal activity—the true co-ordinated life of the
children of God. The principle of regeneration which
is the leaven of the spiritual life, will be implanted as
the active or dominant constructive principle in the
very germ of the new being. Such is the New Life
and order which the Christ was raised up to establish,
but which will never be realized until men become his
true followers, and co-operate with him under the ministry of heaven for its realization in their own experience. "As in Adam [the natural man] all die; even so
in Christ [the spiritual man] shall all be made alive."

The Fall and Redemption.—In the light of this
study the true nature of the fall thus typified in Scripture, and of the redemption opened to the world in and
by the Christ, becomes unmistakably apparent. Like
the Adam and Eve of Scripture, all children are
brought into the world innocent, having the spontaneous instincts of the animal nature in the physical functions, and the equally spontaneous monitions of the
spiritual nature—the voice of God—in the moral sense.
If the promptings of this voice are obeyed, the rational
and moral powers will unfold in the light and freedom
of the spiritual life, under divine inspiration and guidance. If this normal unfolding of the spiritual life is
not interrupted it will go forward to complete and
permanent embodiment, a divine incarnation—the reproduction of the Christ life. If, however, the leadings
and warnings of the spiritual nature are disregarded
and ignored—in the heat of animal desire and the enticements of sense—and the soul yields to indulgence

against the protest of the spirit, she partakes of the forbidden fruit, "the tree of the knowledge of good *and* evil." The law of God in the personal life—which is the right use of the functions and things of life—is violated, and the soul comes under condemnation of the moral law in the consciousness of guilt, and is thus driven out of the Eden of innocence.

So long as the evolution of life has risen only to the level of the natural man, with the higher spiritual nature and life embodied only in germ, and expressed as a prophetic instinct or intuition in the midst of sensuous activity and experience, it was perhaps inevitable that this man of the Adamic order should, under temptation, fall. The heavenly Father, however, never forsakes nor forgets His children though they wander from and forget Him. He keeps an open door of return—through repentance and faith—to the spirit of loyalty and the privileges of divine fellowship and communion. The indestructible and incorruptible germ of His own nature in the spiritual life of His children, is never separated from the eternal spring of His life and the infinite fountain of His love; hence in the very condemnation of sin there is breathed also the whisper of hope, and there springs up a prophetic instinct or intuition of a possible redemption. This possibility will ever be made a certainty by genuine repentance and faith. The redemptive and restoring power of Spirit is as absolute and certain in its workings, as is its creative and life-giving power. "The seed of the woman" shall indeed bruise the head of the tempter and trample under foot his power to harm.

Under the universal experience of sinning and repenting, falling and rising, the spiritual nature has expanded and unfolded in the life of the race, in spite of the enticements of sense and the aberrations of sin. As a result of special conditions individuals have here and there been caught up in this rising impulse, and under the inspiration of the Spirit have become its seers and prophets, living centres of mighty influence for the further quickening of the spiritual life of the world. In this unfolding of the spiritual life of the race and its exceptional development in a few, it was natural that the rising line of seers and prophets thus spontaneously evolved as special workers for the many, should culminate in one complete incarnation of the divine and perfect life. Thus came the Christ taking into himself all power of prophecy, seership and spiritual ministry, the God-Anointed Leader and Redeemer of his race. The germ of the Divine nature and attributes deposited from the Father in the spiritual life latent in His children, is a divine pledge of the ultimate evolution and realization of that nature and its attributes in experience. The final bringing forth of these latent possibilities to full fruition under providential leading and discipline, is the Divine redemption of that pledge. This is the true nature of that redemption foreshadowed in Old Testament prophecy and opened in the New Testament as a promise of final and absolute fulfilment in and through the ministry of the Christ.

The Spiritual Baptism.—It is related of Paul that on visiting Ephesus in his missionary work, "and find-

ing certain disciples, he said unto them, Have ye received the Holy Spirit since ye believed? And they
said unto him, We have not so much as heard whether
there be any Holy Spirit. . . . And when Paul had
laid his hands upon them, the Holy Spirit came on
them; and they spake with tongues and prophesied.
And they were in all about twelve men." We read
also that between the resurrection and translation of
the Master, being with the disciples, "He charged
them not to depart from Jerusalem, but to wait for
the promise of the Father, which, said he, ye heard
from me: for John indeed baptized with water; but
ye shall be baptized with the Holy Spirit not many
days hence," and "Ye shall receive power when the
Holy Spirit is come upon you: and ye shall be my
witnesses." These with many other passages from the
Apostolic history refer to a peculiar, unique and distinct experience which was promised to all disciples in
a certain stage of their spiritual development; and
which, when experienced, was to endue them with
"power from on high," or clothe them with some special gift of the Spirit. This promise was literally fulfilled in the experiences referred to. That it does not
come in the first or earlier stages of the spiritual life
—the unfolding of the spiritual man—is evident not
only from Apostolic experience, as they were not prepared for it until after the translation of Jesus, but
also from the experience of the Master himself, who
did not receive it until about thirty years of age,
though he had grown up from infancy under divine
inspiration and in unbroken fidelity to the law of the

spiritual life. His permanent illumination dated from
that experience when "the heavens were opened unto
him" and "the Spirit descended and abode upon him."
For a specific classification and description of the
"gifts of the Spirit," or the various occult powers thus
conferred, see Paul's first epistle to the Corinthians,
twelfth chapter, which is worthy of most careful study,
as it is the positive testimony of one who spoke from
personal observation and experience. It is enough in
this connection, to call attention to this remarkable
experience as a special illumination of the Spirit, which
lifts the mind to a plane of intuitive perception of truth
at first hand, and a commanding power of action absolutely above and beyond the reach of possible attainment by the most severe and perfect methods of intellectual culture and training.

Nature of the Power Conferred.—The story of
Pentecost and the transformed lives of the Apostles
after that experience, as with the large numbers that
had a like experience under their ministry, furnish illustrations of the nature of the power received and of
the character of its manifestation in their transformed
lives. Peter thus describes it as the fulfilment of the
prophecy of Joel: "And it shall come to pass in the
last days, saith God, I will pour out of my Spirit upon
all flesh: and your sons and your daughters shall
prophesy, and your young men shall see visions and
your old men shall dream dreams: And on my servants and on my handmaidens I will pour out in those
days of my Spirit; and they shall prophesy." The
complete fulfilment of this ancient prophecy includes

"all flesh," and as promised, will bring the illuminated
life and some phase of special mastery to all, as illustrated in its partial fulfilment in Apostolic experience.
Among the "gifts" or special powers bestowed were
the immediate and practically instantaneous healing
of all manner of disease, sickness and insanity by word
or touch; the intuitive command of other tongues or
languages otherwise unknown or unlearned, "the
working of miracles," etc.   The perfect example, however, of the practical omniscience or perfect intuition,
wisdom and occult mastery conferred by full spiritual
illumination, was exhibited in the Master.   "The disciple is not above his Master, but when he is perfected
shall be as his Master."

The Fact and Problem Involved.—Here was a
young man born of humble parents in an obscure
province, who, so far as we can determine from the
meagre record, grew up with the scantiest resources
of external help, the village Synagogue and the oral
traditions of his people being the extent of his contact
with the learning of his time.   This peasant carpenter
on coming to maturity, moved by an all-commanding
impulse and inspiration, took his stand before the
world as a prophet, teacher and reformer; his own
immediate inspiration and illumination from the living
God and Father of men being the authority he claimed
for his message.   "He taught as one having authority
and not as the scribes."   Men everywhere "were astonished at his doctrine, for his word was with power."

He entered upon this public ministry with a wisdom,
an insight, a majesty of character and power of per-

sonal influence unequalled by any of the prophets and teachers preceding him, which confounded beyond measure all who had known his previous history. "And when he had come into his own country, he taught them in their Synagogue, insomuch that they were astonished, and said, Whence hath this man this wisdom and these mighty works? Is not this the carpenter's son? is not his mother called Mary? and his brethren James, and Joses, and Simon, and Judas? And his sisters, are they not all with us? Whence then hath this man all these things?" It is evident, from these exclamations of his neighbors and acquaintances, that they had seen nothing in his previous life which could account for or afford any satisfactory hint as to the source of his sudden endowment of this exceptional wisdom and power. Only enough of his early history is given by his biographers to show that he was an exceptionally devout and spiritually-minded child and youth, ever seeking to know the deeper wisdom of the law and the prophets as held in the traditions of his people and read and taught in the synagogue.

This characteristic became so marked that, at twelve years of age, on being taken to Jerusalem he astonished the Rabbis in the temple by his questions, understanding and answers, which certainly indicated a natural genius of inspiration corresponding with his devout aspiration. This is further confirmed by the only subsequent allusion to his career up to the time of his visit to Jordan and his baptism by John. On his return from Jerusalem with his parents, we

18

read, "And he went down with them, and came to
Nazareth, and was subject unto them. . . . And Jesus
increased in wisdom and stature and in favor with
God and man." Still there was nothing developed in
that intervening history to sufficiently indicate or
account to his neighbors for the exceptional character
of the wisdom and power possessed by him from the
time he entered upon his public ministry. Nevertheless he appeared among them with a little band of disciples, himself, perhaps, the youngest of the group,
though in wisdom and commanding greatness of personality so much above the noblest as to seem another
order of being, which, indeed, he practically was.

Still the Question of the World.—From that day
to this, among those who accept the story of his marvellous life as veritable history, the same question has
arisen that puzzled and confounded the people of his
own country and time. Whence had this man this
wisdom and these mighty works? Some answer by
saying, "He was very God veiled in human form and
flesh." Others say, "He was a re-incarnated Avatar
or Planetary Spirit;" while others still, rejecting both
these claims, recognize in him the supreme Man and
Brother of men, and remain silent over the mystery
of his exceptional life and works as something beyond
present understanding, if taken as literal fact. Others
again, accept the story of miracles as figurative only,
representing the power of his exceptional inspiration
and influence over the moral and spiritual lives of his
followers. Nevertheless the story of his life, "miracles" included, was obviously given as actual external

history. His immediate followers, however, who had the benefit of his most confidential teaching, never dreamed of his being either the "Incarnate God" or a pre-existing being of any kind. What they did think, and testified to, after his ascension, and speaking under the inspiration of their own spiritual baptism at Pentecost, we have in the specific words of Peter, the foremost among those who had followed him through his earthly ministry.

This brave and heroic Apostle boldly testified on that occasion, with the full indorsement of the assembled disciples, and facing those who had participated in securing the crucifixion of their Lord, "Ye men of Israel, hear these words; Jesus of Nazareth, a man approved of God among you by miracles and wonders and signs, which God did by him in the midst of you, as ye yourselves know. . . . This Jesus hath God raised up [from the dead] whereof we are witnesses. . . . Therefore let all the house of Israel know assuredly, that God hath made that same Jesus whom ye have crucified, both Lord and Christ." And again on another occasion at the house of Cornelius, among the Gentiles where he had been sent by a special providence he said, "The word which God sent unto the children of Israel, preaching peace by Jesus Christ: . . . That word, I say, ye know, which was published throughout all Judea, and began from Galilee, after the baptism which John preached; How God anointed Jesus of Nazareth with the Holy Spirit and with power: who went about doing good and healing all that were oppressed of the devil; for God was with him."

We must take this testimony of Peter as reflecting the claim which he knew that the Master made for himself; since he was his chosen ordained and specially instructed Apostle and witness, testifying to that which he had seen and heard. If anything more is needed, we must remember that he spake also, as we have said, from the authority of that higher illumination which he had received subsequent to the Master's ascension in fulfilment of his parting promise. There is nothing in the fuller record of the four Evangelists but confirms this specific explanation by Peter of the nature and source of the exceptional wisdom and power of Jesus. "How God anointed Jesus of Nazareth with the Holy Spirit and with power." "A man approved of God among you by miracles and wonders and signs, which God did by him in the midst of you."

The Open Secret and Solution.—In these words of Peter and the special account of the permanent illumination of Jesus after his baptism, when "as he prayed the heavens were opened unto him, etc.," followed by his victory over temptation in the wilderness, we have, as already intimated, the open secret and solution of his divine achievements and victorious life. From his illumination at Jordan and complete spiritual victory in the wilderness, "He returned in the power of the Spirit into Galilee preaching the gospel of the kingdom of God," and entering upon the mighty work of his ministry as the Leader and Saviour of men. That he was to save men by leading them up to the same spiritual baptism, permanent illumination and victory over the power of temptation and sin, is evident from his words of instruction and promise to his immediate disciples, and through them to all his faithful followers. The perfect demonstration of this, however, was in the practical fulfilment of that promise, not only in Apostolic experience, but in large numbers under their subsequent ministry. Why it has not followed in the subsequent history of the Church, save in a few of its martyred saints and persecuted mystics, we have endeavored to show.

The Christ ideal of attainment and his corresponding method of its realization by all men, were lost to the world through the speculations of the early fathers of the Church, who assumed the authority of "Apostolic succession" without the real Apostolic baptism and spirit. The hated and persecuted Mystics, who rejected ecclesiastical authority and followed only the divine guide within, held the secret of the regenerate life, lost to the Church through its pride and pomp of external authority and power, the spirit of Anti-Christ. To awaken earnest souls to this palpable fact, and call their attention to this open secret of the Christ and Apostolic life and teaching, is the one motive and hope of our effort in these appeals, as through spiritual leading it has thus been opened to us. The recorded life and words of these great teachers and exemplars and especially of the Master, are fortunately open to all. If men can be induced to break away from the arbitrary and fictitious authority of tradition, and trust the interpreting power of the Spirit in their own souls, the new renascence of Apostloic life and power will begin.

In seeking the Apostolic baptism and the Christ illumination of the Holy Spirit, we have not only the example of the Apostles but of the Master also, to emphasize the fact, that much earnest effort and preparatory discipline of experience are necessary to bring the soul and its organism up to this consummation and supreme experience. The reason of this we have endeavored to show and will more specifically illustrate presently. If full, permanent illumination were an immediate possibility upon entering the path of the spiritual and obedient life, such surely would have been the experience of the Christ. Though unquestionably a profound spiritual genius, living a life of unexampled fidelity to the law of truth and purity, and following the divine leading from a child, he was not ready, it appears, for the full, perfect and abiding illumination until about thirty years of age. He doubtless had, as all who are faithful to divine leading will have, seasons of unusual spiritual exaltation and revelation, but the development and perfection of certain specific organic conditions, both mental and physical, were a necessity with him as with all others, before the perfect illumination could find a free, normal and permanent organic expression.

This illustrates the truth of his great doctrine of birth into the spiritual life or kingdom of God, and the growth or unfolding of that life through regeneration, from spiritual infancy to a full-rounded and divine manhood. Once fully attained, however, as the Christ, he was especially qualified to do for his followers what there was no one thus qualified to do for him; to specifically help them, not only by example and instruction, but by the quickening touch and awakening power of his personal influence when they, through understanding, were prepared to open themselves to him. Hence his specific instruction to them before his departure, and through them to us and to all who would follow and share with him in this divine realization, "Where two or three are gathered together in my name, there am I in the midst of them."

It was the faithful following of this instruction by the Apostles after the ascension of their Lord, when "they were all with one accord in one place," and "continued with one accord in prayer and supplication," that opened them to that marvellous influx at Pentecost, when "suddenly there came a sound from heaven as of a rushing mighty wind, and it filled all the house where they were sitting. And there appeared unto them cloven tongues like as of fire and it sat upon each of them. And they were all filled with the Holy Spirit, and began to speak with other tongues as the Spirit gave them utterance." About three years of preparation under the personal ministry of the Master made them ready for the Pentecostal baptism and with it a high degree of, if not the full and perfect, spiritual realization. They were ever after endued with a marvellous power and spiritual insight, which certainly demonstrated the truth of the Lord Christ's claim for the regenerating and transforming power of the Spirit in the life, and which places the Apostolic attainment, at least, within reach of all men.

The Times and Seasons.—It is not needful and therefore it may not be given any to know the exact time when this blessing may come. It is enough to know that regeneration and a season of preparatory discipline is a necessity to all, and that the period of preparation will depend upon the fidelity and consecration to the divine leading. On the eve of his translation the Master, knowing that the disciples were nearly ready for this high experience, counselled them to remain together at Jerusalem—where their Apostolic ministry was to commence—with one accord in earnest prayerful seeking and confident waiting for its immediate realization. Nevertheless he saw that it was not best for them to know the time or season of its coming, the confident expectation, yet patient trusting and dependence upon the Father's will and wisdom, being a necessary condition of the blessing. "And being assembled together with them, he charged them that they should not depart from Jerusalem, but to wait for the promise of the Father, which, said he, ye heard of me: For John truly baptized with water; but ye shall be baptized with the Holy Spirit not many days hence. . . . And he said unto them, It is not for you to know times or seasons, which the Father hath set within his own authority. But ye shall receive power, when the Holy Spirit has come upon you: and ye shall be my witnesses both in Jerusalem, and in all Judea, and in Samaria, and unto the uttermost part of the earth."

The Calling and Election.—We are told in Scripture to make our calling and election sure. From the foundation of the world the Father has provided and ordained this high privilege and destiny for all His children, yet as children of the living God men are endowed with freedom of choice and action, and therefore clothed with the tremendous responsibility which this involves. Every department of the divine Economy is governed by unerring wisdom and immutable law. There is but one pathway to the attainment of the immunities, privileges, freedom and mastery of the perfect life as sons of God, and that is obedience to the law of the Spirit in the life. It is the pathway of the spirit, the strait and narrow way of regeneration through which alone man can rise from the plane of the sensuous to the realization of the spiritual life. The election or starting upon the path rests entirely with himself. Humanity was brought into being, and to the consciousness of personality and responsibility on the plane of the sensuous life or natural man, without any voluntary choice or agency of his own.

With the endowment of moral freedom and the sense of responsibility, the rising to the full realization of his inherent possibilities depends entirely upon his co-operation with the divine provision to this end. Serious consideration is necessary to lead one to take the decisive step of entire consecration to the leading of the Spirit for the realization of the perfect life of a child of God, and thus enter upon the path; but the taking of the step is practically the work of a moment. It is like the planting of the seed after suitable preparation, in confident expectation of a future harvest. When the ideal of the perfect life is fully adopted as the goal of earthly attainment and desire, and the soul has given itself in unreserved abandon to co-operation with the divine ministry for its realization, all needful help and guidance from the Father will be bountifully given. Then all the organic conditions come under the molding influence of the new ideal and the inspiration of the Father's love, and are regenerated and reconstructed after the divine pattern. This is "The washing of regeneration and the renewing of the Holy Spirit," or of that which is wholly spiritual. The time consumed in the regenerative process before the mental and physical conditions are ready for full spiritual illumination will, we repeat, depend largely upon the earnestness and devotion of the disciple in his determination to reach the perfect life, and his faithfulness in following the leading of the Spirit in the path of duty.

Necessity of Discipline.—Much severe discipline seems necessary to effect the complete regeneration of some, yet the compassionate Father will impose no difficulty or burden upon His child which is not best for him, and will Himself walk in helpful companionship through the struggle to victory. As a rule, the more complete the reconciliation of the personal will with the Divine will, the shorter will be the discipline to which he will be subjected, since victory over self-will and personal desire, perfect unity with the will of the Father in all things, is the one object of the discipline. There can be no realization of divine sonship until this attitude of the mind and heart is effected. When this is complete, the laying on of hands in prayer as in Apostolic times will often accelerate the process. This, however, should be resorted to only under the unmistakable leading of the Spirit. It should always be made a special subject of prayer for divine leading, lest the human be thus made to usurp the place of the Divine.

Inspiration and Illumination.—While the distinction between inspiration and illumination is fully implied in what has been said, a statement of what the difference specifically is may help to a better understanding of the whole subject involved. Inspiration leads to illumination, and is a necessity to it; but inspiration is not in itself illumination. When a man is moved to speak or act wiser and better than he knows or intends he is inspired. Many unworthy men have thus at times been made the instruments of truth, justice and heroism, because they were moved for the time by a diviner influence than their natural affiliations would attract, or are lifted by a temporary quickening and exaltation of the better nature by the divine contact. Inspiration is not in itself evidence of personal righteousness, or moral purity. All men are subjects of inspiration in a greater or less degree, and may under the proper conditions have the nobler impulses quickened within them by the touch of a holy influence from centres of divine activity, or the baser impulses quickened by the touch of a corrupting influence from centres of depraved activity. When the heart is centred in God, however, the life is opened only to influences that are divine and heavenly, and thus receives power to exert a corresponding influence

upon all it touches. Every monition of the Spirit in
the moral sense or conscience, prompting to and approving right, protesting against and condemning
wrong, is the inspiration of the living God. There is
no other adequate source or explanation of this moral
sense.

It is this which relates and binds the soul to God.
When man recognizes the divine authority of this voice
of God in his own soul, and desires only to know
and be guided by the divine will and wisdom which
thus prompts him, he opens himself fully to the immediate inspiration and guidance of the Divine Spirit, and
the special ministry of heaven. He thus also effectually shuts the door against all that is opposed to God
and His law of truth and righteousness in the personal
life. The full and permanent inspiration and guidance
of God are entirely dependent upon a moral motive, a
spirit of unshrinking loyalty to the law of truth and
right, duty before pleasure and pleasure only in duty.
Consecration to this life, and the spirit of glad obedience to its imperative law, puts the soul under the
transforming influence and power of the Divine Spirit,
and the work of regeneration begins. This election or
choice is the work of man himself, but he will receive
divine help when it is truly sought, and this help is the
work of inspiration. As the spiritual life is thus awakened and under divine influence made to unfold in all
the faculties of the soul, these faculties take on an intuitive and inspirational activity, and effect corresponding changes in the organic conditions of brain and body,
bringing the entire physical organism, as the instru-

ment of the soul's powers, into conformity with the demands of the spiritual life. This is the work of regeneration which is the necessary preparation for the desired illumination. This involves time and discipline which, as before intimated, will be shortened in proportion to the earnestness and fidelity of the seeker.

The Physical Relations and Changes.—The vital system and motive apparatus are under the control of the nervous system. The nervous structure with its marvellous centres of living energy and co-ordinating power is the immediate seat and instrument of the soul and spiritual organism. The soul, or the living self-conscious personality, has the roots of its faculties in and draws its life from the spirit. The spirit, which is the specialization of the life of God in man, is that inmost and essential part and ground of our being which has identity of nature, and so makes us one with God, in proportion as it unfolds from within and becomes expressed in the faculties and powers of the soul. It is the Divine and Universal Spirit come to limitation in the spiritual and physical organism of man, and through which the life and powers of man are rooted and anchored in the Divine. It is this which makes man in his spiritual nature and organism an indestructible personality and child of God. It is this which makes possible the unfolding of the Divine nature and attributes in man, which as effected lifts him into conscious unity and oneness of life with the Father, and brings the realization of his own divine nature, spiritual supremacy and freedom as the child of God. This when reached in the body is the illu-

minated life of divine realization on earth, attained
only through the entire moral and physical regeneration of the natural man, in the evolution of the spiritual man.

Before this can be effected, the grosser organism,
the seat of animal activity, must be brought into complete conformity with and subordination to the demands of the nervous system, that it may respond to
all the normal activities of that system. The nervous
system must in turn be brought and kept in like conformity with and subordination to the demands of the
soul, so that it shall respond with spontaneous ease
and promptness to every normal activity of the soul.
These to be normal and perfect must be under the law
of the spiritual life and the spontaneous expression of
its inspirations. To secure this, the spiritual life must
be awakened into full activity and brought forth to its
rightful supremacy in the soul, and through the soul
over the entire dependent organism. The soul then
becomes the organic expression of the spirit, the nervous system the perfect instrument of the soul, and the
vital and motive systems are brought under the control and made responsive to the co-ordinated and
healthful activities of the nervous system.

To bring about and establish these as the permanent
organic conditions of soul and body is the true education and only perfect preparation for the real work of
life, the work of achievement and mastery. In effecting this result, a twofold culture is involved; physical
as well as spiritual. There is a physical morale for
the body as there is a spiritual morale for the soul.

The first is expressed in the law already stated; viz., conservation of energy in the animal activities of the vital functions, for expenditure in the higher activities of the rational and moral powers in the legitimate work of life. This is physical morality. That the higher activities of the soul be held and directed to their true work, they must be under the law of the spiritual life and the inspiration of the Divine Spirit, the personal life and motives one with the Divine. This is spiritual morality. For the animal in man to be subordinated to and co-ordinated with his spiritual nature, the personal will must be subordinated to and co-ordinated with the Divine will and purpose in the life. There must be no cross purposes between the finite will, desire and judgment of the child and the infinite wisdom and goodness of the Father.

The spiritual nature is always at one with God, because it is so much of His Spirit in His child; but the personal desire and will are not always at one with the spiritual nature; they are more generally with the animal in opposition to the spiritual. Hence the spiritual nature can be unfolded and brought into activity in the soul's powers and enthroned in permanent supremacy in the organic man, only as these powers are kept under the inspiration and guidance of the Father's Spirit; and this is wholly a matter of personal desire, or choice and will—the desire to be at one with the Father and to know and fulfil only His will and purpose which are infinitely wise and good. "Wherefore, brethren, give diligence to make your calling and election sure: for if ye do these things, ye shall never fail."

Co-ordination a Necessity.—Until all the physical organs are responsive to and under the complete control of the co-ordinated energies of the nervous system, and these in turn are responsive to and under the control of the higher soul powers, the soul itself is neither prepared nor qualified for the full illumination of the Spirit. While the law of physical morality here defined is disregarded, there will be a continual disturbance and depletion of the nervous forces through the excessive and perverted activities of the animal functions, which in due time brings permanent derangement of the nerve centres and weakness and irritability of the nervous system, unfitting it as an instrument for the normal development and exercise of the soul's powers. Until this law is strictly observed in the physical functions, there can be no perfect co-ordination of the grosser organism with the nervous system and this with the spiritual, and, therefore, no regeneration and preparation for spiritual illumination and divine realization. And again, this complete physical and spiritual co-ordination is possible only through the co-ordination of the personal desires and will with the will and purpose of the Father in us. Until this is made the ruling motive of life, no advance can be made toward spiritual illumination. Desire for reconciliation or at-one-ment with the Father is the first step in this direction, and no other can be taken without it.

Divine Realization.—This is the realization of one-ness of life and purpose with the Father in all the personal activities, in which the soul is enabled to see things in the light of truth, or as God sees them.

Dwelling in unity with the Father he stands in the light of the Divine omniscience, and interprets all things in that light, which is the perfect vision of truth and righteousness. This is divine illumination and is one with divine realization.

The Specific Steps Involved.—The soul as a spiritual organism and personal identity, is first individualized and brought to the realization of self-conscious being and personality on the plane of the natural man, under the dominion of the senses and the law of the animal or selfish life. The second crisis or step in its evolution is the awakening to the higher consciousness of spiritual being and personal relationship to God as child to Parent, and the spirit of fidelity to that relationship, determined to follow only the inspiration and guidance of the Father. This is spiritual birth, and entrance into the true life of a child of God.

The third step is the unfolding and perfection of that life in the soul with corresponding transformation of organism under the inspiration of the Father's love. This is the work of regeneration. When the law of the animal life—self-gratification and self-will—is thus wholly overruled and replaced by the law and love of righteousness and truth, and the co-ordination of the physical organism with the soul's powers, under divine leading, is complete, the soul is then ready, not before, for the full and permanent illumination of the Spirit. Before this divine consummation is reached, however, the faithful will have seasons of spiritual exaltation, when there will be a temporary suspension of the activities of the outward man, and the soul will for the

19

time be immersed in the pure light of the Spirit, and realize the beatific supremacy and untrammeled freedom of the spiritual life, in conscious oneness with the life of God. When, through the completed work of regeneration, this becomes the permanent realization or consciousness, all personal desire and will become one with the Divine. The soul is then animated by the one desire to be only the Word made flesh, a personal expression of the Divine will and wisdom, the embodiment of the one perfect life and thought of God.

Spiritual Illumination.—Spiritual illumination is the unclouded vision of truth and righteousness, when the soul is one in spirit and purpose with the Father, and the Divine nature shines through it unobstructed, so that the consciousness of things is one with the Divine Spirit, and the personal equation is submerged and forgotten in the one light of the Divine omniscience. Opinion is then sunk in actual knowledge and the authority of personal judgment is lost and forgotten in the authority of truth itself. Truth is the relation of things as they are in reality, or, as they exist in the mind of God; and righteousness is personal adjustment to this reality, in which pride of opinion, the wisdom and authority of men, and all human standards become as worthless rags. The vision of righteousness comes only with the spirit of this personal adjustment in righteousness. They are simultaneous and constitute the unity and identity of the soul with righteousness or oneness with the Divine. It is the realization of God.

Things are external and objective; the truth of things is subjective; in spiritual illumination, the objective facts, and the subjective truth of facts and of the relations and principles involved, become one in the consciousness, and the perfect adjustment of the soul to this perception, is the personal realization and consequent identity of the soul with the truth, and so with God. In this circle of divine experience the authority of truth stands supreme in the consciousness over all personal opinion and over all authority of personalities. Inspiration is always personal because partial and incomplete. There is and can be no such thing as plenary inspiration. Should inspiration open the soul to the perception of absolute truth, it is no longer inspiration, but illumination; it is absolute knowledge from personal realization. The soul cannot then be informed of the truth, because it is one with the truth in this realization. The object of inspiration is to lead and lift the soul to this realization which begins in and with illumination; but where illumination begins inspiration ends.

While the personal equation remains, the soul is the subject of and dependent upon inspiration, but the inspiration is of necessity more or less refracted by the personal equation. This is overcome only through perfect unity with God in all things, the complete realization of God in the life. Spiritual illumination then is the full vision of truth and righteousness when the soul, standing in the light of omniscience, sees things from the standpoint of the Divine; sees and knows them as they are in the mind of God; when all personal de-

sire and preferences, all pride of opinion, human wisdom and all standards of human authority, all fear
and favor of men sink out of sight in the ineffable
sense of unity with the thought and wisdom of God.
This is impossible to one who seeks divine sanction to
his own preconceived opinion, doctrine, creed, philosophy, or any system of human thought and speculation.
The human must become absolutely still in the recognition of the Divine voice and desire for the revelation
of truth in its divine reality and significance. The
personality must be sunk in the supreme realization
of truth and right, in the one desire that these only
shall speak and be heard.

Unity of spirit and purpose with God in the life
is an absolute necessity for the illumination of His
Spirit, and this unity is possible only through the
supreme love that gives all to be one with the Father
in all things, that God may be all and in all, the
one realization in which the personal equation disap-
pears. Inspiration is given, we repeat, to guide and
lead up to this experience. Inspiration is open to
all and belongs to all. It can help men, however,
to this divine realization, only as personal preferences,
pride of opinion and desire for self-exaltation are
laid down, that the truth and righteousness which are
of God shall rule the thought and life. "Be still
and know that I am God." "And when he had called
the people unto him with his disciples also, he said
unto them, Whosoever will come after me, let him
deny himself, and take up his cross, and follow me.
For whosoever will save his life shall lose it; but who-

soever shall lose his life for my sake and the gospel's, the same shall save it." " Be not therefore anxious, saying, What shall we eat? or, What shall we drink? or, Wherewithal shall we be clothed? . . . For your heavenly Father knoweth that ye have need of all these things. But seek ye *first* his kingdom and his righteousness; and all these things shall be added unto you."

CONCLUSION.

To such as have been helped by the reading of this book to a new or fuller conception of the higher and perfect life divinely promised and possible to man on earth, and who desire above all things to attain, while in the flesh, to its certain supremacy, illumination and power, we would offer in conclusion a few practical suggestions concerning the necessary initiatory steps to be taken.

Nothing, for this purpose, can be more explicit and assuring when understood, than the words of the Lord Christ recorded in *Matt.* xviii. 18, 19, 20: "Verily I say unto you, Whatsoever ye shall bind on earth shall be bound in heaven; and whatsoever ye shall loose on earth shall be loosed in heaven. Again I say unto you, That if two of you shall agree on earth as touching anything that they shall ask, it shall be done for them of my Father which is in heaven. For where two or three [two or more] are gathered together in my name, there am I in the midst of them."

Here are three distinct relations and conditions specified by the Master as involved in the work of spiritual development and realization. The first presents the law which determines the success or failure of all human effort. The second defines the conditions under which special answers to prayer, or divine help to specific ends and purposes, are secured; and the third reveals the conditions under which the special ministry of the Christ in spiritual presence and power is to be secured and enjoyed, which opens man to the Christ life and makes that ministry possible and certain.

The first clause here quoted, assumes that the divine economy and government are perfect and therefore unchangeable, and that these are pledged to the absolute vindication and triumph of every movement in harmony with the divine order, and the ultimate and certain defeat of all that is opposed to that order. So far as man is concerned, everything depends upon the relation and attitude which, as an individual, he assumes toward the divine law and government. Whatever attitude he seems to assume, his dominant ideals and ruling motives determine his actual character and position before God, and the corresponding results in his life. In endowing man with freedom of choice and action, God virtually binds Himself, in His dealings with him, to the results under His perfect economy, of the choice he makes. As a man sows so must he reap. If he sows to the Spirit in his ideal and effort, he is bound to realize his highest ambition. If he sows to the flesh or the selfish life he is doomed inevitably to ultimate defeat. Man thus determines for himself the character of his life in the flesh, by the ideal and motives that dominate that life, whether he shall be the slave of physical conditions, or rise to dwell in spiritual supremacy over them. He binds not only himself but practically binds God also—in

His perfect and immutable law—to the legitimate results of his attitude toward the divine order, whether
it be in harmony therewith or in opposition thereto.
" Verily I say unto you, Whatsoever ye shall bind on
earth [the conditions of the human in its relations to
the Divine] shall be bound in heaven [the position of
the Divine in its relation to the human]; and whatsoever ye shall loose on earth shall be loosed in heaven."
If a man, then, commit himself in faith and effort to
the attainment of the perfect life on earth, he binds
not only himself but the power of omnipotent love to
its accomplishment.

The second step and condition here specified, refers
to the relation and attitude of men toward each other,
implying that all interests and efforts in the divine
order are mutual and co-operative; and hence that
associative action on the part of man is a necessity
to perfect success. Under this law we have the assurance of divine co-operation in every righteous
cause, and the unfailing efficacy of united prayer.
"Again I say unto you, That if two of you shall agree
on earth as touching anything that they shall ask, it
shall be done for them of my Father which is in
heaven." Unselfish union of souls for the attainment
of divine power of service to man, brings union with
God in the realization of that power, and its actualization in service. Hence it is that unity of men in
mutual interest and associative effort for the realization of brotherhood in God, brings them into oneness
with God in the realization of His Spirit and power in
their lives. We have a complete illustration of this

truth in the Apostolic experience at and after Pentecost.

The third step and condition which follows in the
order specified by the Master, is the special ministry
of his spirit in active co-operation with men, which
their union in associative effort in his name secures.
The union of souls for the realization of the Christ-life
of divine sonship and brotherhood, unites them with
his spirit and opens them to the special ministry of
heaven in his name. The Divine sphere being thus
opened to them as it was to the Master and the Apostolic brotherhood, the Christ or anointing Spirit of
heavenly love, sympathy and ministration descends
upon them and becomes an abiding presence and power
in their lives. Conjunction with the Christ-heaven
and conscious communion and fellowship with the
angels of God thus become permanently established.

We have illustrated a practical application of the
primary steps and conditions here considered, in the
action of the Apostles preceding the outpouring of the
Spirit at Pentecost, when, in compliance with the Master's instruction, they met together in his name, " with
one accord in one place." Compliance with these specified laws and conditions leads necessarily, as with
them, to the

FORMATION OF SPIRITUAL GROUPS

as permanent centres of actual brotherhood, for the
conditions of spiritual evolution and associative effort
in attaining divine realization on earth. The Master
formed a permanent group of twelve; and though he

taught the multitude as occasion offered, his special
instruction and training were confined to the select
twelve. Here is a hint and example which it will be
always safe to follow, but they can be started with
two or more.

Let any number then from two to twelve, who can
unite for a permanent group to become one in spirit
and work as a unit, band themselves sacredly together
in the holy brotherhood of Spirit, and in the name of
him who opened the divine and perfect life in its fulness unto men. Let the Apostolic example be their
Model, and nothing less than the fulness of the Pentecostal baptism their ideal of preparation for service.
Let the union in prayer be for this blessing, remembering the last injunction of the Master to the Apostolic group, " Tarry ye at Jerusalem until ye be endued
with power from on high." This prayer-union is your
Jerusalem of preparation. Wait for the sure leading
of the Spirit before entering upon any special work in
his name. "Do not run before you are sent;" but
when you feel the unmistakable moving of the Spirit,
shrink not from faithful obedience to its leading.
"Quench not the Spirit; despise not prophesying."
The Master himself did not enter upon his work until
from his season of preparation in seclusion, he " returned in the power of the Spirit." So the Apostles at
and after Pentecost were " filled with the Holy Spirit,"
and " spake as the Spirit gave them utterance." " How
shall they preach except they be sent?" The simplest effort " in the demonstration of the Spirit and
power," will effect results impossible without it. Let

the place and time be chosen, consecrated and held
sacred to these gatherings in his name, and nothing
be allowed to interrupt or prevent the gatherings
within power to avoid. Let the meetings be as frequent as possible without interfering with the legitimate work and duties of the outward life.

ORDER OF EXERCISES.

It will be asked, how shall the groups be conducted?
The order of exercises should be of the simplest character lest too much dependence be placed upon externals, which will ever, as it always has, defeat the end
in view. The first object of the gathering—the opening and leading of the Spirit in the entire work—should
be kept uppermost in mind. Let there be as little
suggestion and interference from the wisdom of the
external man as possible. The example of the early
Friends, which in the beginning of their society was
wholly a leading of the Spirit, is worthy of study and
emulation. The record of that movement in the day
of its power, and of the marvellous spiritual experiences of its inspired apostles, is a mine of spiritual
wealth and suggestiveness. They followed more closely
the Apostolic method and reproduced more nearly the
Apostolic experience and results than has been done
since that wonderful day. They lost the Spirit in its
inspiration and power, only by making a virtue of their
simplicity and emphasizing the form, which thus became as much a dead formality and external service
that deludes the conscience with a false sense of duty
done, as the ceremonials and ecclesiasticism of the

more pretentious sects. To avoid this mistake, keep the emphasis ever upon the immediate inspiration and leading of the Spirit, seeking only this, and being ever ready to adopt any form of exercise or work which may be spiritually opened to the group.

Better follow faithfully the leading of the Spirit even at the risk of fanatacism than attempt to limit its manifestation to any external standard of authority or propriety. The Apostles were thought to be drunken with wine at Pentecost. One only precaution is needed: If a member of the group feel prompted of the Spirit to offer a suggestion concerning an exercise of the meeting or some ministration of service, let it be submitted to the spiritual intuitions of the entire group. There can be no perfect work without the united action of the group. The very object of its formation is to secure this, and it is more readily effected with a small number of not more than twelve than with more, until, at least, a good degree of spiritual development is attained. The group must become one in the Spirit before the Spirit can become one in it to use it as an organic instrument of service. The object, we repeat, of the group becoming unitized in the Spirit is, that the Spirit may become incarnated or embodied and expressed in it as a unit. When this unity is complete, and not before, the full Pentecostal "demonstration of the Spirit and power" will come. The opening of the spiritual life of each to the others will open the spiritual heavens unto all.

Since the first object is the opening of the spiritual life of the entire group as one, let all external suggestion, criticism and judgment be suspended, and let the slightest movement of the Spirit in each be encouraged. Above all things avoid the danger of any one assuming to be, or of being looked to as an oracle for others. Look for and seek only the divine oracle in each soul, and in due time it will respond in fulness. Remember, however, the diversity of gifts, and that the gifts of each may vary. In a group of twelve we have reason to expect all the special gifts enumerated by Paul. Let each gift be honored and encouraged. "Now there are diversities of gifts, but the same Spirit. And there are differences of administrations [ministration], but the same Lord. And there are diversities of operations, but it is the same God which worketh all in all. But the manifestation of the Spirit is given to every man to profit withal." One may have "the word of wisdom," and thus furnish inspired counsel to others or to the group, as needed, but if it be of the Spirit it will be recognized and responded to as such by the spiritual sense of the entire group, and nothing should be done without this response and sanction. This will not only prove a safeguard against fanaticism, but will also prevent the spirit of the human from stepping forth in leadership, which now, as in all the past, will be the one temptation and danger. "He that would be greatest among you let him be servant of all." "And be ye not called Rabbi; for one is your Master, even Christ; and all ye are brethren." "Where two or three are gathered together in my name, there am I in the midst of them."

The Christ will speak his word of light and power

in the silence of each soul; and this will find external
expression in the spiritual gift of that soul. What has
been said of "the word of wisdom" applies equally to
all the "Gifts." That which is truly of the Spirit will
meet with the spiritual recognition and response of
the entire group. This law of spiritual brotherhood
and fellowship, if observed in its spirit, will preserve
the groups from all danger of perverted activity in
either direction. "How is it then, brethren? when ye
come together, every one of you hath a psalm, hath a
doctrine, hath a tongue, hath a revelation, hath an interpretation. Let all things be done unto edifying."
Each will have some special leading, experience or
revelation, either in or out of the meetings, and unless
spiritually restrained from doing so, should report
them for the edification and encouragement of the
group. The Apostle Paul gives much valuable instruction concerning the meetings of the groups, in the 14th
chapter of First Corinthians.

We will suggest a simple order for the starting of
the groups, after which let it be open to such modifica-
tion and change as the inspiration of each group leads
it to adopt.

Until, at least, some decided degree of spiritual inspiration and power is developed, the meetings of the
groups should be strictly confined to its members, and
their experiences in the meetings or connected with
them, should be held sacred to the group and not made
the subject of discussion and criticism outside. Those
anxious to know of these experiences can easily obtain
them by forming a group of their own. This may

begin with two or three "in his name." The need of this silence is that the work of the Spirit shall not be subjected to the judgment and criticism of the flesh. Silence of the flesh and stillness of the external is an absolute necessity to spiritual revelation and development. When the Pentecostal baptism is reached and the gifts of the Spirit are fully and permanently established, the group will be moved to give its open testimony to the world, and to enter upon its public ministry.

A chairman should be chosen to conduct the exercises, open and close the meetings, etc.; and such other officers also as may be needed to manage the external affairs of the group. The length of time for the regular sessions should be agreed upon, and all the members should be in their places at the opening and remain till the close. Except for special reasons, the meetings should open and close promptly at the time appointed. The best results will be secured by the strict observance of this rule. A short time devoted to the singing of Spiritual Hymns, or Songs of the Spirit, tends to harmonize and spiritualize the sensibilities and promote a spirit of unity and fellowship. Then a reading of brief scripture selections, without comment, or spiritual instruction and experience from other spiritual writing; after which, let there be a season of silent meditation and prayer for the inward opening and revelation of the Spirit. The brief reading of inspired writing or record of spiritual experiences, helps to call in wandering thoughts and unify and focalize the attention upon the object of the meet-

ing, preparatory to the silence for divine communion
and revelation. Ten to fifteen minutes at least, may
be profitably spent in these preparatory exercises,
and not less then twenty minutes or half an hour
should be given to the silence. After this such as have
experienced a movement or revelation of the Spirit,
should each in turn in the briefest time and manner
possible give expression to the same, unless especially
restrained of the Spirit from doing so. Let the time
be thus occupied in such testimony, words of exhorta-
tion, songs, prayers, or ministry of healing, present or
absent, as the Spirit prompts. Better keep still and
silent to the end, however, than to let the human
speak or act without the prompting of the Spirit. Let
there be no discussion nor dictatorial expressions.
These meetings are for the unfolding of spiritual and
inspirational power, and ultimate illumination, not intellectual training. Opportunities for the latter are
everywhere abundant. The spiritual can be unfolded
only through communion with and inspiration from
the Divine. The specific object of these groups is to
open and bring to permanent realization this exalted
experience. To meet in his name is to seek in unity
of effort for the realization of his promised presence
in Spirit and power. The actualization of this in conscious experience is more to be desired than all external accomplishments. It will bring infinitely more
into the life. Conscious fellowship with the Divine is
the realization of the loftiest possible aspiration of
man. "With thee is the fountain of life; and in thy
light shall I see light."

APPENDIX.

20

APPENDIX.

[THE following extracts from letters received from readers of the previous volume, "The Way, The Truth and The Life," are given to show the hearty welcome with which the views therein set forth have been received, and the deep interest awakened in its interpretation of the Christ, and the higher possibilities of man on earth thus opened to faith and effort. Several hundred similar letters have been received from all classes, orthodox and heterodox, so that it would almost seem that a platform is here presented upon which all could unite to work for the realization of the Christ ideal—the Christ promise of the perfect life of divine sonship and brotherhood in universal experience. Some of the most hearty and appreciative letters have been from clergymen of different denominations. Some of the more enthusiastic expressions have been purposely withheld from these selections, but what is given is a fair type of the bulk of the letters received from people to whom the author is a stranger, save through the reading of his book.

Many interesting questions have been received from readers of "The Way, The Truth and the Life," too numerous for individual reply, but which it is hoped have been satisfactorily answered in "The Pathway of The Spirit." Should further questions or difficulties arise, they will be considered in succeeding volumes of this series.]

DEAR SIR:—Having read your book, viz., The Way etc., or Christian Theosophy, for which I cannot find words to express my gratitude to you for so ably elucidating the principles of practical Christianity, I wish that every preacher and teacher of Christianity could read it and adopt its views, which, if generally adopted, would bring about the millennium. Please mail particulars about your school and oblige a seeker after truth."

MY DEAR SIR:—. . . I cannot tell you how thankful I am that your book came into my possession. To me it is the direct inspiration from Christ himself, and you must be the happiest of men to have been led along so divine a path, to the perfect understanding of His mission and method.

"Yours very sincerely,

J. H. Dewey, M.D.

DEAR SIR:—I have just finished reading your handbook of "Christian Theosophy: The Way, The Truth and The Life," and must say it gives me a more comprehensible insight into the teachings of the Christ than anything I have ever read before.

It creates a thirst to persevere in the Scriptures and
a desire to understand more fully the methods taught
and applied by you in your school. . . . Awaiting
your reply, "Yours truly,

———— ————

————

J. H. Dewey, M.D.

DEAR SIR:—I have just finished reading your book,
"The Way, The Truth and The Life," which was
loaned me by a friend. I desire to express my gratitude to you as well as to the Divine Spirit that inspired
you to write a work of such inestimable value. As I
wish to procure the book for the benefit of others as
well as myself, will you please tell me where it can be
obtained and its cost? Have you written other works
on this subject? An early answer will oblige,

Yours respectfully,

———— ————

————

J. H. Dewey, M.D.

DEAR SIR:—Please send me one copy "The Way,
The Truth and The Life."

I think your book is wonderful. It thrilled me with
new light. A new heaven and a new earth are open
to me. I read your book as I have searched the Scriptures in the past. So now I look for treasures in
Christian Theosophy. I shall take pleasure in lending
your book that the light may shine. I inclose $2.00.

With sincere respect and friendship,

———— ————

J. H. Dewey, M.D.

My Very Dear Sir:—"The Way, The Truth and The Life" reached me safely, and is my constant companion, teaching me many things, and above all bringing Jesus the Christ nearer to me than I have ever been able to realize before. . . . Inclosed find $2.00 express order, for which please send a copy of "The Way, The Truth and The Life" to ———, an only sister of Mr. ——— my husband. I have interested her in your book by reading portions of it to her while she was ill, and she desired me to write for it. Wishing you the best there is in life, I am very sincerely,

Your friend,

——— ———

———

J. H. Dewey, M.D.

Dear Sir:—I have been reading a copy of your book entitled "The Way, The Truth and The Life." I sent my copy to a friend, a minister on the Pacific coast and desire to obtain another. I cannot say enough in praise of the book. I consider it inestimable and hope you will fill my order at once, as I shall be lonely without it. Enclosed find P. O. order for $2.00.

Have you other books on this subject?

Respectfully,

——— ———

———

J. H. Dewey.

Dear Brother:—Though we are strangers in one sense of the word, yet I have become somewhat ac-

quainted with you through your book, "Christian Theosophy," which I have just finished reading.

It has opened up many new fields of thought to me,
and I am really anxious to become more thoroughly
consecrated to the work of the Master than hereto-
fore. I have been a minister for several years. . . . I
am glad I have had the privilege of reading your
book. . . . I do so want to be of more service to humanity in blessing the weak and healing the sick. My life
is consecrated to the work, and how best to apply my
talent is the great question of my heart. I want to
be a perfect man and attain the Christ-like life in *this*
body. . . . May God's choicest blessings be ever upon
and within you, is my accompanying prayer.

Your Brother in Christ,

Dr. J. H. Dewey.

DEAR SIR:—Inclosed please find $2.00, for which send
me "The Way, The Truth and The Life." Will say
that with a few others here, I am studying the above
with great interest and satisfaction. We are a class
of four, reading and studying together with a view of
mutual advancement and if possible we want to help
others. . . . We like your book much better than anything we have seen, and heartily indorse your position
regarding ———. Trusting you will find time to give
us the above desired information, and bidding you God
speed in the glorious work, I am,

Very respectfully yours,

Dr. Dewey.

DEAR SIR: — Your work called "The Way, The Truth and The Life," fell into my hands on last Thanksgiving day, and I shall never cease to be thankful for it. The article on "Mental and Faith-healing," comes the nearest to my own belief and what I have tried to teach for the past two years of anything I have ever seen. I *know* from my own experience that it is *true,* and I can never accept of a belief which considers even the most marvellous healing to be any intervention, or setting aside of *law.* It can only be the fulfilling of law. Please send me two copies. . . .

That your work and teaching may be greatly blest and extended for the good of humanity, is the sincere wish and desire of,

——— ———

Dr. J. H. Dewey.

DEAR SIR:—The book which I requested sent to my residence was received. I am glad to get it. We have both read a borrowed copy, and think so highly of the work and its concise teachings that we desire to own it.   Yours truly,

——— ———

DR. J. H. DEWEY:—I have read and re-read "The Way, The Truth and The Life" with satisfaction and delight.

Though only a student I am able to command the conditions of my body, and in considerable measure that of my children and others.

Since reading your beautiful book I have endeavored to enter the condition of mental introversion and develop the sixth and seventh senses. . . . My apology for writing is, I am an earnest seeker of Truth, with a strong desire to *live* it, and so operate with those who work for the advancement and uplifting of humanity.

Respectfully and truly yours,

J. H. Dewey, M.D.

DEAR SIR:—A friend lent me your book for a few hours, she "would not spare it longer"—and I feel I must have a copy of my own, for it is the first thing in mental healing which I could understand. The title is "Christian Theosophy" isn't it? . . . I am sure many people must thank you in their hearts for your beautiful book. Yours, etc.,

DEAR DR. DEWEY:—I have tried to benefit you and others by speaking of your book as I had opportunity. To me this is a life-giving book. I send you $2.00 for "The Way, The Truth and The Life;" please direct the book to —— and oblige,

Yours,

J. H. Dewey, M.D.

DEAR SIR AND BROTHER:—A copy of your work, "The Way, The Truth and The Life" has come into my hands, and I have read it with ever increasing interest and deep satisfaction, the more so because I had seen a part of the truth set forth therein. That mind should be master of matter and of all lower forces should be true, and is so in the universe. . . .

Any suggestions you may make to me will be most gratefully received.

Yours most fraternally,

——— ———

———

Dr. J. H. D.

DEAR SIR:—Your book, "The Way, The Truth and The Life," is the most satisfactory work that I have seen, and I have read many; and I deem it the very best one to place in the hands of my pupils. While it treats all points with perfect candor, it contains nothing to shock or puzzle one who has studied or taken a course of instruction, but it supplements many things which can be touched upon but briefly in classes, and it leads so gently and clearly to the points as to be invaluable in enabling them to impart in a judicious way, something of what they have learned, to those whom they would interest, but whom they fear to approach abruptly.

All that I have written falls very far short of what I would say, nor does it represent my thought even as far as it goes, . . . and I wish to order one dozen copies of the work, and feel that I cannot send the order without some expression however imperfect it be, of my appreciation of your efforts to help mankind.

Yours very truly,

——— ———

J. H. Dewey, M.D.

DEAR SIR:—I have been reading a few chapters of your book entitled "The Way, The Truth and The Life," with great interest. . . . Will you please send me a list of your books on this subject, with price attached, including the one I am reading, and whether you can supply them or how I can get them?

Very respectfully,

Dr. Dewey.

DEAR SIR:—We have greatly enjoyed the perusal of "The Way, The Truth and The Life," and we rejoice with you in the good this work is bound to accomplish. All here who have read it wish to re-read again and again, and finally must get the book as their own. . . . Respectfully,

Dr. J. H. Dewey.

DEAR SIR:—Inclosed find my check for $4.00 for two copies of "The Way, The Truth and The Life." I am indebted to —— for a knowledge of your book, she having kindly loaned me her copy. I consider the book so valuable that I wish to own it and present a copy to a friend.

It is in my opinion the first correct expression of a true system of Theosophy, and it gives me pleasure to find an able refutation of current incorrect doctrines. . . . Hoping you will excuse the liberty I have taken,

I am sincerely yours,

J. H. Dewey.

DEAR SIR:—My apology for writing you is, your book, " The Way, The Truth and The Life," was placed in my hands a few days ago by a friend. I have read it. It certainly contains the clearest statement I have ever seen of man and his possibilities. Have you the book for sale? Have you written other books? . . . I have been interested in these subjects for years, and desire all the light I can get, that I may be useful. . . .

Fraternally,

DEAR DR. DEWEY:—A friend lent me your book on Christian Theosophy, and after an hour's reading here and there, I felt that nothing short of actual owner-ship would satisfy me. I enclose $2.00 P. O. order for the same. Would you kindly forward book at once as I expect to leave the city in a few days, and wish to study the book while on my vacation.

Sincerely,

Dr. Dewey.

DEAR FRIEND:—I have been exceedingly interested in your book, " The Way, The Truth and The Life," and find it full of inspiration.

Yours fraternally,

Dr. J. H. Dewey.

MY DEAR FRIEND:—Please find inclosed money or-der for two more copies of " The Way, The Truth and

The Life." It is the best book of the kind I have found. Have you others?

Yours in the Truth,

———— ————

Dr. J. H. Dewey.

DEAR SIR:—I came across your book, "The Way, The Truth and The Life," the other day and read a few pages in it. I was much interested in it. I am a clergyman. I would like to own the book. Will you send a copy directed as above? . . . I think from the hour I gave to looking over the book, you have done a great service to the cause of Christianity.

Truly yours,

———— ————

J. H. Dewey, M.D.

DEAR SIR:—Please send me by mail or express, as is the cheapest, two copies of your "The Way, The Truth and The Life." I have one copy of the book now, and want these to lend.

The book has been very helpful to Mrs. S. and myself. . . .

Very truly yours,

———— ————

DEAR SIR:—Inclosed please find $2.00, for which send me one copy of "Christian Theosophy."

It is—without flattery—the best book on the subject I have read, and it has been of assistance to me.

Respectfully yours,

———— ————

J. H. Dewey.

RESPECTED SIR:—Please find inclosed $2.00 to pay for your grand book, "The Way, The Truth and The Life." I have read it once, it was loaned me by a friend who bought it of thee. Now I wish to own it myself. . . . Very respectfully,

——— ———

Dr. J. H. Dewey.

DEAR SIR:—I have read "The Way, The Truth and The Life," through several times and like it very much indeed. Please send catalogue with terms for instruction and oblige,

Yours truly,

——— ———

Dr. J. H. Dewey.

DEAR SIR:—I am much interested in Christian Theosophy as set forth in your book entitled "The Way, The Truth and The Life." Have you written other books elucidating Christian Theosophy? . . . Your book is exciting great interest in these parts.

Very respectfully yours,

——— ———

DEAR SIR:—Will you kindly inform me the price of your book, "The Way, The Truth and The Life?" It is the finest thing of the kind yet published.

Yours truly,

——— ———

Dear Dr. Dewey:—I have been greatly interested in your book, "The Way, The Truth and The Life," and think it should be widely circulated. A few weeks ago I sent through a bookseller for a dozen copies for myself and a few friends. . . . I should expect to sell a few of the books when there is opportunity, and to give or lend to those who are unable or unwilling to buy, etc.

Please send addressed to,

───── ─────

─────

Dr. J. H. Dewey.

Dear Sir:—Please find inclosed $2.00 in payment for one copy of " Christian Theosophy," which be kind enough to send to Miss ───── ───── and allow me to express my hearty approval and sincere pleasure in the book. It has been a help to me. I have been practising "Christian Science" for over a year. My endeavor has been to hold *the truth in love,* and regret whatever seemed inconsistent with the simple, natural teaching of the Scriptures. Friends have asked me repeatedly for *some book* which I could *heartily recommend.* And I take great pleasure in saying to you that " The Way, The Truth and The Life " is *the one* and the *only* one that seems to me *really* scientific. Hastily and respectfully yours in the one service and life,

───── ─────

─────

Dr. Dewey.

Dear Sir:—Inclosed please find $2.00 for copy of " The Way, The Truth, and The Life " to send to Mr. ───── ─────. Your work has helped so clearly to see and understand this grand Truth, that I think perhaps it will help my friends to see it also. . . '. Although I have not read more than half of "The Way, The Truth and The Life," I feel that it is doing more for me than anything I have read. . . .

It suits me thoroughly and I hope to master the thoughts therein suggested completely.

Very Truly,

———— ————

————

Dr. J. H. Dewey.

MY DEAR SIR:—I have just read your book " Christian Theosophy." It has truly shown me "The Way, The Truth and The Life," and I thank you for having written it. It has helped me to a practical realization, I may say, of the possibilities as well as the duty of cultivating our higher faculties.

I have for a long time thought in that direction, but you have encouraged and crystallized my resolutions.

———— ————

————

Dr. Jno. Dewey.

DEAR SIR:—About a year ago we bought a copy of "The Way, The Truth and The Life" and read with great satisfaction, interest and profit, and have loaned and recommended it to many friends and acquaintances. The book does not lose in interest, but may be read and re-read with increasing interest. I inclose two dollars for a copy for a friend.

Yours truly,

———— ————

CHRISTIAN THEOSOPHY SERIES.

A New and Original Series of Books Designed to Unfold and Practically Apply the Theosophy of the Christ.

By JOHN HAMLIN DEWEY, M.D.

No. 1 of the Series is entitled:

"The Way, The Truth and The Life:

A HANDBOOK OF CHRISTIAN THEOSOPHY, HEALING AND PSYCHIC CULTURE."

This work of over 400 pages gives an outline study of man in the light of the Christ life and teaching, describes the New Education and the specific processes involved, based upon the Ideal and Method of the Christ, and comprehensively defines, analyzes, and applies the fundamental principles upon which the whole are based.

The succeeding numbers of the series are compact volumes of from 200 to 300 pages each, in which special features of the system are more fully elucidated and applied.

"The Way, The Truth and The Life," Cloth, Gilt, $2.00.
"The Pathway of the Spirit," 300 pages, Cloth, Gilt, $1.25; Paper, 75 cents.
"Spiritual Gifts, or True Christian Occultism," in preparation.
"The Law of the Perfect Life,"   "   "

OTHER WORKS BY THE SAME AUTHOR.

"Introduction to the Theosophy of Christ" (pamphlet), 35 cts.
"Christian Theosophy Defined,"   "   6 "
"Divinity of Humanity,"   "   10 "
"Scientific Basis of Mental Healing,"   "   10 "

Any of the above works sent post free on receipt of price. Address the author,

J. H. DEWEY, M.D.,

367 West 35th St., New York.

CPSIA information can be obtained at www.ICGtesting.com
Printed in the USA
LVOW010042280712

291888LV00019B/110/P